A History of Sherburn (in Hertfordlythe)

Church of England Primary School

*To those special people who have answered the call
to dedicate their lives to teaching children*

A HISTORY OF SHERBURN

(IN HERTFORDLYTHE)

CHURCH OF ENGLAND PRIMARY SCHOOL

━━━━━

ANNE COLLIER

2008

First published in 2008 by
Anne Collier

ISBN 978-0-9544412-2-7

Designed and typeset by:
Croft Publications
The Croft, 8 St James Meadow
Boroughbridge YO51 9NW

Printed and bound by:
Smith Settle Printing and Bookbinding Ltd
Gateway Drive, Yeadon LS19 7XY

CONTENTS

ACKNOWLEDGEMENTS

Raymond Patrick Metcalfe for his generous encouragement and his loan of the Wykeham Military Hospital 1914-18 Autograph Book; Carol Barnes for allowing access to School documents; Scarborough & District Newspapers and York & County Press for permission to use material from old publications; the staff of the Scarborough and Malton Public Libraries for their kindness and help; Colin Longthorpe for his memories of the years spent in Sherburn as an evacuee; John Clarke, Rosemary Dawson (nee Calam), Deidre Nash (nee Newton) and Alison Oulton (nee Bradford), for loan of photographs; Nia Bland of Scarborough for the German translation

Profits to Sherburn Church of England (VC) Primary School

CHAPTER I
A BRIEF HISTORY OF EDUCATION

EARLY HISTORY OF EDUCATION especially in villages is meagre, but we can assume that in the 1700's most schools were rural because the majority of the population lived in country areas where the inhabitants were self-supporting tillers of the land. In 1743, out of East Yorkshire's 168 parishes, 101 did not have a school. Archbishop Herring's Visitation returns for 1737 reveal that *"in Shereburne, there is no publick or charity School"*. Lawson's book *"Primary Education in East Yorkshire"* describes a typical village school of that period thus *"We have a private school where about 30 boys and girls are taught English, Writing and Accompts; the schoolmaster is very careful to instruct them in the Principles of the Christian Religion, according to the doctrine of the Church of England and doth bring them duly to church as the Canon requires"*.

Towards the end of the 1700's, England began to change from a rural to an industrial civilisation as the population slowly shifted from tiny villages into growing towns. The number of factories increased and so did the number of urban children who spent most of their time *"in mischief"* and to resolve this, they were employed in factories for six days a week leaving Sundays for them to *"run wild"*. A man called Robert Raikes tried to address this by appointing and paying teachers to teach on Sundays. Children were taken to church and taught *"to read and learn the Catechism* (see appendix 1), *to know the order of the Church service, when to kneel, sit and stand"* and the idea spread rapidly. By 1786, the York Committee for Education called for all children to attend with the rule that *"teachers shall take care that the scholars come clean to their respective schools, and if any be guilty of lying, swearing, talking in an indecent manner, or otherwise misbehaving, the teacher shall point out the evil of such conduct, and if, after repeated reproof, the scholar shall not be reformed, he or she shall be excluded"*. (*'History of English Elementary Education'* E Smith). These first Sunday Schools initiated the idea of free education and gave Britain's education system its Christian heritage.

Society was divided into rich and poor, and those who governed and those who were governed, and the dominant political view was that if poor people were educated, they would rebel and demand reforms. Rich people employed a governess until their children were old enough to attend a public school whereas poor children were educated by observing and taking part in the activities of life in and around their own homes. Boys learned outdoor skills connected with food production from animal husbandry and crop growing, girls learned domestic skills and how to make clothes and both learned spinning and weaving.

England's places of learning ranged from universities, colleges, private schools to small village schools. Oxford university was founded in 1167, Cambridge in 1209 and their various colleges during the 13th-15th centuries. Eton College for boys from wealthy families, was built in 1440 and since then over the centuries, numerous universities, colleges and schools have been built. Charity schools began to be established in the 18th century in an attempt *"to rescue children from complete ignorance and train them up for a life of industry and proper humility towards their betters". ('History of English Elementary Education'* E Smith). These could be either day or boarding schools where the masters were required to pass an examination in the principles of Christian religion, have an aptitude for teaching, the ability to write well and understand arithmetic, whereas mistresses only needed an aptitude for teaching! Boys were taught to count, read and write, girls to read, knit and sew. Because many village children were poor, the aim of charity schools failed.

In 1833 the Government made its first annual grant of £20,000 towards half the cost of building new schools and the other half came from voluntary contributions. Also in 1833, a national survey revealed that out of every 10 children, 4 did not attend school, 3 went to Sunday School, 2 to an inefficient *'Dame'* or day school and only one received satisfactory education. This led to a demand for a state education system but it was not until the 1870 Education Act that education was recognised as a public service and existing church schools received increased grants and locally elected boards were empowered to establish schools partly maintained by local rates. School attendance was made compulsory for children aged 5 to 14 and if a child was absent too often, except for sickness when a doctor's certificate had to be produced, parents were liable to a 5/- (25p) fine. This was difficult to enforce for various reasons. Some children were unable to attend in bad weather because they had inadequate footwear or none at all; older children often had to stay at home to look after small children while the mother worked in the fields when the father was ill or unable to hold a job and worse still when the mother herself was sick or died in childbirth, the eldest had to be *'mother'*. These problems were eased in 1880, when Exemption Certificates were granted to older pupils allowing them to help at home or be in part-time employment. The 1893 Elementary (School Attendance) Act raised the exemption age to 11 except in agricultural areas where children might, under certain conditions, still claim half-time exemption.

The standard of teaching in Victorian Schools varied from poor to excellent with religion, reading, writing, arithmetic and needlework being principal subjects and in 1888 a Royal Commission set up to take stock of the 1870 Education Act, exposed the need for better school buildings and playgrounds. At the same time, work outside the classroom, like drawing plans, sketching, visiting woods, lanes, ponds, farms and cultivating a school garden became part of the curriculum.

Some village schools were run by a man who had failed to earn a living in other ways and some known as *'Dame Schools'*, were run by an elderly woman in her own cottage, charging 2d/3d a week per child, but because poor families were usually large, the majority couldn't afford to send their children. William Howitt who was born in a Derbyshire village in 1792 wrote: *"My first teacher was Nanny Aldred an old woman who lived in a very little house just by our garden; she wore a large mob cap* (covering all the hair)*, a broad-striped bed gown, a large checked apron, in which she used to go, when school was over, gathering sticks. I remember too, that she took great quantities of Scotch snuff and had three or four large cats, so that in old times she would certainly have been drowned for a witch"*. (*"The Boys' Country Book"*).

The first mention of a school teacher in Sherburn's parish records appears in 1801 when Robert Cooper aged 71, was buried in St Hilda's churchyard after being school master and parish clerk for many years. Robert and his wife Ann (nee Stephenson) had three children John, Robert and Thomas. In 1814, John and Mary Coulson's child Mary Ann was baptised in St Hilda's and between 1815 and 1828, John and Margaret Whitehead had five babies baptised: Jane, William, Matilda, Henry and Betty. Margaret died in 1829 and John married his servant Jane Hugill in 1844, eight years before his own death. These school masters either taught children in their own homes calling them day or boarding schools, or in some sort of school building which could have been on the same site as today's Sherburn school.

Boys from middle class families boarded at the vicarage where the vicar taught them reading, writing and arithmetic to supplement his meagre income. Sherburn's pre-1900 census returns record names of the pupils living first with the Rev John Mason from 1834-73 then with the Rev Richard Ellis from 1873-1905 (see appendix 2). When the Revd James Whittam arrived in 1905, Sherburn vicarage was so dilapidated he didn't know how his predecessors had been able to accommodate these pupils. Nevertheless, he had frequent visits from *"members of the upper ten"* wanting to see again the rooms where they received their primary education.

In 1801, Sherburn's population was 349 and there were 72 *"habitable homes"*. By 1815 the population had increased to 450 and the 1841 census returns (Public Records Office Ref: HO107/1211), reveal that out of a population of nearly 600 occupying 112 dwellings, Sherburn had roughly 200 children aged 11 and under (including the Vicarage pupils) and most were from labouring families living in tiny one or two-roomed cottages. White's

Directory states that in 1840, Sherburn had *"a good School and the Hon Marmaduke Langley allows £20 a year for the education of poor children"*. Langley was Lord of the Manor. The school was being run by widow Hannah Clarkson aged 35, and successive headmasters were James Thompson (1850's), William Clarkson (1855-59) at *'Mr William Clarkson's Commercial Boarding and Day School'*, William Mallory (1859-67) and also during the 1860's, 38 year old Ann Watson a school mistress was living at *'Cottage House'* where she may have been running her own *'Dame School'*. On an old map, *'Cottage House'* appears to be on the site of today's *'Sherburn Lodge'*. In 1871, Alexander Shaw 25, schoolmaster from Huddersfield, was living in Sherburn and in 1873, Anthony Sawkill from Stokesley was appointed school master. That year, the vicar Revd John Mason 68 and his wife Sarah 69 (nee Knowlson) died within six months of each other. They were married at St Michael le Belfrey Church, York, in 1834 the same year he was appointed vicar of Sherburn. They had four children Hannah (b 1835), John (b 1836), James (b 1840) and Sarah (b 1847 died aged 3 weeks). At his death, the vicar owned 21 acres, 1 rood, 8 perches of land bringing in an annual rental of £54..5s..0d. John and Sarah Mason were laid to rest side by side at the east end of St Hilda's Church and their epitaph reads *"they were lovely and pleasant in their lives"*. Their son John was Curate of Stainborough and Worsborough, near Barnsley, for 30 years, and their son James was Canon of St Paul's Cathedral, Leicester, for 40 years.

Little Sarah Mason may have died from a killer epidemic like cholera, because throughout the years 1847-48, 41 children and 15 adults died in Sherburn (see appendix 3) including two other Mason babies, Robert and Charlotte children of the vicar's brother Robert Mason who was Sherburn's doctor for several years. Robert and his wife Ann (nee Stork) had at least seven children, the first two were boys who died in 1841 within days, their next three were girls who died in infancy and in 1851 the Masons were recorded as having two daughters Annie 8 and Charlotte 1. Robert Mason died at Sherburn in 1862 aged 54 and his wife and surviving children Annie and Charlotte went to live in Scarborough where they ran a lodging house.

After 1870, schools were inspected annually and in March 1893, Her Majesty's Inspector (HMI) said that at Sherburn, teaching and discipline were *'creditable'*, but the school was over-crowded and unsatisfactory, and he ordered a new school to be built. Within a week Lady Downe of Wykeham had donated land to extend the site, the late James Kirk owner of Sherburn brewery, had bequeathed *"a handsome sum"*, local farmers had offered to lead building material from the railway station and the Wesleyan schoolroom had been hired temporarily. The official re-opening of the school was celebrated a year later on Friday 20 April 1894 with a Concert and a Ball in the large room, attended by leading members of the community and many others. Talented musicians, including some locals, provided high class music and singing and Mr Bishop's Band from Scarborough provided music for the Ball. Just before dawn, dancing ended with a waltz *"Love's Old Sweet Song"* (see appendix 4). Then everyone stood to attention and sang *'God save the Queen'*.

Up to 1900, if the Board of School Managers did not employ a school cleaner, the school master's wife was expected with the help of pupils, to sweep floors, light fires and scrub out the *'earth privies'* (toilets). These were in an outhouse and had wooden seats with holes through which excrement dropped into an earth pit. Early every morning the cleaner tipped ashes from the school fire grates into the pit to soak up liquid and quell the stench and the pit was emptied regularly during the hours of darkness by the *"parish night-soil cart"*. The school cleaner in 1900 was Mrs Atkinson but at the time there were four Mrs Atkinsons in Sherburn, Annie a widow who lodged with Thomas Dawson, Mary wife of Joseph, Louise wife of Fred and Betsy wife of Thomas. Widow Annie at 46 was the most likely to be school cleaner because Mary was 75, Louise was 26 and of child-bearing age and Betsy was a self-employed dressmaker with an apprentice Elizabeth Currey lodging with her.

In 1902, Balfour's Education Act placed *'board schools'* under borough or county councils (Local Education Authorities) authorising them to develop elementary schools and establish secondary and technical schools. Campaigners warned against councils funding church school saying that most parents wanted religious instruction for their children. A variety of subsequent Acts widened the curriculum and provided more opportunities for all children to have elementary as well as higher education. The 1918 Education Act fixed the school leaving age at 14 and launched a scheme to provide part-time education for pupils aged 14 to 18. Medical inspections, nursery schools and special needs centres were also introduced. In 1926, a Board of Education pamphlet *"Rural Education"* stated that village children *"should be prepared for country life and trained for rural occupations"* and another pamphlet *"The Education of the Adolescent"* ordered primary education to end at 11 and secondary education made available for all children aged 11 to 15. This meant that all pupils were examined at 11 and transferred to either a grammar or a secondary school.

In Laurie Lee's book *"Cider with Rosie"* he describes his school days during the 1920's thus: *"Our village school was poor and crowded, but in the end I relished it. It had a lively reek of steaming life; boys' boots, girls' hair, stoves and sweat, blue ink, white chalk and shavings. We learnt nothing abstract or tenuous there – just simple patterns of facts and letters, portable tricks of calculation, no more than was needed to measure a shed, write out a bill, read a swine-disease warning. Through the dead hours of the morning, through the long afternoons, we chanted away at our tables. So it was, always had been, would be for ever. We asked no questions, we didn't hear what was said, yet neither did we forget..."*.

Marjorie Wise's book *"English Village Schools"* published in 1931 describes some of the appalling conditions she found in rural schools where there were untrained and often unkind teachers. She writes: *"Would it not be better for children to run about in the fields than be forced into this type of schooling? The children sit in stiff, still rows in a galleried room as if they were in the infant room of 50 years ago. A young incompetent supplementary teacher that I saw, getting £35 a year, was exposed by the inspectors. Her head teacher asked the County authorities to help but they replied that her health was good, so she must stay."*

The 1944 Education Act raised the school leaving age to 15 and sub-divided state-aided education into primary, secondary and further education so that *"every child would have an education appropriate to his age, aptitude and ability"*. In 1948, the *"General Certificate of Education"* replaced the *"Higher School Certificate"* and grants were awarded to university students whose family income was less than £600 per annum. Plans also began to replace grammar, secondary modern and technical schools with *"comprehensive"* schools whereby all 11-year olds would transfer from primary to comprehensive education without being tested. This idea came from a spokesman for the Middlesex County Council who claimed that *"at 11 a child may not have an examination temperament and may fail dismally. That failure may penalise him or her for a long time, not only in denying him or her grammar school and university education, but in shattering his confidence"*. Despite apprehension about the size of comprehensive schools and fears that they would become *"a threat to education"*, the first opened in September 1954 in Kidbrooke, London and by 1976 free grammar schools were phased out.

The 1961 Plowden Report claimed that one in five children attended a country school where parents expected as good an education for their children as they would have in a town and primary schools were ordered to have at least three classes each covering two age groups. Corporal punishment in UK state schools was abolished in 1986 and in public schools in 1996. The 1988 Education Reform Act ordered teacher training days, a standard national curriculum, national testing and inspections by Ofsted (Office for standards in education) and handed over control of budgets to schools. This dramatically increased paperwork for teaching staff and especially for teaching heads.

During the summer holidays of 1990, Sir Claus Moser, Vice President of the British Association for the Advancement of Science and warden of Wadham College, Oxford, called for a royal commission to investigate what he claimed

---

Sherburn Upper School c1906 with Anthony Sawkill headmaster standing at right end of back row. William Calvert Bell assistant teacher from 1904-1912 is sitting at the left end of 2nd row from front.

was a crisis in the country's education system. He said hundreds of thousands of children had educational experiences not worthy of a civilised nation caused by ten years of government spending cuts leaving the teaching profession demoralised and under-skilled; only one child in three was staying on at school after the minimum leaving age and even fewer were moving on to higher education.

Anthony Sawkill was headmaster of Sherburn School from 1873 to 1914, and his successors were George Farmer from 1914-16, Harry Potter 1916-38, John Newton 1938-64, Richard Duncan Sykes 1965-83, Geoffrey Howdle 1983-2000, Nigel Mainprize (acting head) and Mrs Aileen Moss served one year each and Mrs Carol Barnes was appointed in October 2003. As well as trying to portray life at Sherburn school throughout the years from 1873 to the present day, the following chapters include records of village people and events and some of the social changes that have taken place over those years.

CHAPTER 2
ANTHONY SAWKILL (1873-1914)

ANTHONY SAWKILL, son of Robert Sawkill a butcher from Stokesley, was a 20 year old bachelor when he was appointed Sherburn's school master and held the post for 41 years. During that time, the school was the hub of village life, for as well as being headmaster, he took an active roll in all village activities. He was the people's warden and church organist and in 1907 after 33 years as choir master was presented with a Chimes Clock, an Aneroid Barometer and a gold signet ring. He was leader of the Brass Band which he founded in 1880, he joined the parish council when it was formed in 1894 serving as chairman and treasurer; for 40 years he was a member of the Court Langley No 784 Ancient Order of Foresters Friendly Society founded in Sherburn in 1840 to help poor families, serving as chief ranger for 16 years and secretary for 23. He was secretary to the cricket club for 26 seasons and umpire for 41 and belonged to the Lawn Tennis Club, Bowling, Hockey and Rifle Clubs. He was secretary to various royal celebration committees, in 1887 for Queen Victoria's Golden Jubilee, in 1897 for her Diamond Jubilee, in 1902 for the Coronation of Edward VII and in 1911 for the Coronation of George V. He was a freemason for 20 years and when he died was Master of Malton Camalodunum Lodge. For 30 years he was correspondent for the *"Malton Messenger"*.

On 21 August 1975, two years after arriving in Sherburn, Anthony Sawkill married Margaret Dickinson in St Hilda's Church and they lived in a terraced cottage in St Hilda's Street. Their son Anthony was born in February 1882 but lived only ten days. Margaret died in 1893 aged 41 after a long illness following a severe attack of influenza in the summer of 1891 when there was a nation-wide epidemic. Margaret was known to be *"a genial, warm-hearted and steadfast friend and an unassuming and excellent neighbour"* and many villagers attended her funeral on Easter Monday 3 April 1893, as well as people from Malton, Scarborough, York, Leeds, and Middlesborough. She had been in the church choir since she was a little girl and her fellow choristers sang her favourite hymn *"Jesu, Lover of my soul"* to her favourite tune *"Emanuel"*. Anthony Sawkill's mother and brother died the same year as his wife Margaret. He married his second wife Clara Ellen Marston of Sherburn Post Office on 4 September 1894 and their daughter Kathleen was born in 1895 and their son Philip Marston in 1901. They lived in a five-roomed house and had a maid called Elizabeth Swan. Kathleen and Philip attended Sherburn School and in

1909 Kathleen went to Bridlington High School for Girls and in 1913 was appointed pupil teacher at Sherburn. Philip Marston Sawkill went to Archbishop Holgate's in York, then to Leeds University where he gained first class honour degrees with distinction in arithmetic, French, geography and science.

Victorian teachers were trained in schools and whilst training were called pupil teachers. In the 1880's, Anthony Sawkill had in his care: Henry Charles Marston 18 from the Post Office, Esther Megginson 17 from Costa Mill, Pickering, who lodged with her uncle John Britain, farmer/miller at High Mill, Albert E Watson, son of Jane Watson a widow, John Thompson, son of George and Frances Thompson, shoemakers and Percy Bielby, son of Tom Bielby farmer. Percy passed the Queen's Scholarship Examination and went to Chelsea College, London, and gained a BA degree.

Anthony Sawkill had a succession of assistants and most were often late or absent or didn't stay long. They included Miss M Shaw, Miss Edith Eyre (Derbyshire) and Rosa Wilson 25 (Sunderland) who lodged at the Vicarage with her uncle Richard Ellis. After the 1897 annual inspection, HMI asked Miss Shaw to resign because of a physical disability which was hindering her teaching and pupil progress and he advised Miss Eyre to attend a Scarborough School to *"observe kindergarten methods"*. During the Christmas holidays, Miss Eyre sent a telegram to say she had sprained her ankle and would be off until Easter and Miss Betsy Lewis was appointed temporarily. Miss Eyre resigned in 1902. Miss Rosa Hillier 29 (Taunton) left after a month, Miss Alice Johnson 25 (Northallerton) after two years and Miss Minnie Bridge (Goole) after one year, Miss Mabel Hutton left after a year to go to St Thomas's School, York and Miss Kate Mackay (Kircardineshire) left after seven months. The managers engaged a *"monitress"* Miss Martha Brown aged 18 who lived at Springfield Farm with her bachelor brother George but she stayed only four months. Miss Ellen Howes 19 (Hull) stayed 16 months and Miss Mary Hodgson 20 (Co Durham) stayed three years. Miss Janet Mackintosh (Bridlington) was appointed in 1904 and lodged with Mrs Frances Thompson and Miss Lilian Botterill (York) was appointed in 1905. Although Janet Mackintosh and Lilian Botterill were often late or absent, they were on the staff when Anthony retired. Anthony Sawkill's wife Clara was also a teaching assistant.

This rapid staff turnover could only be due to bad working conditions, for there is no doubt Anthony Sawkill was well liked. Former pupils and assistants often came back to see him and he carefully logged each visit. Former pupils included William Horsley a farmer who returned to England from Manitoba after 18 years, John Owston, James Dawson and Charles Allanson. Assistants who visited included John Thompson from Blackburn, Albert E Watson from Slaithwaite and Henry C Marston. Even Minnie Bridge's parents called in 1904. Another of Anthony's visitors was Josiah Wilson, an insurance agent in Scarborough, who had been a fellow-student at York Training College.

William Calvert Bell, a former pupil, was appointed in 1904 for an annual salary of £50, and stayed until 1912, bringing stability and improved standards to the lower school. When he left he joined the staff at Scarborough Central school and Sherburn school presented him with a brass 400 days clock under a glass cover *"in recognition of his services and genial and kindly character"* and the Chapel Sunday School gave him a leather travelling bag. William was born in 1883 and was the son of Betsy and John Bell, blacksmith. Betsy was the daughter of William and Ann Calvert (grocers) who moved to Sherburn when she was 9. Betsy's brother John Calvert emigrated to British Columbia and her brother William Calvert to Kansas City. Her sister Rachel married Elmer Bogg, a grocer in Sherburn for 30 years and a well known artist, who produced and sold excellent pictures. At least three of his oil paintings are still in Sherburn. Rachel died aged 64 in 1899 and Elmer aged 72 in 1913 two years after he retired to Scarborough.

Harry Bulmer Marston succeeded William Bell in 1912 but after a year went to York Training College. Miss Lillie Raine came from York in 1913 and Kathleen Sawkill, the head master's 18 year-old daughter, was appointed student teacher at the end of 1913. After two months, Kathleen became ill and left a few weeks before her father retired. When she recovered she was employed as a clerk at Weaverthorpe Station until her marriage on 14 June 1917 to 2nd Lieut Arthur Cuthbert Dunn (Military George Cross). George Harrison signalman, presented her with a silver mounted umbrella on behalf of railway staff and employees at William Page's corn warehouse. John Bogg, Page's manager and Henry Penrose stationmaster, praised Kathleen's *"happy relationship with the staff"*. By this time the Sawkills were living in *"Ivy Cottage"*, the detached house situated at the north-east corner of the school. Arthur and Kathleen had two daughters Kathleen Frances (b 1918) and Janette (b 1922).

Shortly after Kathleen's wedding, John Bogg retired after 40 years as Page's manager. He'd been on the parish council since its formation, was a Wesleyan local preacher and he and his wife Mary Amelia had four children Edward, William, Florence and Catherine. Catherine was a Sunday School teacher and chapel organist and when she married George Skelton of Wold Newton in April 1918, she was presented with a music stool. She wore a pretty cream dress and hat and her bridesmaid was Miss R Milner. After a honeymoon in Middlesborough the couple went to live at Wold Newton. (see appendix 5 for wartime weddings). Mary Amelia Bogg 67 died in 1915 and John Bogg 77 in 1923.

* * * * * * *

The 1893 Education Code required all headmasters to keep a log book and *"enter therein such events as the introduction of new books, apparatus, courses of instruction, plan of lessons, visits of managers, absence, illness or failure of duty by any of the school staff, or any special circumstances affecting the school, that may deserve to be recorded"*. Anthony Sawkill made his first entry on Monday 1 March 1897. Attendance was 128 and although Article 19 of the Board of Education Code called for numbers at Sherburn not to exceed 151, they often reached 169. Scholars were moved from the Infants Class through Standards I, II, III, IV, V, VI, VII, before leaving at 14. In February 1904 out of 133 children, 12 were aged 3-5, 103 (5-12), 10 (12-13), and 8 (13-14).

The vicar checked the registers every Friday and during the quarter ending November 1889, one third of pupils had been absent daily not just through sickness but because of *"parental neglect"*. To address this, managers constantly urged parents to send their children to school and introduced a classification system: *Excellent* for full attendance, *Very Good* not more than 5% absence, *Good* not more than 10%. Despite this, average attendance between April 1890 and April 1893 was 66%. (see Appendix 6). The reason for poor attendance in 1891 was the 'flu epidemic which caused the death of Anthony Sawkill's first wife. That year there were 15 deaths in Sherburn: Richard Pincher 36; Elizabeth Pickering 69 widow of William; Matthew Johnson 80; Flora Owston infant; Mary Owston 74 wife of Joseph; Nora Dobson 14 months; George Clarkson 91; Annie Hugill 30; Charles Dawson 61; Thomas Blythe 74; Ann Levitt 72 wife of William; Thomas Bean 68 and David Shepherd infant. Thomas Quinn 60 (stationmaster) and his wife Hannah 59 died within weeks of each other.

Bad weather frequently affected attendance and on 12 February 1899 half the children were absent. Heavy snow on the Wolds buried 25 of John Foster's sheep and 15 of Valentine Prodham's. Carriers from Sherburn and other villages returning from Scarborough market couldn't reach their destination and had to spend the night wherever they could. Roads were blocked, telegraph poles and wires were strewn across roads and gangs of men were engaged clearing them. That was the only time, Jonathan Milner postman for 37 years between Sherburn and West Lutton, could not make the journey. For the first 17 of those years, he was said to walk 132 miles per week and for the last 20 years he drove a mail horse and cart. Jonathan and his wife Fanny had eight children: Frances Mary, Thomas Wilfred, Robert Edwin, Lawrence Marshall, William, Olive May, Stanley and Ivy.

An Attendance Officer or *"Kiddy-Catcher"* visited school regularly and noted names of absentees and if necessary visited parents. Medical certificates were carefully logged, eg *"William and Herbert Stones suffering from Influenza are not in a fit state to attend school. O Norris 31 March 1897"*, and *"This is to certify that Alice Dunn, residing at Sherburn, is suffering from Eruption of Ear and is unable to attend School. O Norris, Feb 9 1899"*. On Friday 10 August 1900 the head master wrote *"Attendance poor owing perhaps to the weather, but a number of children are kept away two or three times a week on frivolous excuses, e.g. nursing, going for coal, fetching sticks etc".*

There were other reasons for absence. In March 1897 Robert Levitt's children, James, John, Lawrence and Alfred, attended the funeral of their sister Violet aged 14. The Levitts lived in Mill Field Cottages near a Windmill where local farmers brought their corn to grind into flour. Robert was an engine driver at the Brewery and he and his wife Jane (nee Pinkney) had three older children Frederick, William and Edward. On 7 April 1897, twenty children played truant to go to a sale at Manor Farm where Charlotte Clarkson was selling up following the death from pneumonia of her husband George 42. Before moving to the farm, George and Charlotte were proprietors of the East Riding Hotel for 10 years. They moved to the farm when George's grandfather also George died aged 91 after living at Manor Farm for half a century. The Clarkson name first appeared in Sherburn parish records in 1787 and in 1902 when Mary widow of Samuel Clarkson died, the number of her children, grandchildren and great-grandchildren who attended her funeral was said to be over 100.

On Tuesday afternoon 31 January 1899, 25 children played truant to see the wedding of Frederick Hick (tailor) and Mary Jackson. Later in the year when school manager William A Binning's only daughter Mary Edith married Henry Percy Brown of Scarborough, the head master closed the school. The Binnings lived at Hilda House Farm opposite the school and on the morning of Wednesday 18 October 1899, the village was said to be *"quite enfete"* as the bride and her father set off by carriage for St Hilda's Church. She wore a white moiré silk dress, trimmed with chiffon and a white picture hat and her bridesmaids Maude Pruett and Frances Winter, wore cream cashmere dresses and black velvet hats and they all carried shower bouquets. The bride gave her bridegroom a pair of gold cuff links and he gave her an engraved gold bracelet. He gave each bridesmaid a gold brooch set with pearls. After a reception at the bride's home, they caught the 1.30 pm Express train for London, the bride wearing a brown beaver cloth dress and *"heliotrope velvet toque"* (necklace with small cluster of flowers). As the train entered and left the station, a dozen fog-signals exploded and in the evening, everyone was invited to celebrate with sports. The bride had three brothers John, Alfred and Lawrence Binning.

Ganton Golf Course was another cause for truancy. On 15 June 1903, Mr Sawkill wrote *"two or three boys who are not legally qualified are, I am told, at Ganton Golf Links, seeking employment as 'caddies' for the Yorkshire Clubs Tournament"* and on 5 August 1907, John Buttery, William Currey and Lawrence Milner went to the Links instead of school. Ganton Golf Club was founded in 1891 with Sir Charles Legard as president and the annual subscription was two guineas (£2.10p) for gentlemen and one guinea (£1.05p) for ladies. In 1899 golf professional Willie Park junior beat Harry Vardon on the course for a stake of £200. A year later Harry became the first Englishman to win the US Open Championship, a feat won later at Ganton in 1920 by Ted Wray and in 1970 by Tony Jacklin. Between 1913-39, HRH Prince Arthur of Connaught played many times on the course.

On Friday 25 November 1904, the headmaster records *"attendance for the past week is 83% owing to the snow and coughs and colds"*. On that same evening, Thomas Atkinson 49 gamekeeper, was shot by three poachers in a snow covered field belonging to George Lawson, north of the church. Tom died instantly and his body was taken home on a gate through the frosty moonlight to his wife Betsy (nee Posthill). Two other gamekeepers were seriously injured and taken by horse and cart to the Pigeon Pie to recover. The verdict was manslaughter because lack of evidence failed to prove who fired the fatal shot.

One afternoon in July 1911, several pupils played truant to go and see an aeroplane which had landed in a field a mile and a half away and one wintry Monday morning, a quarter of the children went to a wood 2 miles away to collect firewood being given away by Capt the Hon J Dawnay. At noon on Friday 20 March 1914, when Lord Middleton's pack of fox hounds passed through the village, several boys followed and missed afternoon lessons but were later *"severely cautioned"*. On Thursday 6 August 1914, two days after Britain declared war on Germany, several children were absent when volunteers for the Waggoners Reserve left the village by an early morning train.

When pupils arrived late whatever their excuse, they were kept after school for twice as long. Between June 1908 and 1912 there were several latecomers. Ernest Sleightholme was late one summer afternoon and said he'd been to West Heslerton on an errand for his father; Reginald Metcalfe and Charles Pickard arrived in the middle of an afternoon and said they'd *"been to the station for coal"*; Clarice Beecroft and Frances Scurr arrived late one Monday morning and said they'd been to Scarborough for the weekend, Francis Atkinson was brought to school by his mother one afternoon at 3 o'clock and said he'd been gathering chestnuts in Ganton woods and one morning when George Henderson turned up at 10.15, he said he'd been helping his uncle drive a herd of beasts on foot to Gristhorpe.

School closed for a week at Easter, 2 weeks in June for corn weeding, 4 weeks in Aug/Sept for harvest and 2 weeks at Christmas. Afternoon closures included Shrove Tuesday, the Primitive Methodist Sunday School Anniversary Tea in May, the Wesleyan Sabbath School Anniversary Tea in June and the Church Sunday School picnic in July. Day closures included the annual June Club Feast, the joint Wesleyan & Primitive Methodist Sunday School outing to Scarborough in July, the Hirings Fair in November and Polling Day.

Children were allowed to leave early when Scott's or Fossetts Circus came to the village and for special events such as the visit to Scarborough of the *"Buffalo Bill"* Exhibition by Colonel William Cody. Bill was said to have killed 4820 buffalo in 18 months to provide meat for the builders of the Kansas City railroad and after its completion until his death in 1917, he toured the USA and Europe with his colourful exhibition.

On special occasions the children were given extra holidays. The June 1897 corn weeding holiday was extended to include Queen Victoria's Jubilee celebrations and school closed on Monday afternoon 21 May 1900, to celebrate the *'Relief of Mafeking'* a victorious event in the 1899-1902 Boer War when British and Canadian forces broke a seven month siege on the Rhodesian town of Mafeking. On that day crowds surged through London streets, singing, dancing, waving flags and setting off coloured flares and there was rejoicing throughout the land. On 24 May 1900 the children were given the afternoon off to celebrate Queen Victoria's 81st birthday and when she died less than a year later, the headmaster logged: *"Her Majesty Queen Victoria died Jan 22nd 1901 aged 81 years and 243 days"*. He didn't close school but large congregations attended memorial services the following Sunday in Church and Chapel. When Edward VII was crowned during the 1902 harvest holidays, everyone enjoyed a free tea followed by sports. Excess funds were donated to the church's *"Poor Fund"* enabling 5/- (25p) each to be given to *"twenty aged poor and widows"*. The children had the afternoon off on Wednesday 19 August 1903, while their teachers went on a picnic organised by the Sherburn & District Lawn Tennis, Bowling and Hockey Clubs. These Clubs were formed in 1903 by Anthony Sawkill, Dr Oliver Norris, Richard and Charles Duggleby, John Hick, William Bell, John Harland, Robert Hodgson, Basil Halliday and Ainsworth Heath. School closed on 21 May 1910 for the funeral of King Edward VII and the corn weeding holiday was extended to include the Coronation of George V on 22 June 1911.

Local farmers often employed children as young as 8 at busy times and attendance dropped at the end of harvest when children went gleaning ears of corn left by the reapers and in October many went potato picking. Before being granted exemption for part-time work, children had to appear before HMI with their birth certificates and in March 1907, applicants included: Harry Johnston, Arthur C Pinkney, George Bassett, Maggie Henderson, William Staveley, Evelyn Bradford, Sidney Metcalfe, Edwin Milner and Fred Atkinson.

At the beginning of each year, the head master sent HMI his *"Schemes of Instruction"* and as the years passed these became more and more detailed, taking up four pages of his log book. Arithmetic included difficult sounding exercises like *"vulgar, complex and decimal fractions"* and *"long and short division of money"*. In 1910, clay modelling was introduced as *'Hand and*

Eye' training for boys whilst the girls started needlework and in 1913, older girls began travelling by train to Norton Council School for cookery and laundry classes.

The curriculum included nature study walks and on 26 July 1901 the headmaster wrote: *"Field excursion with Stds IV to VII boys this afternoon, inspecting grasses, flowers, trees, growing crops, bees, frogs, moles &c.,"* and in February 1904 *"Out-door work in Mr Prodham's field, learning how, with chain &c., to set out plots of land one acre, half acre and quarter in different dimensions"*; in May 1906 *"examination of half a dozen wild flowers, the comparison of wheat and barley as seen in the blade and roots, three nests (blackbird, linnet and hedge sparrow, 2 with eggs) and the measurement of a small plot of vegetables on George Lawson's farm"*. February 1912: *"Specimens of snails, plants &c gathered. An ant hill partly opened to examine winter condition"*. January 1913: *"Boys brought back to school the skeleton of a rabbit's head, and a bird's egg, an unusual time of year for the last-named"*.

On 5 May 1908 teachers William C Bell and Lilian Botterill and two 14-year old pupils Stanley and William Currey, went with Sherburn Choral Society to compete against 14 other choirs in the York singing competitions. Sherburn won and came second in the Challenge Cup for Combined Choirs (Sherburn & Wykeham). Anthony and Clara Sawkill formed the Society in 1900 with 30 members and he was conductor and she was pianist.

* * * * * * *

At the end of each school year HMI examined teaching standards and pupil progress and in 1897, reported: *"Mr Sawkill again deserves much credit for a good year's work done with but poor assistance"* and a year later *"A distinct improvement is observed"*. Between 1899 and 1903, although epidemic illness and staff difficulties hindered progress, satisfactory standards were maintained. In 1904, HMI reported: *"The school is going on satisfactorily being carefully and intelligently conducted by Mr Sawkill. The children are well behaved but the tendency to talk is too noticeable. The removal of the gallery* and a supply of new desks have made the classroom better adapted for teaching. The rooms are neat and the surroundings cheerful. A school clock is required. The Infants' class is diligently taught and the little children are making promising progress"*. A new clock from B Maw, jeweller, Beverley was hung by the village joiner William Wilkinson Owston. William died three years later aged 54 after being a widower since his wife Sarah died in 1889. (*presumably built-in rows of stepped seats as in Victorian chapels).

Kindergarten desks and dual desks were purchased from Illingworth, Ingham & Co and school materials, books, and slates from Denhams of Scarborough, E J Arnold & Sons, Leeds, A Brown & Sons and Trevor & England, Hull. In 1908 the school's first library was set up with 42 books and

Sir Tatton Sykes donated a teacher's bible and the vicar provided 80 pupils' bibles. Coal for the classroom fires was carted two tons at a time from the Railway Station by either Robert Hodgson, proprietor of the East Riding Hotel or Robert Pickering, a signalman. Paraffin lamps suspended from the ceiling provided lighting but sometimes in mid-winter, lessons had to be substituted with singing *"owing to the darkness"*.

The 1903 Education Bill called for a Body of Managers to have four foundation managers, a Parish Councillor and a County Councillor. Foundation managers were Rev Richard Ellis, Dr Oliver Norris, Robert Brown and John F Lawson, the Parish Councillor was Smith Thos Johnson (shepherd) and the County Councillor Richard Duggleby (farmer). Other managers included, James P Kirk, owner of Sherburn Brewery, Thomas Winter, John Prodham and William A Binning. They met only 15 times between 1903 and 1914 to appoint staff, discuss salaries, purchases, repairs, inspect accounts, consider HMI's reports and examine the headmaster's log book. In 1906, the school was in debt and so the large room was let for dances and evening classes for 10/- (50p) for villagers and £1 to outsiders. Dancing classes earned 2s..6d (12.5p) from 7 to 9 pm and 5/- (25p) if time was exceeded. William Bell gave evening classes in Pittman's Shorthand and in 1909, Harry Johnston gained the Theory Certificate.

The head master played the organ at every funeral and left school in the care of his assistants. He closed school for the funeral in November 1897 of school manager John Prodham a Wolds farmer, and in May 1900 for the funeral of his father-in-law Joseph Marston. Joseph was postmaster and registrar of births and deaths for 30 years, assistant parish overseer for 40 years and a Wesleyan local preacher for 50 years. His widow Maria died aged 87 in 1917 after living at the post office for 60 years. Their children were: Elizabeth Ann, Thomas James, Charles Henry, Frederick William, Clara Ellen and Albert Baker.

On Monday afternoon 27 January 1902, Anthony wrote in his log book: *"a dozen children are absent, believed to be at the funeral of Margaret Norris."* Margaret was Dr Norris's second wife who died in childbirth aged 31. On the baby's first birthday at 2.30 pm, all the school children led by Sherburn Excelsior Brass Band, marched from the doctor's house *"Roseville"* on High Street to school where the headmaster gave the child a silver mug inscribed *"Presented to Oliver E W Norris by the children of Sherburn, Jan 13th 1903"*. The children marched back to the Pigeon Pie for tea served by Charles Laycock and his daughter Isabelle Ringrose and were each given an orange, some sweets and nuts before going back to school to watch a fireworks display organised by William Brown (shoemaker), Thomas Currey (railway carrier) and Richardson Lythe (groom/coachman). Afterwards the children went into school to sing and play games until 8.30 pm when dancing began for adults and continued '*with zest*' until 10.15 pm and ended with hearty cheers for *"little Oliver"* and *"God save the King"*. Three months later, Dr Norris's was forced to stop practising because of poor health and his successor was Dr Rowland Eajon Morriarty LRCP, LRCS, Edin., eldest son of the Revd T A Moriarty, County Cork. Dr Norris's first wife Jemima Ellen (nee Lamplough) died from pneumonia in September 1900 only 18 months after their marriage at Bridlington Priory Church. Jemima was the niece of John Lamplough farmer of Elm Tree Farm (now Elm Grove). White marble tablets are set in the wall of the north aisle of St Hilda's Church in memory of both Dr Norris's wives.

School closed for the funeral of school manager Robert Brown who died on 22 July 1904. Robert married Ann (nee Clarkson) in 1858, and they had seven daughters and three sons. In his early life Robert was a miller at Thomas Smith's Sherburn Mills, then at 28, he went to James Kirk's Brewery where he was manager for 34 years and was said to *"fill the post with remarkable zeal, straight-forwardness, tact and ability, his geniality, kindness of heart and unassuming manner having secured him a wide circle of friends"*. He attended church regularly, was a founder member of the parish council; a trustee of the Ancient Order of Foresters, parish overseer, member of the Sherburn District Conservative Association, member of the Sherburn Agricultural Club and served on the jury for the Manor of Sherburn for 30 years. Brewery employees were bearers and many mourners had to stand in the churchyard.

The old vicar died on Sunday 5 February 1905 and the headmaster wrote: *"Rev Richard Ellis, vicar of the parish, and for 31 years school manger and correspondent, died at 6.20 this (Sunday) morning in the 88th year of his age, born May 24th 1817"*. Richard was the youngest of five sons of the Rev John Ellis, who was vicar of Yedingham for half a century. Two of Richard's brothers were vicars, John at Ebberston and James at Pocklington. Richard was ordained in 1844 and four years later married Ann, second daughter of John Shores of Hull. In 1857 he became curate at Howden and master of the Grammar School there. In 1867, he returned to his native parish of Yedingham then moved to Sherburn in 1873. Throughout his ministry, Richard conducted 250 marriages, 758 baptisms and 533 burials. His last funeral was that of infant Cissy Kellington on 10 October 1904 and his last two baptisms were those of Lizzie daughter of George and Annie Henderson and Francis William son of Frederick and Sonya Atkinson, on 5 November 1904. Only five weeks after the old vicar died and when his little boy was only 3, the 44 year-old doctor died from heart failure early one Friday morning in March 1905. Dr Norris, son of John Oliver Norris of Wakefield, bought the Sherburn practice from Dr A William Deeley in 1888. He was a Parish Councillor and held office in most village organisations. In May 1906, Richard Ellis's widow Ann died aged 82 at Boythorpe in the home of her niece and nephew Mr and Mrs William Gypson and her remains were brought back for burial.

The deaths of the vicar and doctor, long-time friends of Anthony Sawkill, now in his fifties, took their toll on his health and despite being forbidden by Dr Moriarty to teach, he insisted on visiting school several times daily until he was able to return full-time. By April 1905, he was well enough to escort Sherburn's new vicar the Rev James Whittam round the school. James had been Rector of Cumberworth in the West Riding and vicar of Rosedale and stayed in Sherburn until 1915 when he was forced to leave following Court bankruptcy.

School closed in October 1911 for the funeral of school manager John Foster 65. He and his wife Sarah (nee Spink) had two children William and Mary Ella and lived on one of Sherburn's largest farms for 40 years and John who was said to be *"of a genial, unobtrusive and kindly disposition"*, had been church warden, parish overseer, parish councillor and had served on the Manorial Court jury. Sarah died aged 64 in 1915.

* * * * * * *

After 1897 when Anthony started using a log book, school had several closures because of illness. The first was for three weeks in January 1898 when attendance dropped by 50% because of *"epidemic illness"* and school was fumigated. That year, seven children died: Elsie Annie Staveley (15 months), Joseph Bell Knox (15 months), Lillian Elsie Beecroft (11 months), Lillian Eliza Milner (8 months), Norman Holborn (2 years), Robert Henry Buttery (5 months) and Dora Currey (11 years). The next closure was for six weeks at Christmas 1899 because of measles. Epidemic illness was rife all over the country and in London 50 people a day were dying, mostly from influenza, hospitals had trouble coping and grave diggers were working night and day. The next closure was for three months in 1902 not long after the Hood family moved to the village. Their four children were refused admission because they'd come from Weaverthorpe where the school had closed because of scarlet fever, nevertheless the disease spread and during Sherburn's closure from June to September, five children died, Robert Dawson and Miriam Martha Oates both aged 7, Richard Hood 6, Robert Stubbs 3 and William Baxter Pearson 2.

In October 1903, another outbreak of scarlet fever began with Susan and Sarah Cousins, Edgar Brown, Harry Dawson, Mary Hugill and four Atkinson children, and although, school did not close, steps were taken to try to prevent disease. New ventilation grates were fitted in school by Robert Ringrose for 10s..6d, and a course of free lectures on home nursing was organised by the headmaster's wife Clara Sawkill helped by Mrs Richard (Hannah) Duggleby, Mrs Thomas Speck, Mrs George (Ellen) Lawson, Mrs John (Betsy) Bell and Miss Mary Foster. Forty mothers attended the first lecture *"The Sick Room"* when advice was given on cleaning, warming, lighting, keeping the sick room fresh and airy and a demonstration on changing sheets with the patient in bed. The second *"Observation and Care of the Sick"* was attended by fifty mothers and dealt with *"shivering fits, sleeping position, pain, the skin, night sweats, sickness, coughs and expectoration, temperature, pulse, breathing, washing the patient, preventing bed sores, air and water beds"*. The third lecture *"Food"*, had an even larger audience and gave advice on *'when and why solid food should not be given, feeding helpless and unconscious patients; nourishing foods, milk, eggs, beef tea, stimulants, tea, coffee, cocoa, invalid's drink; diet in dysentery, diarrhoea, constipation, consumption, typhoid fever; how to treat convalescents'*, and ended with advice on keeping food charts. Another lecture *"Children"* gave hints on *"nursing, food and medicine, cleanliness, habits, what to do in cases of hip disease, rickets, whooping cough, croup, mumps, ringworm, constipation, ear-ache and infantile diseases: Opthalaria, diarrhoea, convulsions, thrush etc., errors of feeding, infantile mortality, food for infants, milk boiled, sterilised etc., artificial food, feeding bottles and soothing syrups"*.

There was a hospital in Scarborough in those days but few village people, if any would be admitted. The hospital was called *"Friars Entry"* and opened in July 1893. Prior to that there was a Hospital and Dispensary on Vernon Road, set up in 1851 to provide *"medicine and medical and surgical treatment for the sick poor of Scarborough and district"*. The president was John Dale and he arranged for *"Friars Entry"* to be built on the site of the former Wesleyan Day School on land he'd purchased for £1,000. The architects were John Hall and Frank Tugwell trading as *"Medico"* and the builder was John Barry of Westbrook, Trafalgar Street West, who designed and built a 3-storey hospital. On the ground floor there was a waiting room, outpatients, consulting rooms, kitchens, laundry and mortuary, on the first floor there were the women's and children's medical and surgical wards and on the second floor, the men's wards and an operating theatre. A hand-operated pulley lift conveyed patients to the wards, heating and ventilation were *"totally modern"* and lighting was by gas until in 1897, electricity was installed and paid for by the Freemasons.

School closed for two weeks in 1904 when mumps started with the Speck family who had just moved into Pasture House. Five of their children were off school on Monday 25 January 1904 to attend the funeral of their grandfather Mr Hardy and two days later Mrs Speck sent a note to say one of her children had mumps. She was advised to keep them at home but by Friday Cora Dobson, Thomas Hood, May Clarke, Mary Hugill, Arthur Shacklesford, Mabel Hodgson, Charles Levitt, Robert Clarkson and soon one-third of the pupils were absent as well as Miss Alice Johnson teacher. Four children died in the village: Arthur Scurr 6, John Albert Postill 7 days, Marjorie Dobson (infant) and Arthur Dawson Basset 3 months.

In order to improve matters, Dr Wilson, County Medical Officer, wrote to the Sherburn Rural District Council complaining about unhealthy housing conditions. Out of 141 homes, 33 had only two rooms and in some, up to nine people were using the only bedroom and in others, adult male lodgers were taken in. When grown-up sons and daughters returned home from the farms for the Martinmus (Nov) holiday, they had to share the already fully occupied rooms. Richard Duggleby chairman, said the same conditions existed in every village and so Dr Wilson's letter was filed for future reference. There was another long closure from 7 July to 29 August 1904. The children of Fanny and Tom Naylor (drayman) caught measles, the Speck children caught whooping cough and within a few days there were 30 more cases and closure was incorporated with the harvest holidays. During the closure Dr Moriarty married Miss Florence Daft at Christ Church, Harrogate. Florence, daughter of William Daft of Leeds, was given away by her uncle Sir William Alfred Gelder and wore a gown of ivory satin trimmed with Honiton lace.

The School's first Medical Inspection was in 1909 and a parent or relative was invited. Several days beforehand, the managers ordered two children aged 8 and 12 from the same family to be sent home and the father was told to have them *"bathed and made quite clean and tidy"*. Those same children whose mother died aged 37 in 1903, were eventually sent to the Buxton Industrial Home, Norfolk, following their father's prosecution by the National Society for the Prevention of Cruelty to Children. The next closure was in Nov/Dec 1910 for 7 weeks because of whooping cough. The first cases were Edith Dawson, Winifred Pinkney, Gladys Horsley, Albert and Doris Clarke, Ann Foxton, Sidney Scurr, Iris Dobson, Margaret Ware, Ivy Milner, Arthur Cousins, Florence Bean, Olive Posthill and Maud Monkman and soon a third were off and Miss Lilian Botterill. When school re-opened on 2 January 1911, there were 17 absentees, some with whooping cough and others because of stormy weather. Teacher William Bell was sick and John Wm Crossley (Bridlington) came on supply. Four children died, Lois L Pinkney and Annie Ward both aged 7, Ronald Bean 2 and Lena Bassett 16 days.

Just before school broke up for the 1911 Easter holidays, Albert Sleightholme, Fred Woodall and Frances and Herbert Atkinson caught measles and the disease spread rapidly. When school opened on 24 April, all 157 pupils were present but the headmaster recorded *"Ada Henderson still has a rash on her arms and Charles Calam has a broken out face"* and he sent them home immediately! That Autumn, Gladys and Francis Hunter from the Railway Station were off for six weeks suffering from diphtheria.

At their monthly meeting at Scarborough in April 1914, the Sherburn RDC were still discussing poor housing. Dr Hollings of Sherburn reported *"Towards the end of the year, I and the county medical officer of health, made a tour of inspection in your district. In many cases we found grossly insanitary conditions and over-crowding of a serious nature, which conditions if not remedied are bound to affect adversely the health of your district. Several landlords have agreed to make the necessary alterations. The emptying of ash pits and privies is done in a very slipshod manner and the conditions of many is a distinct menace to public health. I would urge the need for some system of scavenging being inaugurated. There is an abundance of good water to be obtained from the Wolds. The conditions of dairies and cow sheds are fairly satisfactory but far from ideal. I would ask you to cultivate a broad-minded and altruistic spirit with regard to sanitation if you would retain the better class of labourers in your village. The knell of the old conditions of cottage life in rural districts has been sounded and it is your duty by unselfish and un-wearied effort to so improve these conditions that the worth of the agricultural labourer as a national asset, shall be increased immeasurably. By a wise use of the power entrusted to you we shall breed year by year a stronger and more vigorous race".*

Accidents caused long absences. In 1899 Dudley Reynolds the station master's son broke his arm whilst climbing a high fence, in 1905 Ernest Heath injured his hand and in 1906 Fred King from the Railway Station injured his leg whilst climbing into a cart to go to school. Fred's father Henry was a railway platelayer and he and his wife Hannah had at least seven children: Edward, Richard, Sarah, David, Eleanor, Mary and Fred. In 1906 Robert Clarkson dislocated his collar bone and Bertha Brown injured her fingers on the Girls' entrance door. In 1907, Eric Speck fell of his donkey and broke his arm; Alfred Sleightholme burned his face with fireworks, Nellie Bassett was knocked down and injured by a horse in the dark and William Hart injured a finger in the school door. In January 1910, Annie Ward 6, was playing in the snow and when she went inside the melting snow on her boot caused her to slip and she broke her leg, Gwendolyn Scurr was pushed off a form end and cut her tongue on her teeth and the wound bled so badly she was sent home. On 6 November 1913 George Belt was severely burned by fireworks. In February 1914 several children escaped injury as they were leaving school at dinner time. Three horses belonging to Burtons of Bogthorpe were pulling a wagon from Weaverthorpe Station and as they entered the village the horses were startled and began to gallop and although the driver hung on as long as he could, he was unable to stop them running into a school wall. The first horse fell and the cart's gearing broke and set the animal free and the other two horses set off with the cart and galloped for a mile before stopping. The driver escaped injury and one of the horses was badly cut.

Fire was a frequent hazard in those days when there were coal fires in every home and in January 1909 Agnes Annie Buttery 2, child of Thomas Henry Buttery of Low Mill, was burned whilst in the care of a neighbour Mrs Ann Elizabeth Barker. Agnes's parents had gone to the funeral of Mrs Buttery's mother at Wykeham and when Mrs Barker left the child and her own little boy, to bring a pail of water from the village pump, she returned to find the little girl in flames. She and a neighbour put out the flames and dressed the burns, but the child died from shock. The Coroner warned that after the 1909 Children's Act, the provision of fireguards in every home would be compulsory. In December 1913, Ernest Dawson aged four, son of Charles Dawson was burned one evening when he was playing with his six year old brother Sidney on the hearth rug. Their mother went upstairs and when she heard the children screaming, rushed down and found the youngest on fire and put out the flames with her apron. Sidney had lit a candle at the fire and when he took it to the window where his brother Ernest was pulling up the blind, the younger boy's night dress caught fire and he died from severe burns and shock.

Children were cautioned regularly about throwing stones and using catapults and in 1898 after an EREA circular warned them to *"desist from the dangerous practice"*, Sergeant Herbert Pottage gave more warnings. Herbert and his wife Annie Elizabeth had three daughters at school Flora, Lillian and Elsie May. In 1904, a school window was broken during playtime by a stone and nine boys were found with catapults, but all denied using them. Eventually, Thomas Hood owned up and was punished with three strokes of the cane on his hands and the other catapults were confiscated. In 1905 Albert Baker had a tooth knocked out during the *"noontide interval"* by a shot from a catapult believed to have been fired by Edward Rawding 18, a farm hand at home for Martinmas. Edward was the son of widow Mary whose other children were Ruth, William, Edith and Louisa and they lived in a two-roomed cottage in St Hilda's Street. Their father William Rawding 42 died in 1892 leaving their mother to work as a charwoman to provide for her young family.

In August 1906 some five year olds were playing with matches and set a hay stack on fire belonging to Thomas P Crosier, coal dealer and carrier. Because it was dinner time several men came out of their cottages and stopped the fire with water from a nearby pump. In 1907, PC A W Beaumont called at school to ask who had set Whin bushes on fire in nearby fields. In May 1912 a large stack of hay was destroyed at Manor Farm by children playing with matches.

Mr Sawkill's first log book entry about bad behaviour was in 1897 when Edward Rawding and Francis Metcalfe were punished for fighting. A book recording *"Cases of Corporal Punishment"* opened in 1901, reveals that the headmaster hit the offender's body with a cane. The first entry was *"Frederick Brown for deception and showing an old map to conceal idleness - several strokes of cane on back not hands"*. Others included *"John Simpson - using pea shooter after several had been collected and destroyed – 2 strokes"* and the same boy *"smoking a cigarette in my sight in school yard – 2 strokes"*; *"Charles Swann – striking a girl over the head with reading book - a few strokes lower part of body"*; *"David Hugill, Sidney Metcalfe, George Buttery – obstructing Miss Hodgson when fastening the yard door at evening dismissal – one stroke each on the hand"*; *"Arthur Duggleby – running across schoolroom floor when coming in from the lobby – cane on back"; "Charles Levitt ° refusing to come to school. His mother requested me to punish him – 6 strokes on back"; "Fred Atkinson - sitting with legs upon desk to make his class mates laugh – 6 on back and hands"; Constance Bradford – turning round to talk to another class mate during reading – a few on back"; "Frank Calam and Alonzo Bell – going to the cupboard without permission during writing lesson – one stroke each on the hand"; "Fred Stones – humming a tune and so breaking silence of an arithmetic lesson – stroke on hand"; "Charles Swann – stealing out of school at 4 pm after being told to stay for being late – 2 each hand"; "George Dawson – refusal to come to school, throwing himself down in street and being carried to school – few light ones on body to frighten rather than hurt"; "Frank Calam – mimicking master's voice during a lesson so loudly as to cause a general titter – 8 smart strokes on shoulders and back"; "Lawrence Milner – writing a foul word on his slate – 3 on each hand"; "Robert Dawson – suddenly screaming out when all was quiet without any reason – 2 strokes on hand"; "John Dobson – leaving his place to go to next desk – 1 each hand"; "William Beecroft, John Metcalfe, Ernest Scurr, William Naylor – climbing and running along Prodham's garden wall this being forbidden by me – 1 each boy on the hand"; and in July 1908 "Reginald and James Metcalfe, Henry and Walter Bradford and Alfred Sleightholme – stopping in Mr H Prodham's field bathing until 1.45 pm – one stroke each on hand".*

In 1908, a 9-year-old boy was charged in Court with stealing a jar of jam and 3 lbs of bacon worth 2s.6d (12.5p) from Henry Youngman's grocery cart. PC Beaumont saw the boy standing not far from the cart and when the grocer went into the East Riding pub, the boy ran and took an item off the cart, ran to the other side and standing on the wheel took something else. When the policeman approached him, the boy handed over the bacon and jam. The boy's father, a widower, said he always left his children plenty to eat. The Rev James Whittam said the father was a hard-working man and offered to keep an eye on the boy. The Court advised the boy's father to engage a female to look after his children, but several months later his 13-year-old daughter was summoned for causing 3/- (15p) worth of damage to school manager Henry Prodham's fence. The family had been warned after being caught three times pulling firewood from the hedgerows and leaving holes for cattle to escape. Henry and Ada Prodham moved into St Hilda's Farm in 1900 after William A Binning retired and went to live at 11 Londesborough Road, Falsgrave. When their son Herbert Prodham was born in 1901 they had 6 employees lodging at the farm: Robert Sanderson 18 (waggoner, Ganton), Bert Perkin 16 (teamster, Rillington), William Fell 15 (teamster, Scarborough), James Reid 14 (teamster, Scalby), William Heseltine 24 (shepherd, Welham), Gertrude Barker 17 (maid, Staxton).

* * * * * * *

On Monday 22 March 1909, the Rev James Whittam invited the older children to be present at the *"cutting of the first sod"* for the proposed new Church Institute (now the village hall) for use as a place of worship whilst St Hilda's was being restored. Stanley Currey and Mabel Hodgson both 15, Sunday School pupils, thanked Viscount Downe and Captain the Hon J Dawnay on behalf of everyone, for providing the building. The official opening was on Sunday 6 July 1909 at 10.30 am followed by choral Holy Communion, at 2.30 pm there was a children's service and at 6.30 pm a service of Evensong. After the church re-opened, the institute was used as a reading room for men and boys, where *"innocent games could be played and a clean manly atmosphere preserved"*.

The vicar's wife Sophia Whittam 62 died four months later on 1 November 1909 All Saints' Day. The Whittams had lived at the Vicarage four years. Sophia was the daughter of Major James Douglas and Mrs Jessey de Wend of Underbank Hall, Penistone and among the robed clergymen who headed the funeral procession was her brother-in-law Rev G Lewis of Burnham. There were many mourners and eleven bearers: John F Lawson and Anthony Sawkill (wardens), Robert Hodgson, Albert B Marston, Henry Prodham, Chas H Woodall and Geo Lawson (sidesmen), Arthur Heath and John Gillery (choristers), Joseph Postill and James C Pinkney.

Two years later in April 1911 at Christ Church, Westminster, James Whittam married Agnes Maud Rasdall the only daughter of William Rasdall, of Lincoln. The bride wore a white satin dress with train, a veil held by a wreath of orange blossom and a gold pendant and brooch given to her by her bridegroom. She carried a bouquet of roses and lilies of the valley. When the couple returned from honeymoon on the Isle of Wight, they were met at Weaverthorpe Station by a crowd of cheering villagers and flag-waving children. Gladys Mary Woodall 12 gave the bride a bouquet as she stepped onto the platform. The crowds followed the carriage to the Vicarage where cheering was renewed and the Brass Band played *"several lively airs"* on the lawn. A few days later the newly-weds provided an afternoon picnic and games for 200 children in Henry Prodham's field.

In 1911, the village streets were decorated with flags and bunting for the Coronation on 22 June of King George V. After a united service in the Church Institute led by the vicar and Wesleyan minister Rev James Sharp, all the children, led by Sherburn Boy Scouts, marched in procession through *'a triumphal arch'* into Prodhams' field for an afternoon of sports. After tea had been served to the children, the old folks and widows, Mrs Whittam gave each child a Coronation mug. Adult sports in the evening ended with a cricket match between Dr Hollings's (married) team and Mr W A Cundall's (singles) team, with easy victory for the singles. (see Appendix 7). After 3 hearty cheers, everyone sang the Doxology: *"Praise God from whom all blessing flow, praise*

Him all creatures here below, praise Him above ye heavenly host, praise Father, Son and Holy Ghost", then the National Anthem.

* * * * * * *

On Monday 15 April 1912, as staff and 161 pupils re-assembled after Easter, news was being received that in the early hours, the ocean liner Titanic had sunk after colliding with a gigantic iceberg and 1500 passengers and crew had drowned in the icy waters of the North Atlantic. The following Sunday, at a special Memorial Service, the vicar preached to a large congregation from Psalm 107, v 30 *"He bringeth them to the haven where they would be"* and Job 13, v 15 *"Though He slay me, yet will I trust in Him"*. A collection of £2..10s..10d was for bereaved families.

One Monday in July 1912, St Hilda's Church re-opened after three years of restoration work. The church was full to overflowing and The Archbishop of York preached from Haggai Ch 2 v 9: *"The latter glory of this house shall be greater than the former and in this place will I give peace"* and said Sir Tatton Sykes's act of faith proved he believed that whatever social and industrial changes might come to Yorkshire, the churches he had restored would remain. Sixteen members of the clergy from surrounding parishes were present and organist Mr A L Arnold, Mus. Bac., played selections from *"Tannhauser"* (Wagner) and *"Softly awakes my Heart"* (Samson). At a luncheon in School, Captain Dawnay praised the vicar's dedication and the Rev Whittam said he'd worked with *"great pleasure and intense delight and now wanted to labour for souls"*. After Anthony Sawkill toasted the architect W H Brierley (York), John Thompson of Thompson & Sons builders (Peterborough), paid tribute to his foremen Messrs Ball and Mills and thanked everyone for their kindness throughout their time in the village. Charles Brassleay of Sherburn was employed by Thompsons for 44 years and as well as working on St Hilda's restoration, helped with other churches restored by Sir Tatton. Charles died aged 74 in 1935 and his widow Alice Maud aged 90 in 1957. The new oak Lytch Gate roofed with Colley Weston slates, was dedicated in the evening by the Archbishop and there was a service each evening throughout the week.

As well as discovering the church to date back to 1150, the builders found that before a restoration programme in 1793, the church had a western tower, nave, chancel and north and south aisles, so the 1912 restoration was in fact putting the church back to its original design. The tower was re-built, new north and south aisles added and the 13thC windows were given delicate tracery identical to the originals and fitted with white cathedral glass. A south porch was added, the interior arch over the church door preserved and new supporting pillars installed and the roof was covered with cast lead. The 13thC windows in the tower were preserved, the Norman *'slit window'* kept intact and the ancient sun-dial was walled into the tower below a new clock supplied by Potts of Leeds. The tower was finished with an ornamental parapet of broken battlement, embellished with panels carrying Sir Tatton Sykes's coat of arms and the crests of St Hilda, the See of York, Lord Downe and the Rev James Whittam. Along the parapet in Latin were inscribed the words: *"How amiable are Thy tabernacles, O Lord of Hosts. My soul longeth, yea even fainteth for the Courts of the Lord. My heart and my flesh crieth out for the living God".* (Psalm 84). A flagstaff was fixed at the summit and eight hemispherical bells *"of pure tone"* installed by J W Benson of London weighing: 3 cwt 2 qrs 7 lbs (8th tenor bell); 2 cwt, 2 qrs, 7 lbs (7th); 2 cwt, 0 qr, 3 lbs (6th); 2 cwt (5th); 1 cwt, 2 qrs, 2lbs (4th); 1 cwt, 2 qrs, 10 lbs (3rd); 1 cwt, 0 qr, 8 lbs (2nd); 1 cwt 0 qr 3 lbs (1st treble). Ropes were arranged so the bells could be operated by one man on the first floor of the tower. The Norman arch under the tower and the three circular Norman pillars supporting the nave, were preserved. On the south side, three pillars and two respods of moulded design, with caps and bosses, and carved labels circling the arches, were restored. The Norman chancel arch remained intact and new support pillars built. New ceilings of beautifully figured English oak were fitted. The floor, except the vestry, was of Yorkshire flags and the solid oak pews, choir stalls, pulpit, and furnishings were fumed and waxed. The hundreds of artistic carvings by George W Milburn (York), made St Hilda's Church known far and wide as one of the most beautiful and interesting in the country. The organ was built by Peter Conacher & Co (Huddersfield) and Stanley Currey was the first to play on the new instrument. The lovely carved chancel screen and tower font was dedicated in 1914. The two Glastonbury Chairs had been bought in 1866 for £3..15s..0d each from W Greenwood, dealer in antique furniture, 24 Stonegate, York and paid for out of church funds with permission from George Clarkson and John Prodham, church wardens.

To commemorate the restoration, Sir Tatton Sykes donated the stone cross sited midway between the church and vicarage. At the dedication in 1913, the robed choir processed from the church singing *"When I survey the wondrous Cross"*. Under the canopy there is the carved figure of St Hilda Abbess of Whitby, and the scenes on the first of the eight panels of the octagonal base show St Aidan, St Hilda and St Wilfred. The other panels show St Hilda's baptism, St Aidan granting lands on the Wear, St Hilda instructing her companions in the monastic life, St Hilda with the ammonite on one side and the hart on the other as depicted on the Shield of Hartlepool where she was also Abbess, St Wilfred instructing St Hilda on the church's dispute about keeping Easter, Caedmon the first British poet reciting to St Hilda and finally St Hilda on her death bed giving last instructions to her nuns. Sir Tatton Sykes paid £30,000 for work on the church and stone cross and St Hilda's was the last church he restored before he died a year later aged 87.

* * * * * * *

In 1906 HMI reported: *"This school continues to do satisfactory work, the drill of the upper group deserving praise. Arithmetic needs to be better arranged and in the lower groups oral work should be more intelligent. Geography in the junior section would benefit by broader treatment. Needlework is steadily improving. Teaching of the Infants is earnest and on broader lines. Reading in the first class is creditably taught and speaking out is a noticeable feature, though indiscriminate answering should be checked and the slower children given time for thought. Altogether much useful preparatory work has been done".*

In 1910, concern was expressed about over-crowding and the harvest holidays were extended to enable workmen to remove the gallery from the western classroom (Infants) and the occupants of the other two rooms were changed around, the Upper Group (Stds V, VI and VII) into northern classroom and Group II (Stds III & IV) and Group III (Stds I and II) into the large room. Three iron fire guards were purchased and the playgrounds levelled with 40 tons of sand and gravel carted from Lord Downe's Wykeham Estates.

When William Bell left in 1912, standards began to fall until the only item worthy of praise was the singing. There was gross over-crowding with attendance far exceeding the recommended 151 and the head master had only three assistants, Lilian Botterill, Lillie Raine and Janet Macintosh. Anthony Sawkill's daughter Kathleen was appointed pupil teacher in December 1913 but had to leave after two months through illness. Not long afterwards, Anthony Sawkill resigned and on his last day Friday 14 August 1914, the vicar presented him with a dressing case for his 41 years of service. Ten days later Britain declared war on Germany,

---

Infants cc 1917. Bertha Potter teacher (back left) and Elsie Beecroft monitress from 1916-1920 *(back right);* 1 Mary Scurr (admitted 1918), 2 Victor Scurr (1919), 3 Lilian Watson (1917)

Others admissions included: 1917: Ethel & Walter Bassett; Len Brassleay; Lilian Buttery; Mary & Robt Collinson; Jack Dawson; John Dobson; Robert Foxton; Marion Gillery; Maggie Henderson; Sarah, Richard, William & Mary Hunter; Leslie Johnson; Emily North; Kathleen Penrose; Albert Pratt; Lilian Watson.

1918: Hilda Ellen Abbey; Lena Bassett; Marjorie Brassleay; Harold & Tom Buttery; Norah Copeland; Jack Cousins; Kathleen Dawson; Francis & Constance Dobson; Marjorie Dunn; Frank Hart; Gladys Hodgson; Ernest Johnson; Leslie & Jack Laycock, Minnie Levitt; Clara North; Margery Pinkney; Kath Ringrose; Mary Scurr; John Stones; Ron & Reg Taylor.

1919: George & Philip Artley; Mary Bean; Ray Beecroft; Anita Brown; George & Roland Carter; Cecilia Clarke (Wreggitt); Olive & Alice Craggs; George & Joyce Hick; Nelson Heseltine; Albert Kitching; Linda Metcalfe; Doris Oxtoby; Tom Pudsey; Eric J Postill; Victor Scurr; Gordon Skelton; Liz Varley; Tom Watson

Anthony Sawkill continued to be involved in school and village life and his successors recorded the times when he and Clara Sawkill called at school. Eleven years after his retirement on Monday night 21 September 1925, Anthony died unexpectedly at the age of 73 while members of his family were out visiting friends. When they returned to *"Ivy Cottage"*, they found him dead in his chair with a book in his lap. Family mourners at the large gathering of mourners were his widow Clara, son Dr Philip Sawkill, daughter Kathleen Dunn and in-laws Thomas, Henry and Frederick Marston and their wives and Albert Marston who was still a bachelor. Numerous wreaths included: *"from his dear ones"*; *"a token of respect from the staff and scholars of the C E School"*; *"in loving memory of a long friendship Mr R Duggleby and family"*; *"Dr and Mrs Thistlethwaite"*; *"with deepest sympathy from Mr & Mrs W A Cundall"*; *"with sincere sympathy from the vicar, church wardens, sidesmen, choir and friends"*. The service in St Hilda's Church where Anthony had been a regular worshipper for over half a century, was conducted by the Rev Charles Rowntree, Stanley Currey played the organ and the choir led the singing of *"Now the labourer's task is o'er"*. The school children gathered flowers and made a wreath and Harry Potter head master, closed the school so that he and his staff could attend.

J Cundall & Son bought 'Ivy Cottage' and their shepherd Arthur Gilbank and his wife Florence Mary lived there for almost half a century. Their children Percy, John (Jack), Thomas and Mary were all pupils at Sherburn school.

CHAPTER 3
GEORGE FARMER (1914-1916)

A NTHONY SAWKILL'S successor George William Farmer was headmaster for less than two years. He lodged in Sherburn and travelled home each weekend and when he began his duties on 14 September 1914, there was grave unrest locally, nationally and world-wide. James Whittam who had been Sherburn's popular but over-generous vicar since 1905, was appearing in Court on a Bankruptcy Charge and Britain was at war with Germany. George Farmer had the same teachers Lillie Raine, Lilian Botterill and Janet Mackintosh and during his first weeks he records the presence of 15 year-old Boris Kirby who may have been a monitor or in training. When the new school year began in March 1915, Lillie Raine's father sent a telegram saying *"Daughter has severe cold, will come Tuesday"*, but when she returned, Lillie had difficulty controlling the children and was asked to resign. Miss Dora Greenwood from Liverpool was appointed. Lilian Botterill sprained her ankle and Miss J Guy assisted temporarily. Janet Mackintosh resigned in February 1916 after 10 years and although the managers tried to dissuade her, she left in May.

There were 152 pupils on roll but by the time George left the number had fallen to 122 mainly due to families leaving the district. Good average attendance was maintained even though he frequently received notes saying *"helping mother"*. On the 19 March 1915, twenty-two children were away during the worst snow storm in 16 years. Wolds roads had 7 foot drifts, travellers had difficulty making their way through the blinding snow and 11 of Irelands' sheep were smothered at Heslerton Wold. Christina Rigby was absent after a crochet needle stuck into her thigh when she stumbled during needlework and because Dr Hollings was away from home, Clara Sawkill from *"Ivy Cottage"* extracted the needle *"with great skill"*. Kathleen Skelton had 3 months off because she had anaemia, Oliver Henderson was off with Impetigo and Rosie Pinkney had Chicken Pox. On 19 August 1915 when school closed for harvest holidays, 17 children were absent in the morning and 22 in the afternoon. On 24 September, the headmaster records *"Attendance this afternoon was not very good 17 children being absent mainly owing to a large number of soldiers entering the village"* and on 30th *"Last night a large number of soldiers slept in the school"*. They may have been on their way to the battle-fields or training centres and intending to catch an early morning train. By mid-November, attendance was badly affected by colds, the head master developed a sore throat and for several days was unable to take lessons. School remained closed all January 1916 because of measles.

The war caused more older pupils to apply for labour certificates. In 1915, Herbert Johnson *"to assist in agricultural work"* and Edward Jerrams to help school manager James Bell Heath at Springfield House. Doris Dobson was granted exemption but when the head master heard she was not employed he ordered her to return to school at once. Agnes Bassett was granted exemption to look after her mother Agnes Ellen 39 who had been sick since the death of her 5-month-old baby Laura Mary in January 1916. The mother died 3 months later. At a public meeting in school Mr Simmonite from the Scarborough Labour Bureau said 200 Scarborough women had volunteered to do men's work and so Anthony Sawkill proposed that *"the meeting pledge itself to further the object of endeavouring to secure the services of females for labour in agriculture.* In Birmingham females aged 14 to middle age were working 12 hours a day, 7 days a week making shrapnel, parts of machine guns and rifles, for an average weekly wage of 32/- (£1.60) for shifts and £3 for nights.

Mr Farmer's log book entries were mainly concerned with repairs, requisites, the time table and standards of pupils' work. John Gillery swept and pointed the chimney stack, George Mortimer, Central Stores, supplied cleaning materials including 2 sixpenny packets of black lead, 10 lb of soap, 2 sweeping brushes, one hard broom, one hand brush, 2 black lead brushes and 2 door mats. William Henry Reynolds, station master, who had been supplying coal from Weaverthorpe Station for 20 years, retired in March 1915 and went to live in Scarborough. Five months later his wife Jane 67 died and was brought back to Sherburn for burial. Four months after that William also died and once again St Hilda's Church was filled to over-flowing. Bearers were railway officials George Harrison, Stephen Bell, Robert Simpson and William Metcalfe, but there were no flowers *'by request'*. Sixteen months earlier in November 1913, the Reynolds' youngest son Lawrence Charles 20 died after being knocked down by a train only yards from their home and people said his parents never recovered from the tragedy. They had two unmarried sons William and Dudley, three married sons Robert (Malton), Fred (Hull) and Edgar (York) and an unmarried daughter Matilda (Scarborough'), a married daughter Elizabeth Ruff (York) and three grand-children William and Maud Reynolds and Lawrence Ruff.

Requisites included 20 dual desks, 40 copies each of Nelson's *"Highroads of Literature Book III"* and *"Highroads of Empire History Book VIII"*; Nelson's Classics *"Oliver Twist"* and *"Robinson Carusoe"*; Blackies *"Lands and their Stories Book III"*; *"Large Type Poetry Books"*, *"English Poetry for the Young"* and *"Picture Composition"* Vols I-III; Jack's *"King Arthur's Knights"*, Macmillan's *"Alice in Wonderland"* and *"Water Babies"*; Cravens *"Simplex Music"*; 2 teachers' books: *"Junior and Intermediate Educational*

Handwork" and *"A year in the Infant School"*, Phillips *"The British Isles"*; 24 McDougall's *"Babes in the Wood"*, a copy of Craig's *"Paper Modelling for Six Year Olds"*; one *"Two Little Dicky Birds"* and 36 *"Nursery Rhymes"*; 1 doz wall maps of Europe and Asia, 3 doz Reeves Colour Boxes, 2 doz clock faces; 1 doz boxes of counters; 1 pkt Giant Letters, one Sewing Basket and 4 waste paper baskets. Despite all these aids to learning, on 1st October 1915 when the master examined the Upper Division in Arithmetic, he described the results with one word *"bad"*! But on the 18th when he set a composition (essay) after a history lesson for the same group on Social Conditions in the 13th/15th centuries, he describes them as *"excellent"*, with many pupils completing 4 or 5 pages of *"well worded sentences"*.

Mr Farmer made 24 entries in the Punishment Book mainly for talking in class, throwing stones, climbing walls, lying, impudence and disobeying Miss Dora Greenwood. Albert Dawson was punished for refusing to sing, Edgar Hick for playing truant, another for stealing and breaking the master's cane, and yet another for *"writing 'filth' on paper and exhibiting it"*.

On 21 October 1915 the head master talked to the upper classes about the British Navy and recalled the Battle of Trafalgar in 1805 when off the S-W coast of Spain, a British fleet of 27 ships and 4 frigates, commanded by Capt Horatio Nelson, were in combat with a Franco-Spanish fleet of 33 ships and 7 frigates under Villeneuve. The British won, but Nelson was killed in his vessel *'Victory'* in their hour of triumph. On the 3 May 1916, the life and work of playwright William Shakespeare (1564-1616) was remembered and on Empire Day 24 May 1916, first celebrated in 1902, the children sang patriotic songs: *"The British Grenadiers"*, *"Hearts of Oak"*, *"Here's a Health unto His Majesty"*, *"Rule Britannia"* and *"O God of Love"*. Elsie Beecroft *"nicely rendered 'Land of Hope and Gory'"* and after The Lord's Prayer and National Anthem, there were *"hearty cheers for King and Empire and the brave soldiers and sailors fighting on their behalf"*.

School owed £11..16s..1d to the destitute vicar and £20 to the trustees of the late James Kirk. A local collection raised £10..1s..od, William Page owner of the corn warehouse at the railway station donated 5/- (25p) and the managers ordered the sale of the piano. When the Education Authority heard of this, they granted £10 towards a new one and a children's concert raised £8. Within minutes of the doors opening, the large room was so full that many were turned away and the performance had to be repeated. The concert opened with everyone singing *"Welcome"*; recitations were by Hilda Dawson *"Bishop Hatto"*, Clifford Calam *"The Owl Critic"* and Sybil Prodham *"Knitting"*; songs included *"Hiring Fair"*, *"Welsh Hats"*, *"Orange Greys"*, *"Loyal Soldiers"* and *"Johnny Smoker"*. Aubrey Brown sang *"The Whistling Coon"* and everyone joined in *"Rule Britannia"* and *"The British Flag"*. A performance of *"Sleeping Beauty"* included Harold Hope as *"King"*, Elsie Beecroft *"Queen"*, Lydia

Clarke *"Nurse"*, Aubrey Brown *"Prince Valiant"*, Clarice Beecroft *"Princess Mayflower"*, Annie Henderson *"Fairy Nettlesting"*, and Maud Bell, Edith Dawson, Christina Rigby, Elsie Webster, Hilda Hick, Bertha Brown, Edna Gillery and Zina Pinkney were *"good fairies"*, Richard Duggleby, Christopher Cousins, Harold Heath, Lewis Heseltine, Richard Dawson and Harry and Herbert Clarke were *"elves"*.

Mr Webster's typewriting/shorthand/book keeping night classes raised funds and Stanley Currey gained the Elementary Certificate in Pittman's shorthand. The school was let on 10 April 1915 for the wedding reception when John Smith Currey, joiner, married Eileen Elizabeth Whiske White who was nursery governess to Marjorie Isabelle daughter of Charles H Close of *"Pasture House"*. The bride wore a cream silk dress, a veil held by orange blossom and carried a sheaf of lilies and Marjorie her bridesmaid wore a cream frieze coat with silk collar and cuffs, a cream and pink hat and carried a basket of pink roses. The bride was given away by Charles Close, the best man was Stanley Currey the bridegroom's brother and there were 100 guests. The honeymoon was spent in Scarborough and the bride travelled in a dress of dove-grey cloth. School was let on 21 June 1915 when Amy Gertrude Heath married Fred Gillery. Amy was the daughter of school manager James B Heath of Springfield Farm and Fred, a clerk at Weaverthorpe Station, was the son of William Gillery. Both Amy and Fred sang in the church choir and their fellow choristers led the singing. The bride wore a beautifully embroidered ivory crepe-de-Chine dress over silk, a veil held by orange blossom. She carried a bouquet of lilies. Frank Gillery was best man and there were six bridesmaids: Olive Heath (bride's sister), Ivy Breckons, Florence and Edith Hick (bride's cousins), and Margery and Beryl Gillery (bridegroom's nieces). They all wore ivory voile dresses with blue sashes, mob caps trimmed with blue and carried baskets of flowers. Amy gave Fred a pair of gold cuff links, he gave her a gold watch and to each bridesmaid he gave a gold broach. The couple left by *"motor"* to catch the 6.22 pm train from Weaverthorpe Station to the Lake District, the bride travelling in a dove coloured dress and hat. Many friends waved them off and everyone was invited to celebrate with sports in the village street.

On Saturday 8 July 1916, Harold eldest son of Richard Duggleby (school manager), of Mount Pleasant Farm, Sherburn Wold married Mary Ella only daughter of the late John Foster (school manager who died 1912). The bride was given away by her brother William and wore a navy travelling dress and carried a *"lovely bouquet"*. Her cousin Elsie Simpson and the bridegroom's sister Flora, were bridesmaids, Stanley Duggleby was best man and Private Edgar George Brown (King's Royal Rifles) played the organ. After a reception at the bride's home the couple went on honeymoon *'by motor'* to Scarborough. In April 1917, Mary's brother William Foster married Frances Halley Cundall in the Wesleyan Chapel, Appleton Roebuck. The bride was given away by

Joseph R Cundall of Tadcaster. The same month, Martha Ann (Patty) daughter of George Lawson (school manger) married Alfred Cyril Trohear at Scarborough, and the reception was at Lawsons' Elm Tree Farm (now Elm Grove).

* * * * * * *

Four days after George Farmer's arrival, there was a war recruitment meeting in school. Anthony Sawkill welcomed Messrs T F Bean, H Beecroft, J M Bradford, T Copeland, F Cousins, J Currey, R Duggleby, F Forge, C Fryer, G Hebden, J & F Hick, E Mallory, T J & AB Marston, J Milner, G H Mortimer, J C Pinkney, L Selby, Dr H T Hollings and many more. After singing *'God Save the King'* Sir Luke White MP, and Messrs Wickham-Boynton, C Smith JP and T Holtby CC, gave addresses on the war and its causes. Some young men had already volunteered, but after that and subsequent meetings, well over a hundred had enlisted (see appendix 8). Many joined the Waggoners' Reserves, a Corps formed in 1913 by Sir Mark Sykes of Sledmere, consisting of 1000 East Yorkshire labourers who used horse-drawn wagons to take supplies to the battlefield trenches in Europe. Most of Sherburn's volunteers were farm labourers or brewery and railway employees. Stanley Currey left his position as book keeper with Wallis & Blake, Scarborough and Harry Y Cundall as junior partner for Joseph Cundall & Sons, auctioneers and estate agents of Sherburn and Tadcaster.

On 6 January 1916, the war office began the compulsory call-up of the half a million men who had not volunteered. Tribunals were held to deal with applications for exemption and at a sitting of the Sherburn Rural Tribunal in the Union Offices, Scarborough, four were granted, one to a joiner/wheelwright from Ganton on medical grounds and because his invalid mother was dependent upon him and three to labourers working on a 550 acre farm at Hunmanby, one because he was *"the most useful man on the farm"*, and the other two because the tribunal considered the farm under-staffed. An appeal was dismissed by a 19 year old who claimed he owned 3.5 acres of land and had a grandmother to support. He was ordered to enlist straight away.

Mrs Harold Hollings the doctor's wife of *"Roseville"* and Mrs Charles Close of *"Pasture House"* held sewing meetings in school to make clothing for soldiers. Fifty ladies attended the first and whilst they were sewing, Messrs Farrier and Currey played piano solos and duets and light refreshments were provided at a small charge towards the cost of materials. George Lawson provided coal for the fires and paraffin for the lamps, the Football Club gave £5, the Cricket Club £3 and subscriptions raised £16..16s..6d. Throughout the first winter the ladies made 61 shirts, 80 pairs of socks, 79 mufflers, 45 pairs of mittens and cuffs, 5 body belts, 38 handkerchiefs and 3 vests, and some went directly to the Sherburn men serving at the front. Sewing classes were also held each

Wednesday evening in the chapel schoolroom where members of the Sherburn Branch of the Young Leaguers Union made dresses, aprons and pinafores to sell in aid of the National Children's Homes.

George Farmer organised the school children to collect eggs for wounded soldiers and one week in May 1915 they collected 213 and another week 178. George Falkard who lived nearby at White House Farm took them to Malton for distribution to military hospitals. These were set up all over the country in public halls, stately homes, large houses, schools, even tents and cricket pavilions, but wherever wounded soldiers could recover in peaceful surroundings far from the horrors of the battlefields. The nearest one to Sherburn was Wykeham Abbey, built on the site of a Cistercian Priory, once the home of the Lord of the Manor of the Wykeham and Sherburn Estates and now the seat of the 12th Viscount Downe. The British Red Cross and Order of St John established Voluntary Aid Detachments (VADs) to recruit and train locals to work in these hospitals as nurses, cooks, laundresses, clerks, typists, telephonists and drivers. By August 1914 thousands had volunteered mostly from middle-class families who could afford to pay for lectures and £1..19s..2d for a uniform. Nurses had to be aged 23-38 and were expected to train for and pass an examination in first aid and nursing. Volunteers from wealthy families gave their services free but there was remuneration. A Medical Officer earned £1/day, matrons, sisters-in-charge and ward sisters one guinea/week (£1..1s) and staff nurses with 2 years training £40/year. The nurses were daily confronted with horrific sights of wounded soldiers, some with amputated limbs or gross mutilation. Bedpans and sputum cups had to be distributed and emptied and the severely wounded had to be fed and washed. Those who had been blinded had to have letters from home read to them and replies written. Throughout all this and long weary hours, the young volunteers were pledged to remain cheerful and helpful at all times. Most military hospitals had autograph books in which patients were encouraged to write a message or rhyme, or draw a cartoon or sketch. One young patient at Wykeham Abbey, Pte W Cast of the 17th Sherwood Forresters, wrote in 1916: *"The happiest moments of my life, were spent in the arms of another man's wife ... my Mother"*. They were after all, far from home and some as young as 17, having lied about their age when enlisting, so eager were they to serve King and Country. Wykeham military hospital closed on the 22 April 1919. (see appendix 9)

After several months on the battlefields, Stanley Currey wrote to his uncle Thomas telling him that his son William Currey had been badly wounded. Sylvester Bean was the first to come home wounded and others who had leave during George Farmer's headship, included Bandsman Arthur Clifford Pinkney (King's Own Yorks Light Infantry), Colour Sergt Frederick George Levitt (E Yorks Regt), William Heseltine and Driver Thomas Jackson (No 16, 5th Reserve Park, British Expeditionary Force). Thomas *"related exciting experiences of himself and others in the early stages of the war at St Quentin and the Mons battle"*. Private George Ward, came from France unexpectedly one Saturday morning in November 1915 for a month's leave and Waggoners Reserves who returned that Christmas included Fred Dawson, Bob Milner, George Buttery, Sid Metcalfe, George Dawson and Sam Clarkson.

After months of local rumour and speculation, the Rev James Whittam was arrested on a bankruptcy charge one Wednesday afternoon in February 1915 as he left St Hilda's Church. James's offer to pay £50 to offset his debt out of his annual income of £207 if he could continue as vicar, was refused. At York Assizes, G F Mortimer (A E B Soulby, Malton) appeared in James's defence and said: *"For many years, he has done his duty as a priest in holy orders, earnestly and faithfully working hard for others on what was after all, a small pittance."* Nevertheless, in a harsh and unyielding summary, Mr Justice Colleridge included the words: *"It is often said, that the punishment which persons in your position suffer from such charges, is so grave as to relieve the Court of the necessity of adding to it. I do not agree. People who occupy high and trusted positions should not be tempted in the way in which poor uneducated ignorant persons are tempted. In my judgement, the same punishment should be meted out to men of high and peculiar positions, as to the humblest and lowliest of His Majesty's citizens. I shall, therefore treat this as an ordinary case, and the sentence upon you is nine months' imprisonment"*. The vicar *"displayed considerable emotion, but received his sentence quietly"*.

St Hilda's Sunday School July Outing was postponed and school was ordered to stay open, but when the day arrived Mr Farmer wrote *"many scholars are absent on account of contradictory rumours"*. Several days later, the Rev Charles Wilfred James MA moved into the vicarage from Westerdale, Grosmont, where he'd been vicar since 1909. He'd held curacies at Llangyfelach (1900-02), Marley Hill, Durham (1902-04), St Paul's, Middlesbro' (1904-5) and Kirby Misperton (1905-9).

On 17 February 1916, Mr Farmer received notice to present himself for war service in accordance with Army Form 3236. When he arrived at Beverley Barracks, he was placed in the Army Service Corps and given 10 ten days to adjust school affairs, but on the 13 March he received this letter: *"Dear Sir, I find you were passed for Garrison Service and not General Service and therefore under Army Council Instruction 274 of 1916, you will not be required to report yourself at Beverley, nor will you be called up. You will remain in the Army Reserve, Class 'B'. Yours faithfully, G H Cayler, Lieut Officer, 15th Rectg Area."*

Church and chapel attendance increased and on Good Friday 1916, there were four services in St Hilda's: Holy Communion 8am, Mattins 10.30am, the solemn service of *"The Three Hours Agony"* from noon to 3pm and Evensong at 7pm. On Easter Day, there were six services: Holy Communion at 7am and 8am, Mattins at 10.30am, Choral Communion at 11.45am, children's service at 2.30pm and Evensong at 6.30pm. All were well attended. The Wesleyan Good Friday rally which had been held in chapel for 40 years, was cancelled in 1915 because of the war but resumed in 1916. Rev T E Westerdale (chairman of the York District) gave a *"stirring"* address on the *'Unity of Denominations'*, Ayton choir led the singing and Wesleyans from Brompton, Knapton, Sherburn, Snainton, Lutton, Weaverthorpe and Wold Newton provided tea for 160 people. In the evening, William Page of York, owner of the corn warehouse at Weaverthorpe Station was chairman and the Rev Joseph Parsons, circuit minister, preached a *"splendid"* sermon. Collections and subscriptions raised £36..17s..9d an increase of £9 on 1914. This was The Rev Joseph Parson's last Good Friday Rally because he died suddenly aged 59 the following June. Only weeks before his death, his three sons came home one weekend unexpectedly and simultaneously, two from serving in France and one from training in England. Two were unable to attend the funeral because they had returned to the battlefields but Douglas the youngest, was granted leave. Joseph had lived in the Manse for barely a year but was said to be *"a good man and thorough in all his dealings"*. Before coming to Sherburn he'd been a missionary for 17 years in India where he founded two orphanages for destitute children.

That month of June 1916, George Farmer handed in his resignation with effect from 31 August and at a managers meeting, the new vicar expressed regret and thanked him *"most cordially on behalf of the managers for his conscientious and able work"*. School usually closed on Whit Monday but that year the weather was so cold, the holiday was cancelled and school fires lit to keep the children warm. Four days later on Friday 16 June when school closed for the corn weeding fortnight, Mr Farmer was given permission to leave before his notice expired. There were three applicants: J W Blenkinsop of Hedon, Miss Frances Grant of Middlesborough and Harry E Potter of Driffield. Harry Potter began his duties two weeks after George Farmer left.

Upper School c 1919: *Back:* Jack Bassett ? , Colin Tacey, Albert Dawson, Oliver Henderson, Sid Dawson, Charlie Dobson
Next: Dorothy Watson, Madge Horsley, Babs Woodall, ? , Mary Bradford, ? , Clare Henderson, Lizzie Jackson, Agnes Hart, Maggie Gillery, Harry Potter (headmaster)
Next: Hilda Hick, Mary Watson, Frank Hart, Herbert Bassett, Les Tacey, Ethel & Lena Bassett, Maggie Henderson, Alice Dobson, Cyril & Rosie Pinkney, Harold Mortimer, Fanny Metcalfe,
Front: Edwin Potter, Marion Gillery, Betty Pinkney, Lil Watson, Joyce Hick, Fred Watson, Jack Dawson.

CHAPTER 4
HARRY EDWIN POTTER (1916-1938)

Harry E Potter's first day on duty was the 3 July 1916 two days after the start of the Battle of the River Somme in France when 420,000 British soldiers died in one of the bloodiest conflicts of the first world war. On the same day Harry's wife Bertha began teaching the Infants and his other teachers were Miss Dora Greenwood and Miss Lilian Botterill. Harry had been assistant teacher at Driffield C of E School from 1904 until 1914 when he was called up to serve with the 5th Yorkshire Regiment. For some reason he was discharged in 1916.

There had been other Potter families in Sherburn. In 1888 Henry Potter a shepherd, married Betsy Anne Ireland at St Hilda's Church and they had two children Bertha and Jane Ann. In 1891 Aeron Potter was groom to Dr Oliver Norris, Robert Edward Potter married Annie Patrick and Hannah Potter from Redcar was visiting John Milner. On Christmas Day 1900, Louisa Potter from Thirsk a domestic servant employed by farmer John Foster, married Frederick Atkinson. By April 1901, they'd all left the village.

Harry E Potter married Bertha Winship in Knaresborough in 1902 and they had one child, Edwin Harry who was 7 when he was admitted to Sherburn School. Harry, Bertha and Edwin lodged in rooms in the village and travelled home to Driffield each weekend by train. On 25 January 1917, their furniture arrived and they moved into a cottage in St Hilda's Street. The County Council bought a piece of land west of the school and with instructions from County Architect B Stamford, Anthony Sawkill and Harry Potter pegged out the foundations for the school master's house. In November 1921, the older school boys planted along the boundary, 600 Beech hedge plants from Longsters of Malton and the Potters moved in for Christmas. In their early years, they had visits from George Farmer, and Anthony and Clara Sawkill who still lived nearby in *"Ivy Cottage"* never ceased to show interest.

Straight away Mr Potter asked for the help of a monitress *"because of the backwardness of the infants"* and former pupil Elsie Beecroft was engaged for a six month trial and stayed four years. Beryl Gillery succeeded her in 1920 and stayed four years. Dora Greenwood left in 1917 to teach at the Blue Coat Hospital School, Liverpool and Lilian Botterill left in 1923. Harry's other teachers included Miss Olive Wray (Kirbymoorside) from 1917-20, Mrs Kate Ringrose 1921-34, Miss Amy E Frowde cc 1929, Richard Harland (Filey) cc

1929, Miss Betty Bray 1934-41 and Miss Violet Levitt 1934-50. Annual salaries in 1917 were: Harry Potter £155, Olive Wray and Lilian Botterill £100, Bertha Potter £70, Elsie Beecroft £17..10s, Annie Ward cleaner £10.

Mr Potter's next task was to deal with a complaint from Beverley about the dirty school. Jack Currey re-painted the interior and whitewashed the toilets and for £5..10s, the ash pits beneath the toilets were exchanged for the *"Pan System"* whereby excrement fell into large grey buckets. Annie Ward was given a Sanitary Cart to take the buckets away for emptying, probably into a large hole in the school garden dug by the older boys. Ventilation was inadequate and in mid-summer on some days, the temperature in school at 9.45 am was 78 degrees, so Mr Potter asked for ventilators for the western (Infants) and northern classrooms and for window blinds for the large room. Heating was a problem and throughout winter several tons of coal had to be burned and in January 1917 although fires were lit at 6.30 am, by the time the children arrived at 9 am the main room and adjoining classroom were still at freezing point. The Infants Room was below freezing and by noon was still only 48 degrees. Children were often absent with colds and one parent refused to send his daughter until school was properly heated. Because of huge fires, the grates had to be replaced, the floors in front of all three fireplaces repaired and the chimney stack and bell tower pointed.

School had a £20 debt and outstanding bills had to be chased. Hornseys of Norton owed £1 for using school for the clothing club, Mr Webster owed 5/- (25p) for his night classes and in autumn the children gathered and sold wild blackberries and elderberries from the hedgerows. At their first Christmas to organise a school treat, the Potters collected £7..17s..0d *"from 21 ladies and gentlemen"* and the children made flags and bunting to decorate the big room. Each Infant received a toy from the Christmas Tree, older children received books, sewing sets, work baskets, writing or drawing materials, parents were invited and Mr Potter recorded *"I consider the whole thing a great success"*. The war was costing £5.7 million a day and there was a nation-wide call for cut backs, income tax doubled and clocks were put forward an hour during the months of May to October to launch *"daylight saving time"* in the hope of saving thousands of tons of coal, the cost of bread increased, meat was rationed and the government appealed to the nation to help by investing in 5/- (25p) War Loan vouchers and within a month school savers had purchased 38. In 1917, a piece of land was bought from Mr Currey and divided into six 14'6" by 7'6" plots and the older boys spent two hours a week cultivating vegetables to sell.

Early in 1918, a whist drive, dance and school concert raised £18..12s..4d. Children's songs included: *"The land we'll ne'er forget"*. *"The Fairies"*, *"Noah's Ark"* and *"The Merry Bakers"* and *"recitations"* were by Jack Dawson, Sydney and Louie Prodham. There were two sketches, *"Granny"* with M Nesfield as

"Oscar Morris (young artist)", Harry Potter *"Colonel Hammersley (his guardian)"*, Miss Kitchen *"Maud Hammersley"*; Bertha Potter *"Mrs Rattenshaw"* and the other sketch *"Beauty and the Beast"* had Sam Pickering as *"Cassim"*, Elizabeth Henderson *"Beauty"*, Annie Clarke *"Emerald"*, Christina Rigby *"Ruby"*, Clifford Calam *"The Beast"*, Jack Dawson and Fred Woodall *"Servants of the Beast"*, Vera Dobson *"Queen of the Fairies"*, Thomas Clarke *"King of the Imps"* and the Infants were *"Fairies and Imps"*.

Gardening continued long after the war and in 1920, in preparation for the school's first course in horticulture, a delivery of gardening requisites included: 7 each of garden spades, forks, hoes, Dutch hoes, and rakes, seeds from Sutton & Sons, potato sets, a safety extension ladder, and a garden barrow. In October 1920, the older boys lifted 62 st 6 lbs of potatoes from a crop they'd planted on 139 square yards of land. The older boys regularly clipped the beech hedge on the boundary and weeded the hedge bottom and path sides. In Spring 1934, the boys prepared seed beds for the girls to start growing flowers and in Summer 83 lbs of Dwarf Defiance peas were harvested as well as other crops. In August 1934, Sherburn had its very first flower, fruit, vegetable and craft show and prizewinners in the children's classes included Ethel Metcalfe for making the best plain pillow case; Gladys Pinkney, Betty Forge, Edna Gillery (all 1sts), Mary Witty, Annie Bell (joint 2nd) for the best embroidery; Reg Bean, Walter Harness for the best cardboard models, Dennis Gillery, Teddy Hutchins for a crayon drawing of a bird, Gladys Pinkney, Thelma Standidge and Dorothy Harness for handwriting. Mrs Bill Henderson made the best pricked hearth rug, Mrs Bill Gillery the best thrift rug and Mrs Gilbank and Mrs Flinton the best baby's frocks. In 1936 the garden inspector reported: *"The standard of vegetable cultivation is high and several vegetables not usually found in gardens are grown. The ground is divided into 6 dual plots, all worked on a good practical rotation. Pest and disease control is studied and pupils show remarkable interest. The flower border provides a succession of bloom over a long period. The utilisation of waste products as a substitute for farmyard manure is of interest and marrows are being grown on this substance. Cucumbers are grown in the frame. Nature study is closely correlated with gardening and all note books are well kept. Additions to equipment are necessary, eg 1 spade, 1 fork 2 rakes"*.

* * * * * * *

In 1920, a jumble sale and Fancy Dress Ball raised £39..4d for new and more efficient ventilators. Dance music for 50 couples was provided from 8.45 pm to 2.30 am by Fred Hick (violin) and Harold Heath (pianoforte), MC's were Henry Prodham and Arthur Duggleby. Prize winners were Miss Olive Heath *"Britannia"*, Miss Elsie Beecroft *"Officer"*; George Falkard *"John Bull"*, George Bean *"Charles Chaplin"*; girls, Eva Rigby *"Prince Charming"*; boys

Edwin Potter *"Cupid"*. The ventilators were a boon in summer and a bane in winter because throughout January 1922, although fires were burning all night, the children often had to keep their coats on and attendance was badly affected by influenza. Snow lying several feet deep in the school yards, drifted in through the ventilators and windows and the older children spent an hour drying desks, bags and books before lessons could begin. On top of that Mr Metcalfe had to clean out the surface drain in the yard to stop flooding. Central heating was installed by Brogdon & Wilson for £74..17s..6d and included an Ideal classic Boiler, 5 two-column 6-section radiators, feed tank and pipes. On the first day the new coke stove was lit at 7 am, as well as small fires in each classroom and by 9 am the temperature was 46 degrees and by noon 60 degrees, even though the temperature outside was 12 degrees of frost. The children raised £14..17s towards this major expense with a concert and other donations included £10 from the Diocesan Fund, £15 from Bettons Charities, £10 from a National Society, £7 from the ERCC and £3..3s from the Bishop of Hull.

School was let for village events at 10/- per evening plus 5/- for use of the piano. During the 20's Harold Heath and Clarice Beecroft paid 7/6d per night for their Monday evening dance classes. Village dances were popular but created problems. In 1919 after a Tennis club dance, some paraffin lamp glasses were broken, at a New Year dance in 1924 two desks were broken and after a Wedding party in 1924, one of the dual desks and the decimal ball frame were smashed, the school was dirty and the girls' yard filthy. On another occasion, the boy's cloak room was damaged, pictures by the Infants were torn from the walls and the classroom was dirty. The same thing happened on Easter Monday 1927. In 1929, the yards were not only filthy but there was an empty whisky bottle in the girls' cloak room, another in the yard and numerous beer bottles. New stage curtains were hung in 1930 and at the next dance, one was badly torn but in 1933 when rude drawings and filthy words were scribbled on the black board, the head master had had enough and sent for the vicar. Thereafter, intoxicating drinks were not allowed, dances had to finish no later than 2 am, the premises had to be left clean and tidy and damages paid for.

This worked for a while and the vicar organised a successful Fancy Dress Dance on New Year's Eve 1934/5, with keen competition and excellent costumes. The decorated schoolroom was filled with children, parents and friends and prizewinners were: Girls' Prettiest: Mary Barr *'Lady of 1850'*, Norah Clarkson *'Star Fairy'*, Rosemary Calam *'Daffodil'*, Original: Annie Bell *'Ovaltine'*, Miriam Mason *'Paint Box'*, Mary Constable *'Keep off the Grass'*, Edna Gillery *'McLean Tooth Paste'*. Boys Original: Douglas Metcalfe *'Red Cross Nurse'*, Edward Calam *'Rabbit Catcher'*, Norman Currey *'Eastern Prince'*, Henry Foxton *'Little man you've had a busy day'*. Comic: Dennis Gillery *'Water Cress Billy'*, Ronald Bean *'Tramp'*, Cecil Pickering *'King Cole'*. Music was by Miss Clarice Beecroft and Miss Mary Currey on piano and

Henry Bradford and Ronald Heath on violins. Then one morning in 1936 after a dance the previous night, the yards were contaminated with urine, several desks had been left out all night and were wet when the children wanted to use them and on top of that, the headmaster fell on the slippery dance floor bruised his shoulder and hip, twisted his back and tore his jacket sleeve.

* * * * * * *

School was hired for wedding receptions but when former school monitress Elsie Beecroft married Harry Hopper from Hutton Cranswick one Wednesday afternoon in June 1923, the service was in the Wesleyan Chapel so the reception was in the adjoining school room. Elsie wore a dress of ivory crepe de Chine, with panels of Chile lace, a veil held with a wreath of orange blossom and she carried a bouquet of white roses, lilies, sweet peas and daisies. Her sister Clarice and the bridegroom's sister were bridesmaids and they wore shell pink crepe de Chine dresses with panels of Chile lace, pink shoes and stockings, black picture hats and both carried bouquets of pink and mauve sweet peas. The bridegroom gave each of them a gold broach. At another Chapel wedding in June 1926, Flora Emmeline daughter of Richard Duggleby school manager, married John Henry Atkinson, son of Henry Atkinson of Little Pasture Farm, Helperthorpe, and the reception was at Mount Pleasant Farm the bride's home. Flora wore a white gown of satin caprice trimmed with pearls and georgette panels, worked with beads and her tulle veil was trimmed with pearls and orange blossom, she carried a bouquet of white roses and carnations and wore a gold wrist watch given to her by the bridegroom. Two adult bridesmaids Blanche Duggleby and Mary Atkinson wore peacock blue silk dresses trimmed with gold beads, rust-coloured condor (wide brimmed) hats and carried bouquets of sweet peas. Two small bridesmaids Mary Heath and Beatrice Duggleby wore dresses of white crepe de Chine, lace caps and carried baskets of roses and sweet peas. Percy Duggleby was best man. The couple left by car for Harrogate and Ilkley, the bride wearing a beige two-piece, a silk crinoline hat and matching fox fur.

On 11 May 1935 when Vera Dobson married William Ness Campbell, a farmer, the reception was at the home of her parents Richard and Jane Dobson, shoemakers. Vera was their only daughter, a former pupil of Sherburn School and had taught at Bishop Wilton C of E School for 13 years. On her wedding day she wore a peach satin dress overlaid with oyster lace, with hat and shoes to match and carried pink roses. Her cousin Doris Dale was bridesmaid and she wore a pink dress of flowered georgette with hat and shoes to match and carried tulips. The bridegroom's niece Lorna Campbell, the small attendant, wore a dress of peach crepe and carried mixed flowers. The couple went on honeymoon to London, the bride travelling in a three-piece fawn suit with hat and shoes to match and their home was in Meltonby.

School was hired on 19 September 1937 when Mrs Edith Pickard of Vicarage Lane married Leonard Brassleay. Edith was the eldest daughter of Mr and Mrs H Stones of West Heslerton and Leonard was the son of Fred Brassleay of 4 St Hilda's Terrace. The bride wore a mid-blue two-piece with cloche (bell-shaped) hat and shoes to match, a pink blouse and gloves and carried pink carnations. One attendant was the bride's sister Miss Mabel Stones who wore a blue satin dress with white trimmings and a hat to match, white shoes and gloves, and carried bronze chrysanthemums, and the other was the bride's daughter Miss Audrey Pickard who wore a rose pink velvet dress and carried mixed sweet peas. They went on honeymoon to the Lake District, the bride travelling in a tweed coat with matching hat and shoes.

* * * * * * *

The school yards were a continual hazard. From time to time they were levelled with a mixture of sand carted from Wykeham donated by Col The Hon J Dawnay and cinders carted from the Brewery and in dry weather the yards were covered with black dust, in windy weather the dust made the children dirty and in wet weather the yards were inches deep in black mud. To remedy this, in 1920, five barrels of tar supplied by the Malton Gas Co were carted by Mr Heath from the station, boiled in Mr Ringrose's copper, mixed with cinders and spread over the surface. This proved unsatisfactory and Messrs Brown, Heath and Lawson attempted to lay a firmer foundation using a mixture of broken stones and 20 tons of slag chippings from Wm Schofield & Son of Grosmount @ 13s..2d (67p) per ton. The chippings arrived at the railway station in trucks with doors in the bottom for easy unloading, and more tar was boiled to bind the ingredients. After a while large cracks began to appear and caused serious accidents. Evelyn Dawson fell and fractured her right arm, Joyce Pickard fell and punctured an artery in her temple and Monica Arnott fell and cut her forehead and upper lip and her father Herbert sent a letter of complaint. The Arnotts lived in one of the Station Cottages and Herbert was a signalman at Weaverthorpe Station from 1923 until his retirement in 1953. The school children were not insured against accidents until 1933 and the yards were not repaired to the satisfaction of the East Riding County Council until 1936.

Harry Potter recorded all accidents and rendered first aid. In 1921 Willie Walker's shin was wounded by a nail, in 1925 George Edmond crushed his fingers when he and another boy were moving the piano, in 1930 Mrs Potter's forehead was cut when a pane of glass was broken in the Infants Room during drill (PE), in 1933 Leslie Pinder injured his finger in the desk top and during one of the Infants' singing lessons, the lower front of the piano fell out and injured Mrs Potters leg, but *"she continued teaching under considerable difficulty and pain"*. In 1937 when Joan Harris fell during games and injured her right shoulder and arm, she was taken to the new Scalby Road hospital which had been officially opened on 23 October 1936 by HRH Duke of Kent. The foundation stone was laid by Christopher Colborne Graham on 27 June 1934, the architect was Wallace Marchment of London and the builders were Foster & Dicksee. The old Friars Entry Hospital closed on 1 October 1936 and the 35 patients were transferred to the new Scalby Road Hospital where there were 116 free beds, 12 fee-paying beds and 12 maternity beds. The new hospital's first patient was said to be Mrs Lilian Cox, 36, a North Side hotelier.

* * * * * * *

Mr Potter only made 14 entries in the Punishment book for offences such as disobedience, lying, stealing, idleness, obstinacy, throwing stones and truancy. He hit the offender's hand or backside several times with his cane and was also known to *"box the ears"* of unruly pupils. In 1921 he smacked a girl three times on her shoulder with his hand for *"disobedience and idleness"*, and this provoked the school's first recorded case of verbal abuse by a parent towards a teacher. The girl's father went into school using obscene and threatening language and Mr Potter read the relevant bye-law to him then escorted him off the premises but the father continued shouting abuse from outside.

Nevertheless, Harry maintained good relationships with parents. Many attended the school harvest festival in 1924, when George Edmond read the lesson and fifty attended a Parents' afternoon at Christmas 1926 when the children recited poetry, sang songs and played musical games. On that occasion, Mrs John Henry (Flora Emmeline) Atkinson, newly married daughter of school manager Richard Duggleby, accepted toys made by the children for Scarborough Hospital. At Christmas 1929, as well as the toy offering for sick children, there was a Nativity Play and the children were given oranges and sweets. Other Christmas performances included *"A Christmas Carol"* and *"Alfred and the Cakes"*.

The vicar checked the registers regularly and absences were noted. During the war more older boys were granted Labour Certificates giving them permission to leave and start work. William Henry Foxton (b1904-d1929) left *"to help Mr Johnson"*, Arthur Cousins to help his father Fred and George Jackson to help a local farmer. In January 1917, Albert and Bertie Jerrams who lived on the Wolds were absent for 3 weeks because of snow. On the 5 April 1917 several children played truant and went to a sale at Westfield Farm where school manager John Foster Lawson had been a tenant since he was 18. Joseph Cundall & Son auctioned 10 working horses @ 99.5 guineas each, several store bullocks @ £17 each and 17 pork pigs @ £13 each. Charles Nesfield succeeded John F Lawson as tenant of Westfield and John's son George Lawson of Elm Tree Farm (now Elm Grove) succeeded him as school manager. John F Lawson served as church warden, parish overseer, parish and district councillor and died in 1935, 18 months after his wife Martha died. They had at least nine children: George, Helena, Elizabeth, John, Hilda, Edith, Agnes, Sarah and Ethel.

* * * * * * *

Throughout the war as well as daily morning assembly, the school day ended with prayer and the national anthem. Former battles were remembered and patriotism continued long after the war ended. On Empire Day 24 May 1925, Frank Hart and Lilian Watson thanked the vicar for his address and Harry Potter wrote *"patriotic songs and recitations were extremely well rendered and the impression created was great".*

There is no mention of HMI visits during the 1914-18 war but on 19 October 1916, Harry Potter records *"This morning I commenced the Term Examination with Stds I & II. The arithmetic is in a deplorable state. In Std I, one child had 4 sums correct, 2 had 1 correct. The remainder had no sums correct, and they appear to have no idea of working them. In Std II the result was very little better".* In September 1919, Norton cookery classes were cancelled because of the national rail strike and when trains started running again, disruption continued. The girls had to leave Malton on the 3.13 pm through-train to Ganton (presumably it didn't stop at Weaverthorpe Station) and walk back to Sherburn. On wet days they were allowed to catch the 4.28 train from Ganton to Sherburn. In 1923, Rosie Pinkney was named the best cook and in 1930, Muriel Groves, Maggie Beal and Mabel Johnson won prizes at Norton Show for their bread entries.

In 1920, a games fund was opened. The school bought cricket equipment for the older boys, £3..0s..8d was spent on basketball outfits and equipment and the tennis club donated equipment for the older girls. A year later the school came 2nd in the first annual inter-school sports event. On 11 February 1921, Harry Potter wrote: *"This afternoon I am taking the upper boys to Weaverthorpe School to play the return football match. The walk there will be occupied by Geographical and Nature Talks. Miss Botterill will remain in charge".*

In 1921, an inter-school sports evening in James B Heath's Paddock raised £37..19d..od. Norton beat Sherburn in the tug-of-war and Sherburn Brass Band played selections throughout the evening (see appendix 10). Officials were: gate keepers: F Cousins, C S Duggleby, J B Heath, A B Marston, G Lawson, C H Woodall; judges Rev J C Vernon, Dr Hollings, H Prodham, R & S R Duggleby, W A Cundall, C H Close, W Brown, R Boyes; stewards: M Nesfield, F R Ringrose, W Currey, A Duggleby; judges' steward T Stanley Currey; programme stewards E Brown and school staff; entries secretary A Sawkill; results clerk G W Pickering, starters R Warcup, H Beecroft, treasurer H Prodham; groundsman John Dobson.

Post-war deliveries to school included dual desks from the North of England Furnishing Co, infants' chairs, 2 teachers' chairs, a folding table, 2 steel scraper door mats, 2 coconut mats, a set of jumping stands, blackboards, 1 doz exercise books, 3 doz cardboard looms, 3 lbs raffia, 4 packets raffia needles, 4.5 lbs of wool; a woodwork bench, an iron plane, 3 hammers and saws, 1 knife, 1 try square, 3 bradawls (small boring tools), 3 gimlets; mugs, plates, oil cloth and dish cloths for the dinner scheme, 1 doz safety straight edge rulers, 30 bibles, 18 copies each of Blackies' *"By the Hedge Row"* and *"Common Pinewood and Bog"*, 24 dictionaries, copies of *"Highroads of History"*, *"Highroads of Geography"*, *"Songs for Little People"* and *"English Folk Songs for School"*. Other titles included *"The King of the Golden River"*, *"The Wonderful Pitcher"*, *"Hubert the Shepherd"*, *"The Story of the Rhine Gold"*, *"Aladdin and the Wonderful Lamp"*, *"The Story of Fairy Foot"* and *"The Strange Adventures of Hans"*. In 1925 for the first time, the County Librarian left a supply of books at school and in 1930 the managers donated a supply of Ancient & Modern Hymn Books for use in daily assembly. During the 1930's recession when there was mass unemployment and hunger strikes, schools were asked to order equipment only when absolutely necessary. Despite the economic climate, in 1934 Mr Potter was commended for encouraging the children to join the National Savings Scheme and that year they saved £116..4s..3d, more than twice as much as the previous year and in 1935 they saved £130..1s..6d.

* * * * * * *

School Inspections re-commenced towards the end of the war and in July 1918, HMI reported: *"A marked improvement has been made during recent years in all classes and branches of the curriculum and the present general condition of school reflects credit on all concerned. Relative weaknesses are receiving attention and on the whole the children are brighter, more intelligent and more responsible than this school has shown for a long time"*. The 1925 report was brief: *"The little ones had quite lost their nervousness, they were good. So were the other two divisions. The whole school is excellent in every way. The work is thorough, writing good and the tone of the whole school is high"*. In 1933: *"Children in the lower and middle classes need special attention and the rate of progress in the Infants is not rapid. The general standard of attainment is satisfactory in spite of staff changes and low attendance at the beginning of the year. The children are bright and interested in their work and special mention may be made of the care given to note books in gardening and nature study. The re-classification of the school into senior and junior divisions should make it easier to provide a satisfactory course for older and more advanced pupils. The school is the centre of many outside activities which adds interest to school life"*.

Religious Instruction (RI) inspections re-commenced and the 1918 report was brief *"satisfactory"*. In 1922: *"It is four years since my last visit. I find a distinct advance made in all classes. The little ones were rather shy but several answered brightly. The 2nd Div were good. The Top Div very good indeed, sensible, thoughtful and attentive. Writing, with few exceptions, good. Tone – high"*. In 1935, the Rev E C Peters reported: *"Infants – instruction is simple and practical and real interest is shown in the children's eager answering. The teacher is continuing her excellent work and is conscious of the responsibility of giving her class good grounding in religious teaching and prayer. The devotional side is quiet and impressive. Group 3 – the class showed themselves well up in the work and the Holy Week lessons brought out thoughtful answers. The Old Testament is dealt with on sensible lines. Group 2 – this class has done good work and seem to have studied the early part of Acts to the same purpose. Group I – these have had careful instruction in prayer book services which are an important part of instruction for older children. The practical interest of the vicar is much appreciated by the staff. Written work reaches a good standard"*.

Some of Harry Potter's pupils went to Grammar and High Schools. His son Edwin went to Bridlington Grammar in 1921, and pupils who went to Malton Grammar included Zena Pinkney (1919), Violet Levitt (1923), Muriel Crawford (1920), Barney Harris (1932), Roy Harle (1935), Colin Charles Taylor (1938). Pupils who went to Scarborough Boys High were George Robert Levitt (1926), John Gordon Pickering (1927), David William Beal, Albert Marston and Cecil Pickering (1934), T Stanley Currey (1935), Walter Howard Bradford (1936), John Derrick Beal and John Constable (1937). In 1935, Violet Levitt's brother George Robert Levitt, after leaving St John's Training College, York, was appointed hand work instructor at Tang Hall Senior School, York, and six months later was informed that he'd passed the final handwork examination of the Board of Yorkshire Training skills for his teacher's certificate with distinction.

* * * * * * *

Four months after his arrival in Sherburn, Mr Potter received Army Form W3236 calling him for war service but six days later, a letter came saying his call-up was a mistake. As part of wartime procedure, on 1 December 1916, the older children were given a demonstration on the use of the *"tube and box respirators"* in case of enemy gas invasion. The war intensified and in February 1917, the area education officer wrote to the head master to say that in the event of him being called up again, he was to tell him at once so that application for exemption could be made. On the 9 March 1917, Mr Potter was declared Class 1 by the Medical Board and became 2nd Lieutenant Harry Potter in charge of a Home Guard Platoon 6th 'C' Company of the 1/3 Battalion E

Yorks Volunteer Regiment with 37 volunteers, 17 from Sherburn, 16 from Ganton and 4 from Heslerton and by August, numbers had increased to 63. At their first church parade, one Sunday evening in August 1917, the platoon marched to St Hilda's headed by the bugle band and officers from Hunmanby headquarters and at a similar service in 1918, the organist was Sergt Stanley Currey who had been discharged from war duties after his left hand was severely wounded by a hand grenade whilst he was demonstrating their use. Stanley served with the 21st Bttn King's Royal Rifle Corporals in Belgium, France and Italy.

Throughout 1917, £208..1s..6d was raised to send postal orders to village soldiers at Christmas. House-to-House collectors were: Mrs Hollings and Mrs Coombs £12..19s..6d; Mrs North and Miss Pinkney £5..1s; Miss Botterill and Miss Wray £3..3s..7d; Mrs Potter and Mrs J Postill £2..15s; W Brown, G H Mortimer and S Currey £4..3s..2d; H Penrose and F R Ringrose 19s..6d; Private Mahon and Mr Berriman £3..3s.6d. Donations included: Hon Norah Dawnay £1; Col Hon J Dawnay £1; Wesleyan Chapel £1..5s; school children's box £1..4s..1d; Sherburn ER Volunteer Platoon £3..6s..6d and *a friend* 9s..2d. Between 31 March and 25 May 1917, the school children collected 1296 eggs for distribution to local military hospitals.

At Christmas 1917, after a Platoon Shooting competition, H Wrigley Esq presented handicap prizes to: Private J R Tinegate, case of pepperettes, 46 points; Lance Corporal Nesfield a sugar basin, 43; Lance Corporal Hardy a butter dish 41; Lance Corporal Clark a bon-bon dish 39; Private Skelton a butter dish 38; Lance Corporal A Ringrose a pencil, 37. The Musketry Course: Private Spencer a mustard pot 59 points; Private F Shield a patent razor 58; Sergeant Allison a butter dish 54; Private J R Reeveley a night light 54; Corporal J S Currey a thermometer 53; Private Cockerill a pencil 52. In No 1 section, Sergeant Beecroft was awarded an engraved sugar basin for averaging 57.4 points. At a singing contest afterwards, cash prizes were won by Private George Snowball of Ganton 10/- which he handed back for the local wounded soldiers fund; Sergeant Harry Beecroft 5/-; Private Fred Shields 2s..6d; Private James C Pinkney 2s..6d and Private Tom Jackson 2s..4d.

In August 1918, Lieut Potter, his Platoon and 39 non-commissioned officers went to Boynton for a shooting test. Transport included Mr Heath's steam tractor, Lance-Corporal Nesfield's and Private Snowball's motor cars and Sergeant Brewster's and Private Pickering's motor cycles and side cars. They set off at 7 am and were joined by 50 men from Wold Newton, North Burton and Thwing and returned at 9 pm. Test shooting was at 200 yards, with 5 independent rounds and 5 rapids and touch firing at 300 yards with 5 rounds.

There were brief news reports about servicemen's leave and injury. In 1917, Fireman William Gillery (Royal Navy) came on leave and Gunner William E Dawson came home to convalesce after spending several months in a Halifax hospital where he'd been treated for a shell wound in his left arm. James and Sarah Pinkney who had three sons in the Army and one in the Navy, heard that their eldest son Private William Currey Pinkney, had been seriously wounded; Thomas Bassett heard that his son Driver Arthur Bassett was in hospital in France after being kicked by a horse; school manager Ben Bassett heard that his eldest son Sapper George Bassett RE aged 26, had died from malaria after two years in Egypt. Before the war George worked for the NE Railway Co of Hull. George Sleightholme heard that his son Sergeant Alfred Sleightholme had been killed shortly after being awarded a military medal. John Baker heard that his sons Rifleman John W Baker and Private Albert W Baker of the Seaforth Highlanders had lost their lives. John had two other sons in war service, Thomas in the Australian Imperial Force and Harry in the Medical Corps. In 1918, Tom and Esther Bean heard that their son Private John Bean was being held prisoner after being reported missing; School manager William Brown's son Private Edgar George Brown (Royal Hussars) came on leave after 19 months in France and Italy, Private Arthur Duggleby came home to convalesce after he and his brother Percy had been exposed to enemy gas, Sergeant Major Sydney Calam returned after two years in France, Sergeant Sylvester Bean after four years and Private L Milner after serving since the war began. In June 1918, John and Hanna Dobson heard that their 20 year old son Gunner John H Dobson RFA had died from gas poisoning at Wimbourne War Hospital. At his funeral on 5 July 1918 at St Hilda's Church, the school children placed a wreath of flowers they'd made on his grave and his epitaph reads *"he served his King and country; we know he has done his best, now he sleeps in the arms of Jesus, a British soldier at rest"*. News was also received that Sapper William Tee a soldier from Hull and former resident of Sherburn, had been killed. Before leaving Sherburn, William was a railway platelayer and he and his family lived in one of the Gate Houses along the line side. His wife Mary died aged 34 in 1915 and his daughter Annie Elizabeth 16 died a year later.

Between 1914-18, ten million soldiers died in combat and three quarters of a million were British. Fourteen were from Sherburn and one of them Sergt Harry Yates Cundall RGA aged 28, died 11 days before the war ended. On the 4 and 5 November 1918, his parents who moved into Sherburn Lodge about the time the war began, received letters from their son saying that the Turks were about to be defeated and he would soon be home. But then they heard from the War Office that Harry had died of malaria in Palestine just as the Turks surrendered. He had served in France, Salonica and Egypt for 2 years. Many relatives and friends including Lieut Potter and his Platoon attended a memorial service on Sunday 10 November 1918 in Sherburn Chapel. The Rev J Coombs (Wesleyan minister 1918-20) preached from Revelation Ch 1, v 18 *"I am he that liveth and was dead"*. The following morning Harry Potter wrote in his log book: *"Nov 11th News having been brought that an Armistice had been signed on the Western Front, I closed the school at 2.30 after singing the National Anthem"*. Giant maroons (explosives) were fired throughout the country, church bells rang, boy scouts cycled through cities and towns sounding the *"all clear"* on bugles and sirens. Factories closed, people ran onto the streets waving flags and by the time Big Ben struck one o'clock after four years of silence, London was a blaze of colour and the King and Queen drove through central London to Hyde Park. In the evening all over the land, street lights were uncovered, blackouts curtains taken down and there were fireworks displays everywhere. Thereafter every year at 11am on 11 November, in accordance with the King's wishes, a two minute silence was observed in all schools and public places.

The next day, School opened as usual but within days, Bertha Potter had to have time off because her father died, Olive Wray applied for several days leave and Harry Potter was taken ill with malaria, a nervous breakdown and Spanish 'flu. No one knows why this virulent global epidemic was given that name and when attempts failed to develop a vaccine, doctors predicted that more people would die from the disease than had been killed in the war. School closed and when pupils and staff re-assembled in the new year, there had been several deaths: Walter North 34 of Manor Farm and his daughter Clara 5, Annie Carr 28 wife of Alfred, shepherd for James B Heath, Springfield, William Greaves Hick 6 months, Alice Hart 3, Mabel Henderson 2 and Henry Speck 7. Three months later, Eva Johnson 13 died of diphtheria.

* * * * * * *

The 1 February 1919 was a day for rejoicing when villagers gathered in school to celebrate the home-coming of some of the *"boys"*. Anthony Sawkill presided and Harry Potter presented War Savings Certificates *"in recognition of their services to King and Country"* to: Harry Adams, John Bean, Edgar Brown, Stanley Currey, William Dawson, Charles and Arthur Duggleby, George Foxton, Alfred Levitt, George Mortimer, Arthur C Pinkney, George and Ernest Scruton, Arthur Taylor. Five months later Henry Bradford, Thomas Forge and Thomas Milner returned. On 18 July 1919, the head master nailed a Union Jack to the centre school window gable and before school closed, the children gathered on the hill, saluted the flag and sang *"Flag of our Country"*, *"Rule Britannia"* and The National Anthem.

As part of the peace celebrations King George V ordered all schools to have an extra week off for the 1919 summer holiday. Celebrations in Sherburn began with sports one day in August when at 1.45 pm, villagers gathered outside School and headed by the Excelsior Brass Band marched to William Foster's Field (see appendix 11). The soldiers beat the civilians in a tug-of-war and the gentlemen beat the ladies at cricket, even though they could only use their left hand. Best scores were: John Calam 33, Edgar Brown 16 and Wm Foster 13; Miss C Beecroft 21, Miss Hollings 14, Miss Kitching 10 and Miss Duggleby 9. After the children's sports, Mrs Hollings presented prizes, everyone sang the National Anthem, then marched back to the village. Mrs J Currey supervised tea in the Wesleyan Schoolroom for children, servicemen, ex-servicemen and *'aged'* residents and the day ended with a dance in school. When lessons ended on the 19 December 1919, Harry Potter and Anthony Sawkill presented 160 Peace Mugs, one to every child under 14. Mr Sawkill urged the children to look after the mugs not for their value, but to remind them in future years of *"the great struggle of right against might"* and of their duty to be patriotic and ready if called upon, to fight for King and Country.

In April 1920, Sherburn's Roll of Honour was hung in St Hilda's Church and began with the names of the servicemen who had *"made the supreme sacrifice"*. On 7 May 1920 a large crowd gathered on the school hill for the unveiling of the village war memorial by Col the Hon J Dawnay DSI, Lord of the Manor. The tablet of Portland stone, designed and made by Milburn & Son, sculptors, York, was set into the school's east wall. The vicar and the Wesleyan minister took part and the hymns *"Stand up! Stand up for Jesus"* and *"For all the saints who from their labours rest"*, were accompanied by the sound of the school piano coming through the window played by Stanley Currey, and the National Anthem ended the ceremony. The memorial was inscribed *"Pro Patria. In memory of the men of this parish who sacrificed their lives in the service of their country in the Great War 1914-1918 - Harry Y Cundall, Sergeant RGA; William E Dawson, Gunner RFA; John H Dobson Gunner RFA; George Bassett, Sapper RE; William Harland, Sapper RE (Tank Corporals); John W Clarke Private Northumberland Fusiliers; Albert W Baker (MM); Private Seaforth Highlanders; Edward Henderson, Private 5th Yorkshire Regiment; Frederick T Scott, Private Highland Light Infantry; John W Baker Rifleman Rifle Brigade; Fred A Atkinson, Private 5th West Yorkshire Regiment, Private Amos Magson 31st Batt AIF; Sgt Alfred P Sleightholme 21st Batt BKRR, Pte Richard Sleightholme 35th Batt. Greater love hath no man than this, that a man lay down his life for his friends"*. After the 1939-45 war, the tablet was replaced by the present tablet which lists the names of the men who died in both wars. For many years on the 11 November before closing school, the headmaster led children and staff in a special remembrance service and hung a poppy wreath on the tablet.

The school children helped with the November Poppy Day Appeal to raise funds for disabled servicemen, instituted by Douglas Haigh after the first World War. Haig was born in 1861, joined the army in 1885 as a cavalry officer and distinguished himself in the Boer War. He served in India, fought at Mons and Ypres in 1914 and was appointed Generalissimo over the Allied Armies in France. After the war, he was created Earl and spent the years until his death in 1928 raising support for disabled ex-servicemen. In 1928, senior pupil Nellie Dowsland was presented with a framed certificate by William Kirby and Percy Pinkney, British Legion members, acknowledging 18/- collected by the children for the Douglas Haigh Memorial Homes. Subsequent poppy sellers included Muriel Butler and Maggie Beal (1931), Joan Baker, Mary Gilbank, Annie England and Betty Forge (1935). In 1935, senior scholars Arthur Stead and Edward Majerrison hung a wreath of laurel leaves and poppies on the school war memorial and the following Sunday, Sherburn Brass Band led a procession of ex-servicemen and members of the Sherburn & Staxton Division of the St John Ambulance Brigade through the village to a service in St Hilda's attended by a large congregation. Harry Potter read the lessons, the vicar read aloud the names of the village men who died in the first war and two minutes silence was observed. A collection raised £1..8s..5d and a house-to-house collection £18..1s..6d for Earl Haig's fund. In 1937, Poppy Day collectors were Margery Clarke £1..10s, Dorothy Dobson £1..10s..10d, Mary Milner £1..1s..2d and the total collected in the area was £16..17s..3d. Arthur Day of Ganton presided at that year's British Legion's annual dinner in the Pigeon Pie, when 40 members enjoyed *an excellent repast* served by Mr and Mrs Harlie Constable. The toast list included *"The King"*, *"Comrades past and present"*, *"The Legion"* and *"Guests"*. William A Cundall and R B Buchannan shared amusing memories and Stanley Currey organised the entertainment with contributions from G Dawson, Brompton-by-Sawdon, F Edwards, Ayton, F Turner and J Flinton Ganton and community singing included old war-time songs. Two years later the second World War began.

* * * * * * *

Harry Potter did not attend all village funerals but when former pupil John Marsk Prodham 16 of Willerby died in July 1918, he and the choir boys and girls attended and the children made and sent posies of flowers. Harry Potter also attended the funerals of Leslie Jerrams 14 who died on Good Friday 1927, Herbert Hugill 22 who died in January 1929 and Eileen Clarkson 6 who died in February 1929. All the staff and children attended Eileen's funeral and took a wreath they'd made. On 13 March 1929, permission was granted to Kate Ringrose, assistant teacher, to attend the funeral of a relative Thomas Pickering Ringrose an LNER guard who was killed in the Darlington train crash. When Margery Smedley 8 died in Bridlington Isolation Hospital in August 1931, the whole school observed a time of silence and when Lucy Stead 5 died in January 1937 during a measles epidemic, all children and staff attended the funeral.

Harry Potter noted the deaths of school managers and when James Pilling Kirk 62, owner of the brewery, died in 1921, he recorded *"a deep sense of regret at the death of James P Kirk who had during his lifetime been an ardent supporter of the school"*. James Kirk died *"from fatty degeneration of the heart"* at his home *"Eastcote",* Esplanade Crescent, Scarborough, where he'd lived for 19 years. Witnesses at the inquest were his nephew Arthur Kirk of Leeds, his housekeeper Miss M Whitehall, one of his maids Violet Hall and Dr Godfrey. Before moving to Scarborough, James lived at Dawnay Lodge, Potter Brompton. His father James bought Sherburn Brewery from the Rivis family in 1867 and the premises were sold in June 1922 to E Walker, York, for £44,750 at the Royal Station Hotel, York, along with 26 fully licensed public houses, 8 beer houses, 3 off-licence shops, wholesale wine and spirit and bottling stores, retail shops, club premises and land at Sherburn, Scarborough, Filey, Bridlington, York, Bedale, Northallerton, Thirsk, Pickering and surrounding districts. The brewery was described as a *"six quarter"* with a capacity of 270 barrels per week.

The whole school attended the funeral of William Brown 52 school manager who drowned in the Mill Dam south of the village in January 1924. His son Edgar saw his father's cap floating on the water and it was believed he had slipped on a stone. William was a retired grocer, vice-chairman of the Sherburn RDC, a member of the Scarborough Board of Guardians and a committed Wesleyan.

When school manager Richard Duggleby 86 of Mount Pleasant Farm, died in March 1927, he was said to be the village's oldest resident and *"beloved by his employees and villagers for his cheery comradeship and ready kindliness"*. Before moving to Mount Pleasant, Richard farmed at Home Farm and was a long time tenant on Col Viscount Downe's Wykeham Estates. In his early life, he was a partner in the auctioneering firm of Speck & Duggleby, was a parish councillor, a District Councillor, a parish guardian, Justice of the Peace, a director of Scarborough College, and an elder of the Wesleyan Chapel. Five of his sons Harold, Edgar, Sydney, Charles and Arthur served in the 1914-18 war and his youngest son Herbert, a joiner, was killed aged 25 in a motor accident at Sherburn cross roads in May 1923. On the night of the accident, Herbert was turning right into High Street from St Hilda's Street and his car collided with another travelling from Scarborough to York. The other driver James A Leeward of York was cleared from blame, but the coroner emphasised that *"motorists should exercise the greatest care in approaching cross roads"*. Richard Duggleby was 82 and too frail to attend Herbert's funeral at the Wesleyan Chapel. Richard's youngest daughter Eva Blanche Grainger 37 died in Scarborough Hospital in 1937.

Another generous and life-long supporter of Sherburn School was William Page who owned a corn warehouse at Weaverthorpe Station for over 50 years until its destruction by fire in the early 1930's. William was a farmer's son from Huntingdonshire, but because he didn't care for farming, set up a corn merchant business in York in 1868. He was a member of the Sherburn Agricultural Club and during the late 1800's when two local poachers were charged at Norton Petty Sessions for trespassing in search of rabbits on Sherburn land over which he had shooting rights, William pleaded for leniency and one charge was dropped and the other poacher was fined 2s..6d with 10/- costs *"to serve as a warning"*. William often attended the Chapel Good Friday Rally and if he happened to be at the station on the day of the Sunday School's annual excursion to Scarborough, was known to give the children pocket money before they boarded the train. In 1891 he donated £2..2s to Sherburn Primitive Methodist Chapel to help offset a £10 debt. William's son John James 50 died suddenly in July 1930 whilst on holiday in the Lake District with his wife and child. John lived at Harrogate and William at York but because they were partners in the firm of William Page & Son, were often seen in Sherburn. When John died, William had reached the age of 90, had been a York City Councillor for 24 years, had declined the invitation to become an alderman a number of times and was the oldest member of York Rotary Club. On his 90th birthday, amongst the many messages of congratulations, there was one from the Lord Mayor of York. Even at 90, William was in his office every morning at 8.30, was still regularly attending the corn markets and was often seen *"with his upright gait and snowy white beard"* travelling by train through Weaverthorpe to Seamer market where, after a snack lunch in the station refreshment room, he would board a west-bound train to more work in Leeds. For many years, Thomas Scurr of 16 Springfield Terrace worked at Pages' warehouse and after the fire, went to work at Sherburn's new Waterworks. He and his wife Nellie had four sons and four daughters and Nellie died in 1940 and Thomas in 1942.

School manager James Bell Heath 72 died in October 1936, two weeks after being involved in a road accident. His wife Ada died in 1934, and they had five sons Ainsworth, Arthur Herbert, Charles Wilfred, Harold George, James Ernest and two daughters Amy Gertrude and Olive Mary. James Bell Heath was a parish councillor, a member of the church choir and a well known Wolds farmer who regularly sent rams and sheep to the Malton and Seamer sales. Other managers included William A Cundall, Arthur Heath, George H Mortimer and Ben Bassett.

In 1937, the whole school and most of the village attended the funeral of Annie Ward 78 who had been school caretaker since the death of her husband Matthew Ward in 1906 aged 46. Annie was taken ill on Friday morning 9 December and her daughter Laura took her to her home in Seamer where she died the following Sunday. Annie Ward (nee Foster) was born at Weaverthorpe, but had lived in Sherburn most of her life. For many years she was in the church choir and at her funeral the choir sang *"Jesu Lover of my Soul"* and *"Let saints on earth in concert sing"*. Chief mourners were George (son), Laura and John Bowman (daughter and son-in-law), George (grandson). Laura was a shop-keeper at Seamer for 25 years and died in January 1949.

* * * * * * *

During the 1914-18 war school did not have to close for epidemic illness, but there were colds and 'flu, and regular cases of ringworm, scabies, mumps and measles and the headmaster often had to send children home because they were dirty or had head lice. During the 1920's school closed several times for diseases such as diphtheria, measles, mumps, whooping cough, chicken pox and scarlet fever and Harry and Bertha Potter were often absent themselves because of illness. In 1920, their son Edwin *"Teddie"* was admitted to the County Isolation Hospital with diphtheria, in 1929 Mary Currey was admitted to the same hospital with diphtheria and when there were several cases in 1934, Bertha Potter was ill for two weeks and Kate Ringrose for two months, a series of inoculations against diphtheria began. In June 1938, when Clive Bean aged 7 collapsed, Harry Potter carried him home and he was diagnosed with tuberculosis and meningitis.

Walter Bradford took children from outlying farms home in his taxi when they were sick. Emily Allison was taken ill in 1926 and Hilda Bean in 1929 and the charge was 2/6d (12.5p) per 3 mile journey. Before the 1914-18 war Walter was a joiner's apprentice at Seamer, a motor mechanic in Scarborough and Leeds and during the war he tested *"those early flying machines"* such as the Salamanders, the Sopwith Camels and the Armstrong Whitworths. During one test flight, the carburettor cap came off and the engine caught fire, flames spread along the fuselage and Walter could see ambulances waiting on the airfield below, but the wind put out the flames and the crew landed safely. After leaving the forces, Walter set up a cycle repair shop west of the cross roads on the A64, then in the 1920's as the motor industry developed, he saw an opportunity to establish a garage and taxi service. When his sons Howard (b1927) and Graham (b1939) left school, the business became W E Bradford & Sons. Howard died at the young age of 50 in 1977 and Walter in 1988 aged 89 two years after he and his wife Alys celebrated their Diamond wedding.

In 1920, because of frequent epidemic illnesses, Dr H T Hollings urged the Sherburn Rural District Council to build 34 houses in the district. Many cottages were damp and unfit for habitation and there was danger to health through lack of a local sewage system, inadequate drainage from houses and yards and the urgent need for movable ash bins. Local farm dairies were inspected twice a year and although the milk supply was sufficient, hygiene was below standard. Dr Hollings also said the village wells were dangerous and a new water supply was needed. That year two blocks of four houses were built in Sherburn on land opposite today's surgery and named St Hilda's Terrace and eight along Vicarage Lane. Ten years later in 1930, B Fell & Sons, builders, built a block of four more houses (opposite today's surgery) for £1,410, bringing the number of new houses to 20. In 1935, the new Norton RDC which replaced Sherburn RDC accepted H Stubbing's quotation of £11,025 for building 34 more. Twelve were ready in Sherburn by the 3 September 1935 and let for 3/- (15p) per week to families living in the worst houses. By July 1937, the Ministry of Health had sanctioned the building of 60 houses in Heslerton, Sherburn, Willerby and Yedingham for £25,256. These included 24 in Springfield Terrace and 20 at the south end of Church View.

In 1932, a new district water main enabled communal water taps to be installed in St Hilda's Street for use instead of the old pumps. The supply came from natural Wolds springs and Lord Downe paid £50 for vegetation to be cleared away and a fence provided to keep out stock. The school water supply cost £14 and a concert raised £6..10s. Songs included: *"Spring Song"* by all, *"Widdicombe Fair"* and *"Little Cock Sparrow"* by the Infants; *"Vicar of Bray"* Douglas Pinkney; *"Old John Braddleum"* and *"Little Black Simon"* Grace Adams; *"Polly Wolly Doodle"* Violet Mintoft and Helena Pinkney; *"Three Little Maids"* Madge Clarke, Gladys Pinkney, Dorothy Dobson; *"I married a wife"* Daisy Watson; *"Three Black Crows"*, Roy Baker, John Clarke, Edward Hutchins; *"Lincolnshire Poacher"* Edward Marjerrison, William Pickard, Herbert Walker, Robert Levitt, Edgar Spanton, Clarence Eyre, Arthur Stead, Leslie Pinder, Edgar Dowsland; *"The Three Sailors"* by Albert Dobson, Norman Currey and William Kirk, *"My Own Country"* and *"Cuckoo Song"* by Class I. There were five sketches: *"The Three Bears"* with Albert Marston, Betty Pearson and Gerald Levitt; *"Red Riding Hood"* with Sheila Butler, Madge Clarke, Ethel Metcalfe, Doreen Lamb, Blanche Marflitt, Kitty Eyre, Ted Henderson, Mary Watson; *"The Lost Wig"* with Ronald Lamb, John Metcalfe, Maisie Majerrison, Walter Harness, Edward Hutchins; *"Guilty or Not Guilty"* with William Pickard as *Judge*, Tom Harness as *Clerk of the Court*, Cyril Metcalfe *Crier*, Edgar Spanton *Policeman*, William Heseltine *Prisoner*, Arthur Stead *Counsel for the defence*, Betty Forge *Counsel for the prosecution*, Edith Dawson, Madge Clarke *Witnesses*; Mary Milner *Prisoner's mother*; William Pinder and Robert Levitt *Reporters*; Leslie Pinder *Foreman of the Jury*; Thelma Standidge, Edna Gillery, Annie Scholes, Lena Pudsey, Edward Calam, Dorothy Dobson, Mary Allison, Clarence Eyre, Herbert Walker, Edgar Spanton, George and Ralph Pickard *Jury members*. The fifth sketch *"A Burning Question"* was given by Joan Baker, Helena Pinkney, Violet Mintoft, Doris Levitt, Daisy Watson, Mary Gilbank, Norah Stellings and Rosie Towse. Pianists were Bertha Potter and Kate Ringrose.

Also in 1932, the newly formed Ganton & District Nursing Association opened an Infant Welfare Clinic in Sherburn. Every fourth Wednesday afternoon all mothers could have their babies weighed in the Wesleyan Schoolroom and consult Dr Wilfred Thistlethwaite or the newly appointed district nurse

Molly Curl. A year later, the free issue began of daily cups of Horlicks to all school children. At the clinic's third anniversary in May 1935, everyone enjoyed *"a splendid tea provided by the ladies of the committee"*, a cake donated by Mrs Dawnay, each child was given a toy and a group photo was taken and a copy given to each mother. Mrs Martha Adams thanked the organisers Mrs H and Miss Wrigley of Ganton Hall, Mrs Cuthbert Dawnay, Heslerton Hall, Mrs Gresley and Mrs J W Elsworth of West Heslerton, Mrs Dukes of Willerby and Mrs C H Close of Sherburn. Throughout 1935, Nurse Molly Curl made 1736 home visits on her bicycle and spent 2320 hours on duty. Molly had a month off in July when Nurse Bumby from Hull took over. The number of babies delivered at home fell after the 1939-45 War when a maternity unit opened in St Mary's Hospital, Dean Road, Scarborough. The hospital opened in 1859 as a workhouse for the destitute and homeless. Olive Arnott of Sherburn was a nursing sister at the maternity unit from 1947 until her retirement in 1979. Olive and her sister Monica attended Sherburn School after the family moved to Weaverthorpe Station in 1924 when their father Herbert was appointed signalman. Olive trained at York County Hospital and passed the preliminary state examination of the General Nursing Council for England and Wales. Herbert was a church warden for many years, Olive and Monica were life-long church members and founder members of the Sherburn Branch of the Women's Institute formed in 1949.

In 1937, the Norton RDC applied to the Minister of Health to borrow £14,891 to build a Water Works in Sherburn above the Mill Dam. The Works supplied water to all homes in the village, but it wasn't until 1960 that the village had its own sewage system and cottagers and council tenants had the luxury of water closets and bathrooms with running water.

* * * * * * *

The children had memorable days off such as 28 February 1922 for the marriage of the Princess Mary to Viscount Lascelles, 26 April 1923 for the marriage of the Duke of York to Lady Elizabeth Bowes-Lyon (later King George VI and Queen Elizabeth), 29 October 1934 for the marriage of the Duke of Kent to Princess Marina, a day in May 1935 to celebrate King George V's Silver Jubilee when each child received a Coronation mug from the parish council followed by tea and sports and 6 November 1935 for the marriage of the Duke of Gloucester to Lady Alice Scott. On 28 January 1936 the day of King George V's funeral, the vicar and the Methodist Minister Rev W Rider led a service in school and the children listened to the funeral broadcast from London on Mr Potter's wireless.

Harry Potter organised several pre-war outings. In April 1934, he and 32 children caught the 7.50 am train from Weaverthorpe to Hull where they noticed Hitler's flag on German ships at King George V Docks. Within 6 years Hull Docks had become one of Hitler's prime bombing targets. One Friday in September 1934, a party of 34 caught the 10.10 pm train and arrived at King's Cross at 4.55am. They had a day's sight-seeing by coach, stopping for breakfast at Lyons Corner House, Coventry Street, where 1000 people could be catered for on each of its 6 floors. They were joined for lunch by two village boys Fred and Jack Metcalfe and for tea by Mr Potter's son Sgt Edwin Potter. They travelled by Underground to Madame Tussaud's, then back to King's Cross to arrive home at 5 am on Sunday. In June 1935, 3 coaches took 50 people on a day trip to Richmond for lunch at the Fleece Hotel then *"over miles of beautiful moorland"* to Northallerton for tea at Russells Cafe. In July 1935, 36 villagers had a day trip to Edinburgh from 6 am to midnight, travelling on the *"Tourist Train with 2 restaurant cars"*, picking up at stations along the line to Malton. The fare was 18/- (90p) for adults and 9/6d (47p) for under 16's. There were day trips to Hull Fair and Liverpool.

In April 1935, Harry Potter organised a Flag Day for the National Playing Fields Association. Collectors were Rosie Towse and Annie England 5s..9d, Gladys Pinkney and Miriam Mason 8s..4d, Annie Bell and Joan Baker 8s..6d and from a school collection 11/-.

School closed for the Whitsuntide holiday on 11 May 1937 and the following day was George VI's Coronation which was the subject of the BBC's first TV outside broadcast. A committee raised £24..8s..7d and the parish council donated £6 towards a souvenir mug for each child up to 14, free tea for all 600+ parishioners, packets of tea and tobacco for pensioners and a social and dance to end the day. Sports were cancelled because of rain, and held the following Monday evening, when practically the whole village followed the Brass Band to Mill Field. Children who competed received cash prizes and there was keen competition in adult races. Officials were Albert Marston, Alfred Levitt, judges; George Jackson, George Grice, starters; Tom Baker, David Harris, Percy Pinkney, Henry Bradford. A surplus of £5..19s..6d provided two commemorative parish seats.

* * * * * * *

The Rev Charles James who became vicar in 1915 after James Whittam's imprisonment, gave scripture lessons twice weekly in school and from time to time during the war, all the children and staff marched to church for a *"Children's War Service"* or an *"Intercessional* (prayer) *service"*. Charles offered himself as an army chaplain in April 1917 and before leaving, called to say goodbye to the children. The Rev G A Greenside (Thorpe Bassett), Rev T E Hughes (E Heslerton), Rev W Rowley (W Heslerton) and Rev W Helm (Yedingham) shared his duties. In February 1918, Charles came on leave and on the first Sunday preached in St Hilda's from 1 Thess Ch 5 v 17 *"Pray without ceasing"* and shared some of his battlefield experiences. After the war he went to be vicar of

Huntington. His successor was the Rev James Campbell Vernon, who had been vicar of Maltby, Rotherham for 25 years. Each summer, James and his wife Esther entertained the Sunday School children and teachers to tea and games in the field adjoining the Vicarage. James died peacefully on 22 July 1924 aged 69 after being confined to his bedroom for several weeks. The children gathered flowers and made a wreath and several posies and school closed so that everyone could attend the funeral. James' widow donated to the parish in his memory, a hand-driven funeral bier which ran on four large iron wheels and was used until motor hearses took over in the 1960's. Esther Elizabeth Mary Vernon died aged 85 at Cliffe Grove, Harrogate in October 1940.

James C Vernon's successor was the Rev Charles H Rowntree and on his first visit to school he told the children about the years he'd lived in Spain and at Sunday School parties, he and his wife provided musical entertainment with their gramophone. At that time there appears to have been a dispute about two Rivis memorial windows removed from St Hilda's during the 1912 restoration. The windows were described in a parish directory dated 1892, as *"the east window of three lights filled with stained glass representing the institution of the Blessed Sacrament erected by Mary Rivis of Wykeham and William Rivis of Sherburn in 1859"* and a *"three-light window in the south wall of the chancel, bearing six well-executed scenes from the life of Christ, inserted by T W Rivis Esq in memory of his sister Mary Rivis who died in 1873"*. The family were rich land owners and built and owned Sherburn brewery. An extract from the September 1929 issue of the church magazine states: *"after many meetings involving much discussion and having had expert advice, St Hilda's Church Council is now able to issue an ultimatum respecting the Rivis memorial windows. They will not be replaced in the church but will be claimed by a surviving member of the Rivis family. The medieval glass, with the approval of the advisory committee at York, has been inserted in the west window over the ancient font. This is the only stained glass window in the church"*. Charles Rowntree arranged for the list of vicars to be hung in church in 1930. In February 1932, Charles left to become vicar of N Grimston and Wharram and at a farewell service, chorister Louis Kirby presented him with a hymn book with music from the choir and Mrs Rebecca Postill presented him with a striking clock from the congregation. He thanked the choir for their *"uplifting influence"* and the congregation for their *"loyal devotion"*. Mr Kirby, vice-chairman of the Church Council, paid tribute to the vicar's *"unfailing kindness, deep devotion and intense religious fervour under whose leadership they had reached a high standard of worship"*. As the vicar and his wife shook hands with everyone, many expressed regret at their departure.

Sherburn's next vicar was the Rev Christopher H Stockdale who had been rector of Wheldrake for 5 years and on his first visit to school in July 1932, he was invited to dedicate a new concert platform paid for with £7 raised by a children's concert. Christopher left in 1936 to become vicar of S Milford, and his successor was the Revd Thomas Wray, former vicar of Scorton with Cold Kirby. Thomas was inducted in December 1936 by Canon England Archdeacon of York who urged the large congregation to support their new vicar and his wife Alice. Clergy present included the Rural Dean Rev T M Burnitt, Settrington, Rev C H Rowntree, N Grimston, former vicar of Sherburn, Rev J E P Cable, Rillington, Rev P Campling, W Heslerton and Rev Lawson-Smith, Wykeham.

The Wrays quickly became involved in village activities and in May 1937, when Thomas presided over the monthly meeting of the Scarborough Hospital Contributory Scheme committee formed a year earlier, it was reported that the annual house-to-house *"Hospital Pound Day Collection"* organised by the doctor's wife Mrs Wilfred Thistlethwaite, included: 105 lbs sugar, 4.5 lbs tea, tins of oxos, tins of Vim, 6 bars soap, 4 pkts cereals, 4 jars jam, 8 lbs rice and tapioca, 337 eggs, jellies, corn flour, beans, bread, tinfoil and 13s..2d.

At the Wrays' first annual Vestry and Parochial Church Council meeting in 1937, George Lawson was elected vicar's warden and Henry Mortimer people's warden. The year's income included £59..1s..10d from collections, £24..17s..9d from Sir Tatton Sykes' Bequest and £14..1s..8d from other sources. Members elected were Mesdames A Wray, Blanchard, R Postill, P Pinkney, A Heath, J M Beal, H Adams, O Pickering, S Stead, W Henderson and Miss Close, Messrs H Arnott, R P Pinkney, D S Jessop, C Forge, F Ringrose. On Shrove Tuesday 1937, Thomas and Alice attended a dance in school when £3..16s..6d was raised for Sunday school funds and music was by Mrs S Pickering and Miss C Beecroft (piano), Fred Hick and Ronald Heath (violins) and Arthur Heath (cornet). Thomas Wray went regularly into school and in October 1937, presented 29 candidates to the Bishop of Hull for Confirmation into the Christian faith. The Wrays formed a Branch of the Mothers' Union and members signed an Act of Dedication promising to keep the Union's objectives: *"To uphold the Sanctity of Marriage; To awaken in all Mothers a sense of their great responsibility in the training of their boys and girls – the Fathers and Mothers of the Future; To organise in every place a band of Mothers who will unite in prayer and seek by their own example, to lead their families*

Infants c1920 *Back:* Fred Walker, Ray Beecroft, Jack Cousins, Robt Foxton, Geo Levitt, Francis Dobson, Tom Pudsey
Middle: Bertha Potter (teacher),   ?   Betty Pinkney   ?   Lilian Watson, Geo Hick, Lena Bassett, Minnie Levitt, Linda Metcalfe, Maggie Jackson, Elsie Beecroft (monitress)
Front: Harry Cousins, Ernest Johnson, Joyce Hick, Madge Simpson, Jack Dawson, Victor Scurr

in purity and holiness of life". Monthly meetings were on a Tuesday evening and started with a service in St Hilda's followed by light refreshment at the Vicarage. On their first annual outing members travelled by coach to Whitby for lunch, Redcar for tea then through Bilsdale and home via Kirbymoorside. When they celebrated their 21st anniversary in June 1958 with a special service followed by a party, the cake was made by Mrs W Atkinson and iced by Mrs W E Bradford.

* * * * * * *

Harry Potter's son chose a military career and on the morning of 14 October 1927, his parents were absent for an hour to see him off by train on his way to China with the 2nd Battn Coldstream Guards. When he came home un-expectedly from Aldershot in January 1929, Mrs Potter was granted a day's leave. In May 1938, he was appointed Company Sergeant Major to the Federated Malay States Volunteer Force. After a short leave, he and his wife sailed on 6 May 1938 from London on the P & O Liner *"Ranchi"* to his new post at Penang. Two months later his parents handed in their resignation.

Their last RI report ended with the words: *"Mrs Potter has done admirable work with her little ones and we wish her many years of healthful retirement. This report is the last of Mr Potter's headship and I would like to place on record the most conscientious and efficient way he has always prepared the religious work and brought it into the whole atmosphere of school life. His 22 years at Sherburn and his kindly welcome to inspectors will be a memory that will not soon pass".* Harry Potter wrote his last log book entry on 29 July 1938 before school closed for the harvest holidays: *"Today I retire from the teaching profession having been headmaster of this school for 22 years. Mrs Potter Infants mistress is retiring also. This morning we were presented with a coffee service on behalf of the staff and children by senior scholar Harold Watson".* The school correspondent wrote: *"This is to certify that I signed the log book. I also feel sure that everybody here has appreciated the services that Mr and Mrs Potter have rendered at Sherburn School and I wish them much happiness as they retire from this sphere of work, signed B Bassett, School manager".*

The Rev Thomas Wray praised Harry's and Bertha's excellent service. Their school duties had always been their first consideration and they carried them out quietly and conscientiously often under harsh difficulties. Their retirement

Upper School c 1921: *Back:* Jack Bassett, Sid Dawson, Lizzie Jackson, Fanny Metcalfe, ?
Middle: Madge Horsley, Babs Woodall, ? , Oliver Henderson, Elsie Bradford, Harry Potter (headmaster)
Front: Albert Dawson, Colin Tacey, Herbert Bassett

ended a long and faithful scholastic career during which they won the children's affection and respect and the parents' esteem and gratitude. The Potters moved from School House to their retirement home *"Forsythia"*, Scalby Road, Scarborough, but there is no record of their deaths in Scarborough. Their son Edwin was landlord of the New Inn in Falsgrave for several years in the late 1950's/early 60's and died in 2000 aged 90 in Boston, Lincs.

CHAPTER 5
JOHN NEWTON (1938-1964)

HARRY POTTER'S SUCCESSOR John Newton was chosen out of 36 applicants and served for 26 years. He had been headmaster at Sledmere for seven years and before that he taught for six years in Cottingham. He and his wife Lydia first met when they were children attending the old Municipal School at Scarborough. There had been other Newtons living in Sherburn. Francis and Priscilla Newton had two babies baptised at St Hilda's, one in 1773 and one in 1778, another Francis Newton married Priscilla Oliver in 1797, Ann Newton 68 was buried in Sherburn churchyard in 1818 and Hannah Newton 64 from Scarborough, was lodging at the Vicarage in 1891 with Rev Richard Ellis. John and Lydia Newton were married in 1929 and had two children John Michael 7 and Deidre Louise 4 when they moved into School House. John Newton's first day was on 1 September 1938 the same day that Miss Lily Hutton from West Heslerton began teaching the Infants.

There were 105 pupils, 22 in the Infants, 28 in Stds I & II (Class III) taught by Miss Violet Levitt of Sherburn, 30 in Stds III & IV (Class II) taught by Miss Betty Bray from Hunmanby and 25 in Stds V, VI, VII (Class I) taught by the headmaster. Lydia Newton was supply teacher then later was appointed full-time. Miss Bray left on the 31 October 1941 to go to Burton Flemming after teaching at Sherburn for seven years. Miss Kilby and Miss Moore came on supply in April 1942 to help cope with an influx of evacuees and the absence of Lily Hutton who was recovering from an operation. Lily was often ill and in 1941 felt threatened with a nervous breakdown and in 1943 was suspected of having diphtheria. By 1950, numbers had fallen to 77 and Violet Levitt went on supply to Foxholes then Wintringham and didn't return. Miss Muriel Robinson and Mrs Dubovsky assisted temporarily and subsequent teachers were Mrs Halston from 1954-55, Tony Brewster 1955-57, Mrs Beal (1957), Miss Margaret Staveley (1958) and Mrs Tindall (1959). Annual salaries were: Betty Bray £236..5s..od, Lily Hutton £115..10s..od, caretaker Martha Adams who succeeded Annie Ward £26 and because Martha also had to clean the Wesleyan schoolroom where evacuees were being taught, Thomas Thompson began cleaning out the toilets for an annual salary of £5. Martha Adam's successors were Hilda Thompson (1940's), Julia Foxton assisted by Reg Phelps (1950's), Eliza Stead (1960's). Reg Phelps came to Sherburn from Birmingham just after the 1939-45 war and when he became a pensioner, took on the role of *"village handyman"* and was often seen wearing his flat cap and pushing an old pram containing tools and equipment.

Long before John Newton came to Sherburn, rumours of War abounded with increasing fears of gas invasions after Italian aircraft had been seen in 1936 dropping canisters of mustard gas on civilians and troops in Abyssinia. On 30 September 1938, 103 gas masks were delivered to school and instructions on their use took all day. The following Spring, a First Aid party of five men with an ambulance was established in Sherburn and there were four air raid wardens with Thomas Stanley Currey as leader, covering Foxholes, Weaverthorpe, Luttons, Willerby, Ganton, Sherburn, Heslertons and Yedingham. Nation-wide and in preparation for enemy invasion, on 31 August 1939 at 5.30 am, the evacuation began of 1.5 million children from cities into rural areas with schools as reception centres. Sherburn School was due to open after the summer holidays on the 4 September 1939 but had to open on the 1st to receive 24 evacuees and 7 teachers from St Joseph's Roman Catholic Infants School, Hull and the next day, 17 more arrived and the day after that 3rd Sept, Prime Minister Neville Chamberlain announced through a wireless broadcast: *"This country is now at war with Germany. We are ready"*.

The Wesleyan Schoolroom was hired and 18 desks ordered and even more evacuees arrived. Dr Wilfred Thistlethwaite and a nurse examined them, some stayed in Sherburn, some went to other villages and some went back home. On 10 and 11 September 1939, 105 children and 5 teachers came from Sunderland and on 7 July 1940, 44 children and 4 teachers came from St Patrick's Roman Catholic School, Hull. At that time, there were 47 Infants and 85 children in Stds I-VII. After a heavy period of bombing over Hull from 7-9 May 1941 when over 400 people were killed in the city, 29 more evacuees came and one of them was 9-year-old Colin Longthorpe who can remember spending many nights with his family in an *"Anderson Shelter"* at the bottom of their garden in Langtoft Grove, Hull, listening to the guns and bombs and his mother's terrified screams and sobbing. The shelters were 6 ft 6 ins long by 4 ft wide, had a curved corrugated steel roof and sides, the floor was the earth, they were put together in a 4 ft deep hole and the roof was covered with 15" of soil. They were cramped, damp and frequently flooded, but they saved thousands of lives. Colin Longthorpe and two of his neighbours Malcolm Wilson and Maurice Jackson *"three little boys in short pants, labels on lapels and carrying cases and gas masks"* left the shelters behind when they were put on the bus to Hull Paragon Station then onto a train bound for Malton where the evacuees were given food and drink then split into groups to go in different directions. The Rev Thomas Wray asked the children bound for Sherburn their *"denomination"* then looked after them on the train journey and during the walk from Weaverthorpe Station to the village. Charles and Clara Henderson of 4 Vicarage Lane took Colin and Malcolm and Mrs

Henderson's daughter-in-law Linda took Maurice but he became so homesick he had to be sent home. Valerie Brinkley lodged with a family in one of the two Gatehouses east of Weaverthorpe Station along the railway line side, Gordon Sparks at High Mill and Mary Duddy with Jessie Edmonds at 20 St Hilda's Street a tiny south-facing cottage that used to stand at the entrance of Sycamore Grove.

Colin remembers that Lydia Newton was *"good looking, kindly but firm and didn't need to raise her voice"* whereas John Newton was very strict. Before drawing lessons began, he ordered pupils to place their hands palms upwards on the desk then with *"cane in hand and thumb on lapel"* he walked up and down each aisle and if he spotted dirty hands *"the cane flashed down onto grubby finger tips"*. Evacuees had to attend church twice on Sundays in their best clothes and any restless or bad behaviour was corrected by having to sit beside Alice Wray the vicar's wife who Colin remembers was *"formidable and authoritarian"* but Thomas Wray was *"a kindly person, slightly absent minded, but a typical vicar"*!

John Newton only used the Punishment Book during his first nine months and made 14 entries. A certain pupil was given four strokes of the cane on his hand for possessing cigarettes and on another occasion the same pupil was given the same treatment for forcing a younger boy to go into the school garden for a ball. Although records ceased, Mr Newton continued to use the cane as a deterrent, Miss Levitt used her pencil to wrap knuckles and Miss Bray who was said to be almost as strict as the headmaster, usually clipped the offender's ears with her ruler, but one elderly gentleman remembers when she pulled him from his desk for disobedience, his well worn jacket tore in half! Next day, a relative took the garment to school and told Miss Bray in no uncertain terms to *"restore the jacket to it's former glory"*!!

John Newton did not enter evacuee names in the admissions book but sometimes logged arrivals and departures. In September 1941, arrivals were: R & T Martin, R Saye, T Faulkner, B A Hunt, B Bailey, J Stather, E Smallwood and 3 returned to Hull: Albert Thompson, June Lumb and Maurice Jackson. In 1942, evacuees who returned to Hull were W and F Fallon, M Feeney, J Pettman, P Butler, N, G and I Oddy, A Thompson, B Bailey, M Wilson, P Wardell, H and J Barnes, J Nicklas, Pat and Rita O'Gorman, June Lumb and John Stather. Michael Mangan was admitted to *"the Sick Bay at Malton"* with scabies. After the 1942 Summer holidays there were 103 village children and 29 evacuees in school.

Walter Bradford, one of Sherburn's wardens, received air raid warnings over his garage telephone, often after dark so he and his wife Alys had many sleepless nights. When a warning came on 29 January 1940 at 9.30 am, the children were sent home immediately. At 10.45 am the *'all clear'* sounded but school did not re-assemble until 1pm. Following an air raid warning at 10.30

am on the 8 January 1941, the Infants and Stds V-VII pupils gathered in the girls' porch and Stds 1-1V pupils in the boys' porch until the *'all clear'* sounded at 11.15 am and this became the usual procedure.

On 10 September 1940 John Newton took a group of children to the Carrs a mile and a half north of the village, to see a Whitley bomber which had made a forced landing in the field south of the road leading to Derwent Farm. The aircraft was situated in the corner of the field near the Derwent River Bridge but some elderly people claim the aircraft was a Blenheim and not a Whitley! On another occasion, a Wellington bomber crashed on top of East Heslerton Hill after returning from dropping leaflets over Germany (see appendix 12). Colin Longthorpe, former evacuee, can remember a Hurricane fighter landing west of East Heslerton Grange Farm in a field which had been the base for a pre-war flying club and where concrete posts had been placed to stop enemy aircraft landing. As the noisy aircraft passed over the village from the east trailing smoke, Colin and a group of children ran past the vicarage, across wet uncut corn fields just in time to see the pilot land the 'plane skilfully in a field alongside the road. As the children drew closer, a policeman signalled to them to stay away from the aircraft.

All windows throughout the land, had to be blacked out during the hours of darkness so that lights could not be seen by enemy aircraft and in November 1940, a dance in school raised money for the School Blackout fund, Percy Pinkney was MC and Fred Hick's Dance Band provided music.

In the early hours of 18 July 1941 five high explosive bombs dropped in close proximity to the village and thereafter school did not open until 9.30 am. After a time of heavy bombing over Scarborough, Miss Edith Norman and her sister came to live in one of the Station Cottages. Their home in Falconer's Square was completely destroyed and they lived at the Station until July 1950 when Edith died aged 83. Those who attended her funeral at Sherburn Chapel included her neighbours Herbert, Laura and Monica Arnott, and villagers Alys Bradford, Rose Hick, Bertha Brown and Jack Currey. Interment was at Dean Road Cemetery, Scarborough.

Throughout the war, there was a Royal Observer Corps (ROC) base at *"the listening post'* in the field east of Sherburn alongside the A64, where members worked round-the-clock in shifts looking out for enemy aircraft and relaying vital information to York headquarters. They included Harry Adams, John Atkinson, Jack Bell, Fred Brassleay, Ted Calam, Charles Close (secretary to Ganton Golf Club for 20 years), Bill Currey, Ted Dobson, Richard Duggleby, George and Tom Hugill, Tom Jackson, Herbert Johnson, Bill Kirk and William Roberts. Tom Jackson 66 who had been a shepherd for 40 years, died suddenly in August 1940. Herbert Johnson won a Spitfire Badge in 1944 for gaining 226 marks out of 250 in the Master Test in Aircraft Recognition, for identifying allied and enemy air craft from 200 photos. The ROC disbanded in 1945 but continued on a voluntary basis and Tom Hugill was one of the longest serving members.

John Newton was an instructor in the local Air Training Corps (ATC) and reached flying officer rank. The corps was called the 2140 Ganton Flight, but they used the club house behind the Pigeon Pie Hotel as their headquarters where cadets gathered for training from Sherburn, Flixton, Foxholes, Ganton, East and West Heslerton, Rillington, Staxton and Weaverthorpe. Sherburn's cadets included Howard Bradford, Norman Currey, Francis Forge, Roy Grice, Albert Marston, Raymond Metcalfe, Colin Taylor and Bill Witty. They practised the Morse and Semaphore Codes and regularly visited Staxton Wold RAF Station, a base for the Chain Home Defence Radar System where they had to climb a 360 feet high radar mast via a series of open ladders and platforms and the descent took 45 minutes. They held their parade services in Sherburn and starting at Springfield Terrace marched east along the A64 and north down St Hilda's Street to St Hilda's Church. In July 1944, Cadt Sgt Raymond Metcalfe 15 and Cadet K E Atkinson passed all subjects in the Official Air Crew Proficiency Examination. Raymond was selected to represent the Ganton Flight at an ATC Rally in London on Sunday 13 May 1945 as part of a national tribute to the RAF.

* * * * * * *

In July 1939, HMI's pupil and teachers' progress report read: *"The present head master was appointed in September 1938. School has four groups, the two senior ones are taught in the largest room under somewhat trying conditions, the classes being separated by a flimsy curtain. Senior boys and girls receive instruction in Handicraft and Domestic Science respectively at a neighbouring School and all senior pupils and some juniors take part in garden cultivation. In the essential subjects, the children make progress as they move through school and on the whole, work in the highest class reaches an acceptable level. Work of these classes however, is hampered by weakness in the groundwork of the lower juniors and some revision of method seems necessary particularly in Arithmetic and English. Sound preliminary work is being done in the Infants which should make it possible to strengthen these subjects in the lower classes and so enable the upper school to extend scope and widen outlook. In oral work some children show commendable eagerness to answer questions and though the response is not yet sufficiently general, a few of the older boys and girls are beginning to reason clearly. The habit of collective answering which is rightly being discouraged, and the inability of a number of children to arrange their ideas in an orderly way, makes it difficult to discover the extent of their knowledge. There is need for systematic speech training and fuller use should be made of singing and recitation. The recent introduction of book craft and the modernisation of the Art scheme, are giving fresh impetus and should offer good training in colour and craftsmanship. The school has a large garden in which much interest is shown by seniors and juniors of both sexes. Garden diaries might well show evidence in greater detail of individual interest and research. The interest which the children take in physical training, for which many have provided themselves with suitable clothing, calls for favourable mention".* In June 1939 the school tied for second place in the Norton & District Sports with 30.5 points and Norton Girls won with 32.

In June 1940 Raymond Metcalfe passed the County Minor Scholarship examination for entry to Malton Grammar School. On 15 March 1945, school closed for ten entrants to take the first annual Special Place Examination (later called 11+), but there were no passes and none in 1946. In April 1946, Ronald Bassett won a scholarship for a place at Hull College of Arts and Crafts. Successful 11+ pupils were Geoffrey Currey, Cedric Gillings, Christopher Grice, Susan Clarkson, Elna Stead (1947); Ambrose Caunter (1948); Elizabeth Bassett, Robin Grice, Arthur Caunter (1949); Valerie Heath, Elizabeth Stead, Anne Pickard (1950); Angela Stead, Mary Caunter and Maureen Pratt (1951); Verena Clarkson, Margaret Caunter (1952); John William Pinkney (1953); none 1954-55; Pamela Heath (1956); David Hugill (1957); Angela Mattinson, Ann Stead, David Pinkney and Andrew Cousins (1958); none 1959; Keith Dexter, Bernard Joyce, Shirley Moss (1960); Carol Bean, Michael Sanderson (1961); none 1962-1963; Joan Lockwood, David John Thistleton (1964). Pupils who went to Scarborough Convent Grammar School, included Deidre Louise Newton (1941), Evelyn Mary Leary (1942), Elizabeth Mary Bardsley, Judith Dawson (1947). In 1948 Violet Levitt's brother George Robert who was teaching in Bournemouth, was chosen to play as goal keeper for the Bournemouth football team. In 1949, the first group of 14-year-olds to transfer to Filey School, included Clifford Thistleton, Brian Bean, Kenneth Dawson, Alan Pickard, Brian Coultas, Ann Church, Dorothy Wray and Kathleen Dobson.

Gardening was vital during the 1939-45 war when the whole nation was called upon to *'dig for victory'* by using every available piece of land for food production. The 1940 school garden report said *"Small plots have been grouped together for ground economy. Owing to the war, the experimental plot will not proceed and the revision of the flower plots will not be so ambitious."* In 1941: *"Particular attention has been paid to crops for which this land is well suited; carrots and parsnips are showing good promise. A plantation of bush fruit is being established and particular care taken to build a stock of virus free black currants. Instruction appears to be very sound".*

There were lessons in rabbit keeping and in May 1942 following a public lecture *"Why every village should have its Rabbit Club for the production of food"*, Sherburn Rabbit Club was formed. Wild rabbit was also part of the wartime diet and soon everyone was singing: *"Run, rabbit, run, rabbit, run,*

run, run. Don't give the farmer his fun, fun, fun. He'll get by without his rabbit pie. so, run, rabbit, run, rabbit, run, run, run".(Noel Gray and Ralf Butler). The Sherburn & District Produce Association was also formed and at their 2nd annual vegetable and flower show in August 1943, Mrs Richard Fawcett (Ilkley) was the opener and Evelyn Mary Leary 12 year-old daughter of Thomas Leary of the Waterworks, presented her with a bouquet. Committee members were John Newton (secretary), Tom Leary (chairman), L Potter, George Foxton, Bob Simpson, Bill Gillery and Eddie Bell. The children entered bunches of wild flowers and the winners were Nora Clarkson and Betty Hugill. Exhibits auctioned by William A Cundall raised £5 for Scarborough Hospital. After the war, the Sherburn & District Produce Association became the Sherburn & District Agricultural & Horticultural Association and their first open show was in July 1946 in the field alongside the A64 across the East Beck. The president was Richard A Fawcett, Ilkley, owner of Sherburn Estates, and officials were George Richardson (chairman), John Newton, John Sinclair (secretaries) and Percy Pinkney (treasurer). The show attracted over 400 high standard entries and despite showers, attendance was good. Each year more classes were added and in 1949 the show opened with a children's fancy dress parade headed by the Sherburn Excelsior Brass Band. Awards were: *Fancy:* Adrian Broome, Janet Currey, Anne Pickard; *Original:* M Foxton, A Roberts, Marjorie Thistleton, Valerie Heath; *Comic*: Peter Cousins, Terry West, Andrew Cousins. In the children's classes: *Wildflowers:* M Foxton; *Grasses:* M. Foxton; *Hand sewn garment (schoolgirl's)* Elizabeth Stead*: Painting and drawing (boys):* Cedric Gillings. The Ilkley Silver Challenge cup for best horse was won by T Mudd, Brompton, the Fawcett Silver Challenge Cup for livestock, horses and foals by Southburn Estates, the Sherburn Silver Challenge Cup for the best beast by R A Fawcett & Sons who handed it over to runner-up J Jeffrey of Brompton; the Richardson Silver Cup for best sheep went to T A Stephenson & Son, Market Weighton, and the Machin Silver Cup for the best pigeon to G Robson & Son.

Sherburn Excelsior Brass Band had re-formed in 1948 with Percy Pinkney as band master, and all the old instruments that had been silent at least for the duration of the war, were thoroughly over-hauled and three second-hand instruments were bought for £60. Members included Lawrence Duggleby, Frank Forge, Percy and Bill Gilbank, Arthur, Harold and Ronald Heath, Bob Levitt, Percy Pinkney, Bob Reeveley. At Christmas 1948 the band made £17 playing carols in the village and neighbourhood. Sherburn's first Brass Band was formed in 1880 by Anthony Sawkill and under his leadership gained *'considerable local reputation'*. Those who enrolled at the first practice on 26 January 1880, were Richard Harland 37 carpenter on 1st cornet (d 1921); Thomas Fred Bean 21 a farm servant (d 1939) and George Clarkson 26 inn keeper at the New Inn later called The East Riding Hotel (d 1897) both on

2nd cornets; John Lightfoot 17 apprentice tailor (d 1920) on 3rd cornet; Jonathan Currey 20 church sexton (d 1945) and Simeon Lightfoot 30 a groom (d 1934) both on tenor saxe-horns; R Taylor (no record of death) on baritone and William Lightfoot 27 shoe maker (d 1909) on euphonium. Joseph Fox (no record of death), a cooper and former innkeeper at the New Inn from 1879-87, played an enormous bass drum called a bombardon and Thomas Stones 25 a blacksmith played a smaller drum (d 1930 at 18 Dean Rd, Scarborough). The Band flourished but disbanded cc 1914-18, then reformed in 1928 with a complete set of instruments, uniforms and a small amount of cash left from the old band and John T Hick was appointed band master and played the bombardon, Percy Pinkney was secretary and William Kirby chairman.

* * * * * * *

Between 1939 and 1947 there were no HMI inspections then in 1948 the report read: *"The 90 pupils aged 5 to 15 are in four groups. The head master who has charge of the seniors, has three assistants* (Lydia Newton, Violet Levitt, Lily Hutton). *A pleasant environment is provided in the infants' room, despite space limitation. Children are keenly interested in their work and activities and talk freely. Progress in reading and number is satisfactory. Unfortunately the upper juniors and seniors have to work in the same room. No steps have been taken to arrange for a partition and this is to some degree responsible for the classes tending to be too directed by the teachers with insufficient activity by pupils. The Head Master realises the value of oral expression but the majority of older pupils do not speak fluently. In formal English and arithmetic, juniors and seniors make steady progress. Reading is enjoyed. Exercise books are neatly kept. A percussion band is providing enjoyable and useful musical experience for lower juniors. Art lessons are a means of expression and a fair standard of work is achieved in book craft. The girls' sewing is good and attractive garments have been made. The value of needlework will be increased when cutting out and planning are more definitely done by the girls. Boys and girls have gardening lessons. Older girls attend a House-craft Centre and boys have handicraft. Throughout the school it is pleasing to note the conscientious work of the teachers and the good behaviour of pupils."* In 1952 Miss Hall from Scarborough began a series of country dancing lessons each Friday morning.

After the war a new Singer hand sewing machine and ironing board were delivered to school and older girls learned to sew pillow cases, pinafores, skirts and night-dresses. Other post-war deliveries included a GEC wireless, two dozen 2.25" rubber balls, one cricket ball, 2 pot moulds, 60 pairs of physical training plimsolls, 16 swords @ 4/- each for Sword dancing, 2 size 4 football cases and bladders, four 20ft and six 9ft skipping ropes, 2 sets of cymbals, 2 tambourines and one drum, 24 Songs of Praise, 12 chairs from Kingfisher Ltd, West Bromwich @ £11..8s..6d and 6 infants' tables @ £9..6s..0d, one

The Pension Service

Part of the Department for Work and Pensions

Your reference is ZM694904A
Please tell us this number
if you get in touch with us

The Pension Service 1
Post Handling Site B
Wolverhampton
WV99 1AL

Phone   0345 6060265
TEXTPHONE for the deaf/hard of
hearing ONLY 0845 6060285

MRS DORIS COSGREAVE
2 BECKHAMPTON COTTAGES
THE GREEN
FROGMORE
CAMBERLEY, SURREY
GU17 ONT

Date 04/02/2017

ABOUT THE GENERAL INCREASES IN BENEFITS
This is to tell you that from 10 APR 17 the amount of benefit you
receive will change. The new amount will be included in the payment on
or after this date. It is important to tell us about any changes, such
as a change of address. If a change of circumstances has occurred,

ABOUT THIS LETTER

If there is someone else in your household who also gets State Pension or Widow's/Bereavement Benefit, they may not have received their letter yet; it will be sent to them soon.

ABOUT OTHER BENEFITS YOU MAY RECEIVE

If you are paid other benefits or allowances separately (such as Attendance Allowance/Bereavement Benefit or Carer's Allowance) you will be sent a separate letter telling you about the rate you will receive from April.

HOW YOUR STATE PENSION OR WIDOW S/BEREAVEMENT BENEFIT IS MADE UP

Your pension/benefit can be made up of one or more components (as shown over the page). More information on components is shown in the leaflet sent with this letter.

ABOUT CHANGES OF CIRCUMSTANCES YOU MUST REPORT

You must tell us straight away about any changes that may affect your pension or benefit (such as a change of address). The enclosed leaflet tells you more about this.

ANY QUESTIONS YOU MAY HAVE

There is a section in the leaflet called 'Answers to frequently asked questions' you may find helpful.

IF, AFTER READING THE LEAFLET, you have a query or you wish to report a change in your circumstances, please get in touch with us. Our phone number and address are shown over the page. Our opening hours are 8.00am to 6.00pm Monday to Friday

PLEASE KEEP THIS LETTER FOR INFORMATION - you may need to use it if you have to submit a tax return.

caused.

HOW YOUR BENEFIT IS MADE UP

basic State Pension		£73.30
Pre 97 additional State Pension	£122.32	
less Contracted-Out Deduction (COD) of	£76.77	
	Total payable	£45.55
Graduated Retirement Benefit		£1.33
Age Addition		£0.25

The amount each week is £120.43

BR5899

Please turn over

teachers single pedestal desk 4'6" x 2'3" x 2'6" with 4 drawers, 4 tubular steel infants stacking tables with 36" x 15" polished plywood tops with pencil grooves, an 11ft drop leaf table for fixing to the main room wall @ £9..12s..od, a Record Player from T Beadle & Co, Hull @ £13..2s..4d and in 1961 a climbing frame was fixed in the girls' yard.

The troublesome school yards were covered with tarmac at the end of the war, during the summer holidays of 1953, water lavatories replaced the *'pans'* for £772, pointing of the school yard boundary walls cost £69 and a new path from the road to the school entrance cost £75. In 1954 electricity installed by Dale Electrics for £56..3s..od, was paid for by Frank and Wilf Ward, farmers and factory founders. The brothers opened the factory in 1949 and began to provide work for school leavers just as farm mechanisation was reducing vacancies. In 1954, new classroom floors were laid for £119..15s..od and a new kitchen was fitted for £248. Doris Allison was the first Kitchen Assistant and in the first term was serving dinners to 23 children and 5 adults. When Doris retired in 1959 her successor was Mary Kedge.

* * * * * * *

The 1939 Religious Inspection report read: *"Infants: the class is ready to talk about stories they know and their teacher has made an excellent start. Hymns and verses are simple and attractive and keep a wonderful pitch considering singing is unaccompanied. Group 3: In both Old and New Testaments, the group made a poor showing and it is clear the teacher has to deal with a discouraging class where many children are dull and unimaginative. Written work is neat, accurate and an altogether more satisfactory attainment. Group 2: children were ready with answers and gave a good account of the New Testament and Catechism. In written work the children reproduced the miracles and parables in their own words. Group I: The duties in the Catechism are well explained and the New Testament portion shows good work. Singing is cheerful and enunciation good. The head master has our best wishes for a successful time."* In June 1940: *"The Infants were happy and responsive, knew their Bible stories well and were eager to answer. The other three groups seemed to be on the same level, response in each was fairly general. Opening prayers were reverent and devout and singing a good average. Repetition work was well known and expression work highly satisfactory. The tone of the School is high and discipline very good."* In 1944: *"There has been a most welcome improvement. The children are much more interested and answered questions willingly. Improvement was especially noticeable in Stds VI and VII. I was pleased with the written work and their compositions were marked by care and in some cases by beautiful handwriting".* In 1945: *"I found this school very satisfactory. Good work has been done. I was favourably impressed by children from 8-10 and those of 11 and 12. Std VII was not quite as good and showed too much hesitation in answering but made up for this in good written work".* An extra comment by the Diocesan Inspector read: *"There is no mention of private prayers being taught. I should feel grateful to the teachers if they would please instruct the children how to formulate private prayers. It will bring forth great results in the life of the child."* And in 1946: *"Good work has been done. There is a happy atmosphere and the children are responsive".* In 1948: *"I inspected all four classes and was pleased with the responses given to my questions. The Infants were eager and had done some excellent expression work. The tone and atmosphere of the school are most satisfactory. The teachers have instructed the children carefully. Written work of the elder scholars was good and covered a good deal of ground".*

Throughout John Newton's headship, the Revd Thomas Wray went into school at least once a week to take daily assembly and pupils were given long pieces of scripture to learn by heart. One elderly gentleman who was a pupil at the time admits that he often gains comfort by recalling some of the words he learned. There were four services in St Hilda's every Sunday: 8 am Holy Communion, 10.30 Mattins (Morning Prayer), 1.30 pm Sunday School and 6.30 pm Evensong (Evening Prayer). At the annual Sunday School prize-giving in New Year 1941, there were 74 children on the register and many of them would also attend one of the other church services with a parent. Both chapels had a Sunday School with a similar number of children. On Friday 8 July 1960, a special service of thanksgiving in St Hilda's Church commemorated 1000 years of worship and work. The bidding included the words *"Beloved, we are gathered here as one Christian family, from the Archbishop of York, our Father in God, to the youngest children, to commemorate the 1000th anniversary of this Church. Let us thank God for so many centuries of the Faith of his Son Incarnate, crucified, risen, ascended; and for all the love which that Faith hath brought to this place and to those who have dwelt here".*

* * * * * * *

Almost every new year, snow and blizzards reduced attendance and in 1940, Wolds roads were blocked and long distance children and Betty Bray were absent for several days and Lily Hutton walked to school from West Heslerton. On 26 February 1947, during one of the severest winters ever recorded, John Newton wrote *"Owing to a fierce blizzard only 5 children turned up for school. I sent them back home whilst there was still a chance for them to return safely and closed the school. Afternoon 24 present out of 82; marked registers and kept school open. Miss Hutton and Miss Levitt both absent all day".* Snowstorms and subzero temperatures caused power cuts all over the country and stopped trains, thousands of homes were without heat and light and Buckingham Palace, the Ministry offices, banks, law courts and department stores were candlelit for days. Isolated farms used sheets as distress signals for the RAF to drop food parcels. Despite heavy snow and high winds in December 1949 and 1950 school concerts raised £15..0s..6d and £16..1s..0d respectively. Snowdrifts prevented milk deliveries on the 4 days 25-28 February 1958.

School did not have to close because of epidemic illness but John Newton always recorded the first cases thus: November 1938 Gilda Stead (scarlet fever), October 1939 Joyce Dawson (scarlet fever), February 1940 Douglas Pickard, William Clarkson, Ernest Marflitt, Margaret Sadler and Dorothy Thistleton (measles), October 1940 Kathleen Dobson (chicken pox) and Aubrey Church (scarlet fever), January 1941 Sheila Dawson (scarlet fever), April 1941 Gilda Stead and Jennifer Grice (measles). In February 1942 there were 9 cases of chicken pox and in June 1947, the measles cases included Moyra Dexter, Susan Lythe, Rita Foxton, Margaret Caunter, Esme Robson, Gordon Thistleton, Michael Bolland, Susan Dixon, Anthony Proudfoot, Michael Drayton and Alison Bradford. In 1949 during a severe outbreak of influenza, Lydia Newton, Julia Foxton (caretaker) and 46 pupils were ill and Elizabeth Basset was unable to take the Grammar School selection exam, but did so later and passed.

In 1940, free milk was supplied to needy families and from September 1942, one third of a pint was issued daily to all children during morning break. Deliveries were by Grangers Northern Dairies, Spavens and Scarborough Co-Op respectively. A 1968 survey revealed that only one child in 100 was in need of free milk and the scheme was abolished. In 1971 the Family Income Supplement replaced the weekly family allowance of 5/- (25p) which began in 1945 for each child except the first.

Following a nation-wide outbreak of poliomyelitis in 1957, all children were vaccinated against the crippling disease said to be caused by the thalidomide drug prescribed during pregnancy for morning sickness. The first pupils to be inoculated included Roy Allison, Geraldine and John Bean, Analisa Brandt, John Calam, Anne Clarke, Andrew Cousins, Janet Foxton, Hazel Hardie, Pamela Harrison, Peter Holiday, Teresa Jackson, Ian McClung, Kenneth Pratt, Rodney Penter, Michael Pickard, Jean Smith, Anne Stead, Heather Wray, Keith Worthy. Also in 1957, there was a national outbreak of Asian 'flu and when school re-opened after the summer holidays Lydia Newton and 41 pupils out of 83, were still absent. By mid-Sept in over 160 large towns and cities of England and Wales, average deaths of 8 per week had risen to 47 because of the 'flu.

John Newton recorded all accidents and rendered first aid. In 1939, a book press fell on Cynthia Spanton's toe and after treatment she was taken home by Miss Bray. In 1942 evacuee Rose Taylor fell and broke her arm whilst playing leap frog and Nurse Curl sent her to Scarborough Hospital in Walter Bradford's taxi. In February 1943, Sergeant Huddleston began a series of lectures in school on *"Safety First"* and there were regular visits by the dentist.

In 1948 Elizabeth Bassett dislocated her elbow and Anthony Proudfoot burnt his face in the school yard but the cause was not recorded and in 1953 Bretton Ellis wounded his scalp during games. One morning in June 1955, Andrew Straughan 9, who lived at the East Riding Hotel from 1954-57, was admitted to hospital with serious gun shot wounds and remained on the danger list for some days. His father Alf Straughan pub landlord, said his son had taken a cartridge from a cupboard, loaded the gun and it went off. In 1961 Paul Rackham fell from one of the outside bars and needed a doctor, in 1962 Timothy Pickard and Ian Umpleby bumped into each other and Tim bit his tongue and needed stitches and in February 1964 David Thistleton badly cut his forehead on a fire extinguisher.

* * * * * * *

General call-up of all men over 20 began immediately war was declared and by the end of October 1939, 158,000 soldiers and 25,000 army vehicles had crossed the English Channel and the RAF was regularly carrying out reconnaissance flights over France. Because thousands of casualties were expected, the government ordered hospitals to be cleared and mortuaries were stacked with cardboard coffins. This excessive preparation proved unnecessary but other precautions were demanded. Information Leaflet No 1 urged every-one to carry a luggage label showing their name and address, street lighting and windows had to be blacked out, headlights dimmed and giant posters urged the population to save, dig, work, buy war bonds, don't travel, don't waste and most important, don't spread rumours for *"careless talk costs lives"*. Householders were told that if they could all burn 5lbs less coal in one day, this would provide enough coal to make 13 bombs! There was a national call for scrap metal to be re-cycled for ammunition and John Newton and his senior boys made a village collection. Food rationing was enforced on items such as meat, bacon, butter, cheese, sugar, tea, sweets and clothing and some remained rationed for several years after war ended.

  Sherburn's parish councillors discussed the re-commissioning of the village pumps as a reserve water supply against enemy action. Fred Stones reported that two would be expensive to repair but two could be repaired at moderate cost. Councillors included Miss Lumley, John Newton, Albert Marston (Library Committee), George Lawson, Ben Bassett and Tom Kellington (Footpath Committee), Charles Taylor and Joseph M Bradford (Rating Authority reps), Alfred E Levitt (Clerk).

  Barney Harris, son of David Harris of 20 Church View was said to be the first militiaman to join up and in June 1940 was promoted to staff sergeant in the RAOC. In July 1942, Charles and Annie Elizabeth 'Lib' Walker of 7 Springfield Terrace heard that their son Pvte Fred H Walker had been captured in Libya and was in a prisoner of war camp either in Italy or Germany. He was released in June 1945, two months after his father died. Fred's brother Pvte John Walker (Leicester Regt) served 4 years in the Middle East, India and Burma and came home in January 1945 along with Pvte George Jackson (Pioneer Corps) and Pvte Cecil Pickering (Royal Marines). Cecil's parents Oliver and Florence Pickering, were proprietors of the East Riding Hotel from 1940-54 and his grandparents Robert and Priscilla Pickering were proprietors of the same pub from 1905-09. Robert and Priscilla (nee Pinkney) were married on 17 December 1870 and he was a signalman at Weaverthorpe Station for many years. He died in 1933 aged 86 and Priscilla died at the East Riding in January 1942 aged 92. William and Ruth Cundall heard that their eldest son, Lieut Harry Y Cundall (Green Howards) had been wounded in Italy. In 1945, LAC Colin Taylor, son of Charles and Dorothy Taylor, grocers in St Hilda's Street and LAC Douglas Currey, son of William and Edith Kate Currey of Ganton, met unexpectedly in Burma. Fifty-six Sherburn men and women served in the forces and two died: Private Thomas Foxton (Green Howards) and Gunner John Shields-Levitt 28 (Royal Artillery). A memorial service for John was held at St Hilda's Church in April 1945 (see appendix 13).

A soldier died in Sherburn on New Year's Eve 1942 outside a cottage in Metcalfes' Yard off St Hilda's Street, opposite Central Stores. At an inquest, Dr Wilfred Thistlethwaite said that just after midnight, he was called to a semi-conscious soldier who was lying on a couch with head injuries and a wound in his stomach. The doctor went home for some morphia but when he returned the soldier had died. The body was taken to the Old Brewery which had been standing empty for some years and Sergt Billing identified the body there on 2 January 1943, as that of William Kennedy 24. Albert Johnson (Royal Armoured Corps) also 24, pleaded *'not guilty'* at York Assizes to wilful murder but *'guilty'* to manslaughter and was sentenced to 12 months hard labour. The wound from which Kennedy died was caused by a sheath knife belonging to Johnson who after the stabbing, threw the knife into the river. Johnson told the police he remembered fighting with Kennedy but said *'it was not deliberate, but more of an accident.'* The men had gone outside to settle an argument, there was a scream and Kennedy ran back inside the cottage bleeding profusely. The knife had penetrated 4" into his body. Johnson who was described as *"a fine man when sober but addicted to violent habits when drunk"*, was from Bolton where he had worked at various mills and his employers described him as a good worker. He had been friendly with Kennedy for 12 months and they were seldom seen apart. Both had been drinking earlier in the evening and for some reason, antagonism had arisen. Mr Justice Croom-Johnson said *"One tragedy is that a good soldier, instead of doing his duty, will have to remain in prison. Another tragedy is that having put an enemy in your mouth to steal your brains, you and drink, killed your best friend. I am sure that to a man of your character, this is as bitter a punishment as anything that my duty compels me to impose. You killed a man with a horrible weapon and there is evidence that on at least two occasions you had drawn this very knife. I am certain you never meant to kill Kennedy and doubt whether you meant to hurt him, I think it possible that there was provocation, but taking all into account, I am obliged to send you to prison, much as I regret having to do so".* Legend says the two young soldiers had quarrelled over the favours of *"a dark and lovely lady of the night"*!

After the war, the empty brewery was used as a meeting place for the St John's Ambulance Brigade led by Margaret Ridsdale (nee Beal) who joined the brigade in 1942. Cadets can remember the life-size skeleton Margaret used in her instruction and on dark nights people hurried past the empty brewery, not because of the skeleton but because of a rumour about a ghost believed to be the restless spirit of the young soldier murdered by his best friend!

Margaret Ridsdale attended Sherburn School from 1923-31 and was a niece of Alfred Burnett of 10 Springfield Terrace. She married Herbert James Ridsdale, son of Thomas Ridsdale of Staxton, in St Hilda's Church in April 1943 and was given away by Mrs Helena Fryer of Westbourne House. Margaret wore a blue crepe dress with matching hat and shoes, and carried a spray of carnations and an ivory backed prayer book. The Ridsdales moved to Staxton in 1952 where Margaret started a St John's Ambulance Division for 11 to 16's, she also served in the ambulance section of the Civil Defence, and although she had eight children, found time each week to wash shirts for the Staxton Football team. When anyone was injured and because the nearest doctor was 4 miles away at Sherburn, a call would go out to *'Maggie Ridsdale, Staxton's Good Samaritan'*. In 1965, Maggie went to London to receive a *'serving sister award'*, in 1981 she received an *"officer sister award"* and in 1987 she retired after 45 years. Two other long serving members were Percy Gilbank for 30 years and his brother Jack for 25 years. Percy left Sherburn School at 14 in 1921 and Jack in 1929, and both worked for Cundalls of Sherburn Lodge where their father Arthur Gilbank had been a shepherd since 1914. Percy's son Bill was born at Cundalls' Wolds Farm and when he left school in 1945, became chief tractor driver after 12 horses had been replaced by two tractors.

In 1965, Joseph Cundall & Son were presented with a championship trophy by H Burton chairman of the Sherburn branch of the National Farmers Union at their annual dinner at the Grand Hotel, Scarborough. They had produced a first class crop of wheat after draining water from Carr land that had been derelict for years, and they also won the mangold competition and came second in the turnip and potato competitions.

* * * * * *

John and Lydia Newton helped raise funds for local soldiers and at Christmas 1940 each member of the forces received a postal order for 7s..6d and a parcel. In August 1941, Sherburn took part in *"War Weapons Week"* when £2,024..11s..6d was raised in the district. School children Rosemary Calam, Mary Cavill, Greta Mintoft, Norah Dobson, Christine Henderson and Brenda and Esther Foston raised £3..9s..9d at a concert. During *"Wings for Victory Week"* in June 1943, £3,733 was raised for ammunitions. The main event was a Sports evening in Millfield organised by John and Lydia Newton, Violet Levitt, Norman Currey, Tom Baker, Percy Pinkney and George Johnson. (see appendix 14).

During *"Salute the Soldier Week"* in June 1944, £2,2410 was raised starting with a dance in school on Saturday night, a United Service in St Hilda's on Sunday, another dance on Monday, a cinema show in the Methodist School room on Tuesday, a sale on Wednesday, a whist drive on Thursday and sports on Friday organised by John Newton and Violet Levitt, with a Home Guard demonstration and running commentary by Major Parks. On Saturday the Seaforth Highland Band headed a fancy dress parade and school children organised stalls and competitions and the week closed with yet another dance. In 1945, Charles Taylor chairman of the parish council, received a framed certificate for the parish's contribution to the War Savings Campaign. Dances continued to cause problems and in 1942 a desk was damaged, in 1943 a widow smashed and in 1946 the lock and key to the Infants classroom were broken.

The day after war ended on 7 May 1945, church bells rang all over the land and people flocked into the streets singing and dancing and doing the *"Hokey-Kokey"*. By mid-day Whitehall and the Mall were packed with cheering crowds as Winston Churchill was driven past for lunch at the Palace. When Big Ben chimed at 3 pm the vast congregation of excited Londoners fell silent to listen to the Prime Minister's broadcast over loudspeakers and as he ended with the proclamation *"Long live the cause of freedom! God save the King!"*, wild cheering was renewed. Rejoicing spread throughout the land in a blaze of flags, fireworks and floodlights and Sherburn school, like all others, closed for two days. Three quarters of a million homes had been destroyed or severely damaged by German bombs, the nation was in debt by £3.5 billion, there was less food than ever, the people were exhausted, shabby and undernourished, but with courage and pride they set about picking themselves up out of the dust and rubble to re-build their lives.

A *"Welcome Home Fund"* was set up and Sherburn's service men and women were each sent a hand-written letter saying: *"We have never forgotten you at Sherburn and constantly remembered you in our prayers. We thank you for all you have done for us and we will never forget the sacrifices you have made in so many ways, or for the dangers and discomforts you may have endured. We all welcome you home and trust you will have many years ahead of peace and happiness. The way has been difficult and hard but together with God we have won through. As a small token of appreciation of your services, we have pleasure in enclosing £5 from the above fund. 'God bless and keep you and yours' is the wish of all at Sherburn. I am, yours faithfully, Oliver Henderson (hon treasurer).*

Ten years after war ended, first-hand activities of the Dutch Resistance were related to Sherburn Women's Institute at their June 1955 meeting by Mrs Molyneux of York who was living in Holland during the war. District Nurse Marion Charter, Molly Curl's successor, presided and winners of a competition to find the highest number of words from the letters in *"Women's Institute"* were Vera Campbell, Mabel Cousins and Alys Bradford. Hostesses were Olive Arnott, Evelyn Park, Madge Percival and Mrs Bill Preston. The branch celebrated their 10th anniversary in November 1958 in the Methodist Schoolroom with a cake made by Mrs Alan Featherstone and iced by Alys Bradford and Elsie Currey. In July 1961, Lydia Newton opened a WI Garden Party at *"Whitegates"*, home of Stanley and Elsie Currey, and 7-year-old Diane Oxtoby presented her with a box of handkerchiefs. School girls Jean Sedman, Pamela Heath and Christine Featherstone sold buttonholes and handkerchiefs.

* * * * * * *

At their first Christmas, the Newtons raised £3..4s..6d at a whist drive to pay for a school party and this became an annual event, with tea, games, dancing and 1/- (5p) for each child. The Church and Chapel Sunday School also provided children's parties and at Christmas 1939, St Hilda's raised £4 for their Sunday School with a Fancy Dress Parade and Dance. There were many entrants and Alice Wray presented prizes to: Susan Clarkson *'Fairy'*, William Clarkson *'Dick Whittington'*, Frances Stones and Helen Shaw *'Valentine and Japanese'*, Cynthia Middle *'Cornflake'*, Jean Pinder *'Mary Ann'*, Brenda Taylor *'Woolcraft'*, Elna Stead *'Lady Pompadour'*, Miriam Adams *'Milkmaid'*, Cyril Adams *'Early Victorian'*, George Johnson *'cow boy'*. Dance music was by Edith Pickering (piano), Fred Hick (saxophone), Ronald Heath (violin) and Harold Heath (drums). Throughout the war, the annual July Church Sunday School day trip to Scarborough by train was replaced with a tea party.

During post-war years, all village children up to 16 enjoyed a Christmas party in the Methodist School room and because there were so many children, had to be held on two evenings. In 1959, there were 178 children and each received an orange, a packet of sweets and 3/- (15p). Organisers included: Mrs J Atkinson, Mrs A L Duggleby, Mrs G Foxton, Mrs E Pinder, Mrs J Thistleton, Mrs A Pickard, Mrs H Metcalfe, Mrs G Kedge, Miss E Metcalfe, Arthur Duggleby, Oliver Henderson, Peter Dunbar and Frank Green. The role of Father Christmas was taken by Charles Taylor or Jack Metcalfe.

School excursions included a day trip to the Royal Show at York on 8 July 1947 by the headmaster and 20 children; a day trip to Bradford on 9 May 1950, a visit to York Minster and the Kirk and Railway Museums in June 1950 by the headmaster and 26 children and on 13 July 1950 school closed for the Yorkshire Show at Malton. On 1 July 1955 there was a train excursion to Liverpool.

* * * * * * *

The Newtons joined in all village activities and as well as being a member of the church choir and parish council, John was an ardent supporter of both the football and cricket clubs. In January 1939, he organised a whist drive and dance to raise money for a football player who had fractured his leg. Sid Dawson and Charles Walker were MC's and music was by Fred Hick and Ronald Heath (violins), Harold Heath (drums) and Edith Pickering (piano). Football Club officers included president Jack Calam and no less than 10 vice-presidents, Dr Wilf Thistlethwaite, Messrs Holmes, Blanchard, Dawson, Heath, Bassett, Constable, Taylor, Gatenby and Tom Leary, chairman Ernest Baker, treasurer George Hugill, secretary Sid Dawson and committee members: Oliver Henderson, Herbert Johnson, George Hick, Charles Pickard, C Holdridge and Cecil Foxton. Mr Newton was still on the Cricket Club committee in 1961 when at the AGM, it was reported that the club had finished 5th in the Beckett League and the Juniors won the Bright Bowl. Officials were: president Harry Cundall, vice-president Rev Thomas Wray, secretary Michael Hotham, treasurer Richard Metcalfe, chairman Raymond Metcalfe, vice-chairman Roy Sadler, committee: Ernest Baker, Arthur Stead, John Newton and Ted Henderson. There was a balance in hand of £217 and the subscription fee was raised from 7/6d to 10/-. Special thanks and a memento of appreciation went to 12 year old Keith Dexter for scoring throughout the season.

John and Lydia Newton helped with church events and in 1939, the annual Vicarage garden fete was opened by Mrs Grotrain of Knapton Hall. Stallholders were: Mrs Williams and Mrs J Edmonds (jumble), Mrs J Newton, Mrs S Stead and Mrs A H Heath (confectionery), Mrs W Pudsey and Mrs C Taylor (vegetables), Mrs E Pinder and Mrs W Henderson (ice cream), Mrs W H Adams and Mrs O W Pickering (drapery), Mrs H Heath (bran tub), Mr R P Pinkney and Mr Cresswell (games). Miss Dorothy Dobson (buttonholes); Miss Betty Forge (tea tickets). Prizewinners were: Mrs W H Adams (doll), Mrs S Stead (cake), Mrs W Pudsey (home-made clip rug). Teas were served by Mrs E Levitt, Mrs J Witty, Mrs C Pickard, Mrs J W England, Mrs D Harris and Mrs W Pickard. Gatekeepers were George Lawson and Sidney Stead. The 1961 Garden Fete was opened by Viscountess Downe of Wykeham Abbey and 10-year-old Pamela Skelton presented her with a bouquet. Rosemary

Dawson ran the children's Wheel of Fete and schoolgirls Anne Clarke, Shirley Moss, Kathleen Pickard, Analissa Brandt, Kay Hotham and Vanessa Skelton sold button holes and tea tickets. Moyra Dexter and Bobbie Dobson won competitions. In 1962, rain forced the event indoors, Miss Howard-Vyse was the opener and Ann Davison presented her with a bouquet of roses. Flower girls were Kathleen Pickard, Ann Umpleby, Carol Dobson and Dorothy Scholes. In 1963, the fete was opened by Mrs M T Barstow of Springfield Farm and Susan Scholes presented her with a bouquet. Flower girls were Diane Oxtoby, Vanessa Skelton, Kathleen, Susan and Jean Pickard. At the Wrays' last garden fete in 1964, 3-year-old Louise Dexter presented a bouquet to the opener, 12-year-old Peter Thistleton sold button-holes and school girls who helped serve tea included Ann Rackham, Kay Hotham, Kathleen Pickard, Carol Dobson and Ann Umpleby.

The Newtons organised the May collections for Scarborough Hospital and in 1955, the children collected 655 eggs, 80 lb groceries and 10/-, in 1956, 562 eggs, 100 lbs groceries and 15s..1d cash and in 1961, 488 eggs, 79 lbs sugar, tinned food, mixed groceries and £1..6s.0d in cash.

John Newton helped with the Reading Room where men and boys had been enjoying recreation every evening since 1912, but because the presence of two large billiard tables restricted the room's use, a pre-war committee raised £200 towards a new hall. They disbanded until after the war then increased funds to £700, Frank Ward, was so impressed, he promised to make funds up to £1000 when another £100 was raised but before that was achieved, the committee disbanded again. The Reading Room was part of the Sherburn Estates owned by Richard Fawcett & Sons and on 25 September 1957, the estates were auctioned at the Talbot Hotel, Malton, by Bernard Thorpe & Partners. The sale included 1284 acres of land, 3 farms, a small-holding, 2 dairy and arable farms, an agricultural holding, a building site, 5 cottages and allotments. The Reading Room and an adjoining piece of land was gifted to the parish by the exhors of the Fawcett estate and at a public meeting, the decision was made to renovate and extend. To this end, the Village Hall Building Committee was formed with members Frank and Wilfred Ward, Colin Taylor, Albert Marston, Arthur Stead, Ronald Elliott, Betty Flinton, Nora Sedman, Iris Poulter, Madge Pigg, Michael Hotham and others.

Throughout 1960, they raised £1700. In February there was a fancy dress dance in the East Riding Long Room judged by Percy and Ethel Webster (Yedingham). Prizewinners were Ann Goodall *'Dr Babs'*; Peter Cousins *'The Abominable Snowman'*, Chris Rackham *'Clown'* and Roy Allison *'Sportsman of the year'*. Winners of a Waltz competition were Raymond and Lucie Metcalfe, Les and Dorothy Dexter and Albert Marston and Mary Rackham. Winners of a Rock 'n Roll competition were Billy Allison and Norma Johnson. Music was by the newly formed Panthers Skiffle Group who made their debut at the Ward Brothers (Sherburn) Ltd staff Christmas party in 1959. Group members were 18 year-old Geoff Harrison on electric guitar, 15 year-old Derek Boyes on piano and 21 year-old Sid Beal (Muston) singer and guitar accompanist.

In June 1960, £150 was raised at a Garden Fete at *The Beeches* and *Broadacres*, the homes of Frank and Wilf Ward. Over 500 people attended and stall holders were; *Tombola* Raymond and Lucie Metcalfe and Moyra Dexter; *Bagatelle* Oliver Henderson and Sylvia Fawcett; *Balloon Race* Francis Forge, Ron Elliott and Steve Goodall; *White Elephant* Betty Flinton; *Treasure Hunt* Mrs Ron Elliott; *Hoopla* Mrs Ron Moss; *Skittles* Les Johnson; *Cakes* Mrs Taylor and Mrs Charters; *Guess the Weight Comp* Shirley and Beryl Moss; *Crockery Smashing* Michael Hotham; *Coconut Shy* Les Stockill and George Stocks; *Football* Richard Metcalfe and Billy Pinkney; *Darts* Arlie Stead; *Photography* Chris Tindall; *Ice Cream* Mabel Cousins. Button holes were sold by Ann Davison, Christine Elliott and David Ward. Doorkeepers were Percy Gilbank, Arthur Duggleby and Percy Pinkney. A fireworks display was organised by Francis Forge, Steve Goodall and Ron Elliott. Catering Staff were Colin and Marjorie Taylor, Ron Moss, Madge Pigg, Beatrice Thistleton, Madge Percival, Marjorie Thistleton, Anne Pickard, Ann Goodall and Nora Sedman. There was open-air dancing until midnight with music by the Panthers.

The village hall committee entered Sherburn in the Village Beauty Queen Competition and Celia Thompson was chosen Sherburn's first Beauty Queen at a Dance at Yedingham in 1960 and was runner-up in the finals at the Olympia Ballroom. By October villagers were losing interest in the committee's efforts to extend the reading room and build a new hall, and following a public meeting they disbanded. The WI organised the 2nd Village Queen Dance in 1961 when Sylvia Pinder was chosen and Susan Dixon was runner-up. Sylvia was chosen again in 1962 with Susan Henderson as runner-up, and yet again in 1963.

In 1963 there was a national Freedom From Hunger Campaign and in May, Sherburn Church and Chapel raised £12..10s in a house-to-house collection. By this time Wards had built their own social centre for their 200 strong work force and they joined in the campaign by organising a garden party in the grounds of *Broadacres* and *The Beeches*. Although torrential rain drove the event under cover, £170 was raised. Ron Bassett introduced the opener Miss Ann Harriman who was appearing as *"Margo"* in *"The Desert Song"* at Scarborough Open-Air-Theatre. Ann spoke of the tragedy of world-wide poverty and expressed her pleasure in being asked to attend such a worthy cause. Children's fancy dress winners were Heather Robinson *'Cleopatra'*, Timothy Mitchell *'Busy Bee'* and Katharine Thompson *'Freedom From Hunger'*.

By this time Sherburn villagers had decided they would after all like a village hall, but not necessarily a new one because although the 50-year-old Reading

Room hadn't been used for years, it was structurally sound. Another committee was formed and plans made for the addition of a kitchen and toilets and general repairs using the £1,700 already raised. The chairman was Jack Skilbeck, treasurer Albert Marston, secretary Anne Collier and members Arthur and Sid Stead, Ron Moss, Bob and Clarice Stewart, Arthur Wilson, Nora Sedman, Betty Flinton, Olive and Monica Arnott, Dorothy Taylor, Madge Percival, Cynthia Skelton, Ruth Matthews, Mabel Cousins, Dorothy Dexter, Doris Allison, Lena Oxtoby and Cissie Heath. Chairman Jack Skilbeck and his family had just moved into the village and Jack worked for Dickie Jackson at St Hilda's Farm. In 1964, his eldest son John who had been head boy in his last year at Scarborough Boys High School, was awarded the Heath Harrison Scholarship in German and the Markhein Prize in a three hour French speaking examination at Queens College Oxford where he gained 1st Class honours degrees in French and German.

School closed on 20 November 1947 for the wedding of Princess Elizabeth to Prince Philip and when Elizabeth became Queen in 1953 John Newton chaired the celebrations committee. By April 1953, £126..3s..7d had been raised and Coronation week began with special services in St Hilda's Church and the Methodist Chapel. The school children planted 5 cherry and 5 almond trees bought for £8..0s..8d plus 3s..2d carriage from Rogers Nurseries, Pickering. On Coronation Day 2 June, there was heavy rain all day all over the country and Sherburn's fancy dress parade had to be in school and the sports postponed. After tea, the children each received a souvenir mug and sweets from John and Lydia Newton and the over-60's had tea in the Methodist School Room. As soon as it was dark, a bonfire was lit on *"Dickie Jackson's Wold"* and the day ended with a dance in school with music by Scarborough's New Rhythm Band.

The Queen gave permission for the Coronation to be televised but few households had a TV, so as many people as possible squeezed into about four homes in Sherburn to see live pictures on a tiny 12" black and white screen of the young Elizabeth being crowned. As more families acquired TVs, members of the Scarborough Amateur Radio Society, nick-named *"hams"*, complained about TV interference and over-crowded air waves. Ernie Brooks, a railway signalman, was one of Sherburn's *"hams"* and between 1954-61 had radio contacts from his *"ham shack"* in the larder of his home at Station Cottages with 94 countries using his international *"RT Q Code G3HFW"* which bridged all language barriers. Ernie built his own aerial, had two receivers and two transmitters one running at 150w maximum power and he gained five certificates including one for *"Working the Empire"*. Ernie's children John and Mary were pupils at Sherburn school in the 1960's. Colour television reached Scarborough in 1967.

* * * * * * *

Mr Newton did not attend all village funerals but on 19 October 1939, recorded that Violet Levitt attended the funeral of her grandfather George Dale 81 of West Heslerton. During the 1800's George was employed in building the Scarborough to Pickering railway line and later worked on the Dawnay Estates until his retirement in 1920. Known to have *"a quiet and unassuming nature"*, George and his wife celebrated their golden wedding in 1935 a year before she died. They had ten children and seven were living when George died. Another of Violet Levitt's family Frederick George eldest son of Robert and Jane (nee Pinkney) Levitt of Mill Cottages, died in April 1945 aged 68. He served in the Boer War and was a sergeant-major in the 1914-18 War and many ex-servicemen attended his funeral at St Peter's Church, Howden.

Mrs Catherine Elsie Ringrose assistant teacher at Sherburn from 1921-34 died in August 1946 aged 68. Chief mourners at St Hilda's Church where she was a regular worshipper were her husband Francis Richard Ringrose a school manager, and their daughter Kathleen Boyle.

Violet Levitt's father Alfred Ernest Levitt of Mill Villas died aged 59 on in August 1950. When he left Sherburn school, he was office boy at Kirk's Brewery and was later promoted to manager. In 1916, he joined the King's Royal Rifle Brigade and was severely wounded and taken prisoner. After the war he returned to the Brewery until its closure in 1923. Alfred was Clerk to the Parish Council for 23 years and secretary to the Court Langley Friendly Society for 26. He was Electoral Officer, auditor for the St John's Ambulance Brigade and vice-chairman of St Hilda's Parochial Church Council and local newspaper correspondent. During 1939-45 he served in the ROC and was treasurer to the Ganton, Sherburn & District Branch of the British Legion for 25 years. At the funeral Legion members formed a guard of honour, the Last Post was sounded and the coffin was draped with the Union Jack. Chief mourners were his widow Sarah, son George Robert (Bournemouth) and daughter Violet (assistant teacher at Sherburn School).

School manager and church warden George Lawson 80 died in January 1951 at his home Elm Tree Farm. His widow Ellen was unable to attend the funeral and died a few weeks later aged 79. Chief mourners were their son George, and grand-children Alfred George Trohear and Ellen Patricia 'Patsy' Trohear.

Other school managers included Ben Bassett, William A Cundall, Tom Leary, Laurence Levitt, Percy Gilbank and Alice Wray who was the school's first female manager. In 1948, when Ben Bassett of Springfield Terrace had reached the age of 81, he was awarded the British Empire Medal. Ben was born in Suffolk and when he left school, was hired as a farm labourer for a crown (5/- or 25p) a week plus his keep and worked on Yorkshire Wolds farms for 60 years. Ben married Agnes Dawson on 29 September 1896 but she died in April 1916 only months after her baby girl died. Ben's second wife was

Annie Shipley and from both marriages there were 18 children and several grandchildren. Ben loved gardening, was a teetotaller but enjoyed a pipe of tobacco and was said to look younger than his age and ascribed this to *"temperate habits and plenty of hard work"*. Ben was presented with a gold medal and silver watch for his 30 years service as secretary of the Sherburn Branch of the National Union of Agricultural Workers and for many years he was a preacher and organist at the Primitive Methodist Chapel. Ben died in 1952 aged 84 and Annie in 1961 aged 64.

* * * * * * *

By the 1950's, Sherburn's oldest people were saying the village was *"a varry different spot"* from the small isolated self-supporting village they'd known. Instead of having to walk a mile to Weaverthorpe station to catch a train for the nearest town there was a regular bus service carrying workers daily to jobs in Scarborough and Malton. Wards' engineering firm was rapidly expanding and the Old Brewery where from 1840-1922 villagers were employed in producing Sherburn's famous Ale, was housing chickens and corn drying equipment and Brewery House had become Cundalls' offices. Across the road a fire station had appeared manned by Walter Bradford, his son Howard, Herbert Hotham, John Pickard, John Matthews, Ernest Pateman, Alan Broome, Tom Gilbank, George Jackson, George White and Harry Kedge. South east of the cross roads, the old Primitive Methodist Chapel where there had been many bright and lively gatherings, was awaiting demolition.

Several shops had disappeared, but Hannah Beecroft 80 was still selling sweets and cigarettes in the front room of her tiny cottage adjoining the west end of the Pigeon Pie. Albert Baker Marston in his 80's, his wife Clara and only son Albert, were running the post office and general store where the Marstons had lived for a century. Albert B Marston's parents Joseph and Maria moved to Sherburn from Snainton in the 1850's and he was the youngest of their six children. From 1890-1900, he studied and practised law in America then after his father Joseph died in 1900, was appointed postmaster. He and his wife Clara had one son Albert. As well as being postmaster for 55 years, Albert B Marston was chairman of the parish council for 20 years and as a young man he sang in the church choir and in a minstrel troupe. He was an antique dealer and collector and an accomplished painter in oils and watercolours. His siblings were: Elizabeth a music teacher, Thomas James a railway clerk, Frederick William, Charles Henry a Sculptor/landscape painter and Clara Ellen a music teacher and wife of Anthony Sawkill, Sherburn's former head teacher. Albert B Marston died aged 88 in 1955 and his widow Clara who was a well-known soprano soloist and member of Dr Ely's Musical Society died aged 75 in 1961. Two doors from the Wesleyan Methodist Chapel, Charles and Dorothy Taylor and son Colin were still running the General Store where they'd lived since before the 1939-45 war. Charles delivered daily newspapers door to door and collected grocery orders for Colin to deliver by van later in the day. Four doors from the East Riding pub, George and Bridgett Jackson lived in a tiny cottage and for many years, George worked for the East Riding County Council as the driver of an old steam-roller Invicta No 11200 made by Avelin and Potter Ltd, of Rochester. By the mid 1950's, these rollers which weighed 10 ton when empty had been replaced by diesel-rollers.

On the same side of St Hilda's Street northwards, Jack Currey's joinery/painting/decorating and undertaker's shop was still serving the community, assisted by Roy Sadler who had worked there since leaving Sherburn School in July 1944. George and Muriel Stead were about to move out of Central Stores and hand over to Ronald and Beryl Moss and children Beryl, Shirley and Keith. Next door, Arthur Herbert Heath in his 70's was still running the butcher's shop he'd inherited from his father James Bell Heath school manager. For many years Arthur played the cornet in the Sherburn Brass Band and his brother Harold played the drums. Harold died aged 50 in 1959 and Arthur aged 77 in 1964 when Arthur's widow Lizzie and only son Ronald, were left to carry the business into its fourth generation.

Opposite Wards' factory, Edgar Mintoft's blacksmith shop had gradually gone out of business as tractors replaced farm horses. Edgar kept homer pigeons and in 1902 at the age of 15, gained his first medal and went on to win many national and local prizes. Just before he died aged 71 in 1958, the Exhibition Homer Society invited him to judge at the 1959 Olympia Dairy Show, London, but he was prevented by ill health. For 49 years, Edgar was a Methodist local preacher and his wife Clara was organist. Next door at Gladstone House, Harry and Martha Adams were running their carrier/coal business and their post-war fish and chip shop. The were still three working farms in St Hilda's Street, White House Farm (Cherry Tree Cottage) farmed by Annie 'Gramzy' Stead (died 1953 aged 80), St Hilda's Farm opposite school farmed by Dickie Jackson (d 1983 aged 94) and Elm Tree Farm (now Elm Grove) farmed by George Lawson (d 1980 aged 79).

Near the Restoration Cross, Alfie and Bev Park were running the Corner Shop built by the Council to accommodate nearby council houses. Alfred died in 1960 aged 80 and Evelyn (nee Bradford) in 1981 aged 87. Fourteen more council houses had been built in West Garth to add to the 84 built since 1920 and plans were in hand to build flats and pensioners' bungalows on land adjoining school premises northwards. These plans were delayed because John Cundall a keen archaeologist, found the remains of walls beneath ground level and pieces of Staxton pottery fired at Staxton and Potter Brompton during the 13th/14th Centuries. Within hours of starting to dig in August 1957, archaeologists found three chalk walls believed to be of a medieval manor, 60ft long, 30ft wide and 12ft high, with partition walls, doorways, buttresses and evidence of a thatched roof. Pottery, bronze pins, beads, and numerous nails were found on the floor of the manor. One of the diggers was Tony Brewster 42, a schoolmaster from Pocklington and previously from Flixton, who had just finished a spell of teaching at Sherburn school. Another was Fred Brook a teacher from Pocklington, who for 4 years during the 1939-45 war, was imprisoned in 7 different German camps where he'd spent hours digging and trying to escape. Other helpers were Christopher Gregory (West Riding), John Atkinson (Mill Cottage) and Terry Smith (Brompton-by-Sawdon).

On the 18 February 1951, one of John Newton's pupils, 7 year old Adrian Broome was killed in an accident on the Scarborough to York road, east of Sherburn cross-roads. The headmaster and 10 senior children attended the funeral in the Wesleyan Chapel. Another former pupil, Lance-Corporal Bernard Foxton 20, was killed in a road accident in Cyprus in April 1957 when his armoured car escorting Field Marshall Sir John Harding, Governor of Cyprus, overturned on a road near Nicosia. Bernard's remains were buried in Cyprus but a memorial service was held in St Hilda's Church on 15 April. He was the second son of Cecil and Beatrice Foxton of 1 Springfield Terrace. Compulsory National Service for men aged 18 ended in 1960.

Violet Levitt's uncle William Levitt died in 1963 aged 85 in The Hawthorns Nursing Home, Malton where he'd lodged for 5 years. He was a bachelor and had occupied the same cottage in Mill Field all his life and could remember Sherburn's working windmill being demolished in 1912 and the last annual Club Feast in June 1914. In February 1964, another of Violet Levitt's uncles Lawrence *'Loll'* Levitt of West Garth, Sherburn died aged 76 in a Whitby hospital. He'd served as school manager, church warden, was leading chorister and always led the choir from their vestry to the chancel stalls, carrying the processional cross.

* * * * * * *

In July 1957, John and Lydia Newton heard that their son Captain John Michael Newton of the Duke of Wellington's Regt, was among those mentioned for gallant and distinguished service in Cyprus. Captain Newton married Alison Brenda Burnett only daughter of Mr & Mrs Norman Burnett, 193 Cottingham Rd, Hull in October 1955. The bride wore a full-length dress of white net and lace and carried a bouquet of tea roses, lilies of the valley and white heather. Her bridesmaids Deidre Newton (bridegroom's sister), Gillian North Smith (bride's cousin) and Judy Ackroyd a friend, wore full length dresses of honey coloured nylon. After a reception at the New York Hotel, Hull, the couple went on honeymoon to Majorca, the bride wearing an off-white tweed suit, mushroom-coloured coat and accessories. Michael and Alison lived in Ash Vale, Surrey and Michael eventually attained the rank of major at the Camberley Staff College, Surrey.

Deidre Newton married Jeffrey Nash of York at St Hilda's Church on Tuesday 27 December 1960. She wore a classical gown of parchment and gold brocade with short train and low back waistline, trimmed with roses of the same material. Her parchment veil was held in place by a brocade rose head dress and she carried red roses and lilies of the valley. The bridesmaids Miss Ruth Mitchell and Miss Gillian Leadley wore day-length dresses of flame red Duchesse satin with stiffened petal overskirts, matching shoes, gold leaf head dresses and gloves and carried matching carnations. Deidre's little niece Helen Jane Newton, wore a dress of parchment net with red sash, shoes, and a flower head dress. The reception was at The Green, Brompton-by-Sawdon and Jeffrey and Deidre went to live at York where he worked as a display manager with a York firm and Deidre was a teacher at Northfields School for Delicate Children.

Within the year, John Newton's health began to fail and by October 1961 he could no longer continue as headmaster. Mr E A Jackson took charge and between 1962 and 1964 there was a succession of teachers, Mrs S J Halder, Mrs Slater, Mrs Hume, Mrs Shaw, Mrs Munroe, Mrs Rivis, Miss Sanderson and Mrs Patricia Hall. At Christmas 1962, Lily Hutton retired after 24 years and at a gathering in school of pupils, former pupils and parents, John Newton was invited to present her with a cheque for £21..15s collected by school children. John thanked Miss Hutton for her loyalty and conscientious work and wished her many years of healthy and happy retirement. John Cundall expressed good wishes on behalf of the school managers. Lily said she would not say goodbye but would always find time to visit Sherburn and she moved into one of the old people's bungalows built near school in the mid-1960's, where she could see the children's outdoor activities from her lounge window. Lily died in June 1975 and Sherburn's headmaster represented pupils and staff at her funeral at West Heslerton.

Lily's successor was Judy Tomlinson from Shipley and because she was only 21, the children called her *"big sister"*. Carl Brandt 7 said *"She's just like my big sister"*! A month later Judy married David Pickard, a market gardener, but after two months had to resign on medical grounds. Her successor was Miss Joan Valerie Alison Bradford who commenced duties on 9 September 1963 when there were 63 pupils on roll. Miss Bradford, the only daughter of Walter and Alys Bradford, garage proprietors, was one of John Newton's former pupils and transferred to St Andrew's School, Malton, then trained at Derby College. On 6 January 1964, Alison married Aubrey Brown. Less than a fortnight later, she was given permission to attend the funeral of her uncle Thomas Stanley Currey 70 who died at his home *Whitegates*. Stanley was an auctioneer and valuer with J Cundall & Sons for 43 years and president of the East Yorkshire Land Valuers' Association. In the 1914-18 war he was a sergeant in the Yeoman Rifles (21st Bttn King's Royal Rifle Corps) and served

John and Lydia Newton 1947 and Deidre, Lydia and Michael Newton 1947

in Belgium, France and Italy. His left hand was badly injured during a demonstration on the use of hand grenades. In the 1939-45 war he was leader of the local ROC and secretary to the War Agricultural Committee. He played the organ at St Hilda's Church, sang with both the Sherburn and Wykeham Choral Societies, and during the 1930's conducted the orchestra at the Methodist Mens' Sunday Afternoon meetings, and for many years conducted the Derwent Male Voice Choir. Stanley had also been organist at St Saviour's Church, Scarborough, for some years. At the funeral in the Methodist Chapel, Rev W H Pittam was assisted by Rev W V Wrigley, Vicar of Hutton Buscel and Wykeham, where Stanley had also been organist. Chief mourners were his widow Elsie and two sons, Geoffrey, a teacher at Pocklington Grammar

---

Football Team 1959: *Back row:* Dave Pinder, Barry Dobson, Ray Johnson, Keith Worthy, David Allison, Pete Cousins, Ray Sedman (John Newton headmaster) *Front row:* Andrew Mattinson, Roy Allison, Barry Rackham, Norman Bean, John Calam

School and Norman, a designer with the Lockheed Aircraft Company, Atlanta, USA.

On the 24 July 1964, John and Lydia Newton retired and in the presence of a large gathering of friends, pupils, former pupils and special guest Richard Duncan Sykes John's successor, Raymond P Metcalfe, one of the first pupils to pass from Mr Newton's class to grammar school, presented them with a £30 cheque collected from villagers. Raymond wished the Newtons a long and happy retirement and paid tribute to the high percentage of their pupils who had passed to higher education during their 26 years in Sherburn. He also praised Mr Newton's keen interest in village life outside school, especially in sporting activities. Lydia received flowers from Andrea Seager (7) and Ann Davison (11). The Rev Thomas Wray expressed best wishes on behalf of the school managers then invited Mrs Newton to present certificates to the children who gained places in the inter-school sports at Filey when Sherburn School retained the sports shield for the 4th year in succession. They were Susan Pickard (5 yrs); Janet Pickard, Julia Nesfield, Gary Axham (8); Raymond Johnson (9); Vanessa Skelton, Dorothy Scholes, Stuart Dawson, Philip Dobson (10); Neil Stead and Paul Rackham (11).

John and Lydia moved from School House into their retirement home 137 Stepney Road in 1961 They bought the house because from the rear windows they could look over the countryside where Lydia had spent her childhood and could watch the birds with the binoculars they'd bought with the money given to them by the people of Sherburn. John died eight months later and the new headmaster, Infants' teacher and senior pupils Richard Heath, Philip Dobson, Dorothy Scholes and Ann Davison attended the memorial service at St Hilda's Church. (see appendix 15).

Middle Class 1961: Back: Richard Heath, Peter Holiday, Michael Pickard, David Scholes, (Lydia Newton teacher)
Middle: Mick Sanderson, Andrew Mattinson, Judith Mayer, Anne Clarke, Barry Foxton, Chris Brandt
Front: John Walker, Pam Skelton, Kathleen Pickard, Linda Taylor, Sheila Walker, Carol Dobson, Glenda Foxton, Ron Carney

CHAPTER 6
RICHARD DUNCAN SYKES 1964–1983

RICHARD SYKES was a bachelor and began his duties as headmaster on 7 September 1964. He was born in the tiny village of Park Hill near Ripon, the only child of a farming family, and when Park Hill School had to close, he and his fellow pupils were taken by taxi to finish their primary education in Ripon 3 miles away. He passed the County Minor Scholarship examination entitling him to a place at Richmond Grammar to where he cycled daily and after he left, he worked in a bank. In 1946 he reported for duty at HMS *"Royal Arthur"* at Butlins Holiday Camp, Skegness, entered a naval training base at the foot of the Malvern Hills and after six months was drafted for Foreign Service aboard HMS *"Indomitable"*. Richard's great aunt was married to Sir James Paton (1868-1948) who was born on *"The Great Eastern"* the largest vessel afloat at the time. James was knighted for his services in the First World War. After demobilisation, Richard Sykes was a temporary unqualified assistant teacher at Beverley Park Camp School, Nidderdale, was an assistant teacher for 6 years in Knaresborough, then was appointed headmaster of Etton village school near Beverley from where he moved to Sherburn with his father Harold, his mother having died in 1961. During his years in Sherburn, he was church warden, secretary to the Parochial Church Council, a parish councillor, a member of both the village hall and playing field committees, organiser of the youth club and a keen supporter of the football team. His father Harold was also a member of the Church Council and secretary to the Over 60's Club. Harold died suddenly at School House on 5 June 1966 aged 71 and in his memory, Richard donated to St Hilda's Church, an oak pedestal table which stands in the sanctuary on the north side of the high altar. At the dedication service the table carried a flower arrangement in yellow and red, the colours of the 5th West Yorkshire Regiment in which Harold served in the 1914-18 war.

At the same time that Mr Sykes began teaching the upper juniors (top class), Mrs B Halliday began teaching the middle school (lower juniors) and Mrs Alison Brown continued teaching the Infants. Mrs Halliday stayed two terms and subsequent teachers of the juniors were Mrs V Watson from 1965-66, Mrs Pat Brewer 1966-67, Mrs Barbara Smith 1967-76 and Mrs Maureen Hernandez 1976-79. Supply teachers included Mrs Ruth Botterill part 1969 and Mr H W Barnes part 1973. In October 1975 Alison Brown married Leslie Oulton. In 1977, primary school head teachers became entitled to clerical assistance and Anne Collier was engaged for 5 hours per week. Each Spring two students came on teaching practice from the North Riding College of Education, Scarborough and in 1982, Linda Flinton former pupil of Sherburn School was the first of many Filey School pupils to spend one week's work experience in school.

Eliza Stead who had been school caretaker since 1956 retired in 1968. At a special assembly, 5-year-old Trudy Marflitt presented her with a bouquet on behalf of the school. Mrs Stead was also given gift vouchers and a beautiful framed colour photo of White House Farm which stands within yards of the school and where she and her husband Sidney Stead had been running a small holding and milk business since the death of his mother Anne Elizabeth *"Gramzy"* Stead in 1953. Anne and Watson Stead and their family Emily, Arthur, Frank, George, Sydney and Fred moved into White House Farm in 1923. Eliza's successor as caretaker was Harry Kedge whose wife Mary had been Canteen Assistant since 1960. Meals were brought by taxi from Filey County Junior School and in 1975, because 44 out of 66 pupils were taking school dinners, Gill Nettleton was engaged as an extra dining room assistant. The Kedges retired in 1979, Mary after 19 years and Harry after 11. Richard Sykes recorded: *"Harry has been a most loyal and efficient member of our school team and he and Mary have served us well".* They were given a cheque for £36 and Mary was presented with a bouquet by the youngest pupil. Harry Kedge's successors were Wendy Pickard from 1979-81 and Moyra Stockill from 1981-2003.

There were 65 children and numbers fluctuated roughly between 31 and 76 and dropped to 32 by the time Richard Sykes left. Throughout his 19 years as headmaster, average attendance was 97% apart from short periods of epidemic illness. In the New Year of 1966, despite a severe 'flu outbreak in surrounding villages and several weeks of heavy snow, average attendance was 98% and to compensate for cancellation of outdoor games and activities, the headmaster took the children sledging on the Wolds. There were no closures because of illness, but in January 1968 and March 1969 respectively, 75% of pupils were off with 'flu and gastric stomachs, during the first week in February 1972, 50% were off with 'flu, during a week in October 1974, 75% had chicken pox and just before school closed for half term at the end of May 1975, 75% had measles. When school re-opened on 2 June, sleet and snow and very cold temperatures called for the heating to be turned back on and snow was falling in London for the first time in June since records began. By the 13th, temperatures had soared and were exceptionally high and attendance was badly affected by sickness. Throughout October and November 1975, out of 66 children there were several cases of mumps and at the end of January 1976, 50% had 'flu. There were regular medical examinations and dental checks and in 1977 Rubella vaccinations against German Measles began for girls. In February 1978 there was an outbreak of chicken pox, in December 1980 attendance was badly affected by *"a virulent illness"* and in April 1983 there were several cases of chicken pox. The only time the head master was absent through illness was from the 27 November 1972 to 8 January 1973 when Mr H W Barnes took charge.

Straightaway Mr Sykes had the school painted inside and out and the drab browns and creams were exchanged for brighter colours, the grey/blue Victorian tiles over which generations of pupils had passed at the entrance to both the boys' and girls' playgrounds, were replaced by tarmac, a new floor was fitted in the hall, the other floors were treated with Bourne Plastic, and the coke heating system was converted to oil-fired. Grass was sown on the school vegetable garden and the school house lawn extended and adapted to create a stage so that drama could become a regular part of the curriculum.

* * * * * * *

In 1967, there were plans to extend the school and 1.5 acres of land north-west of Beech Cottage were ear marked after a planning application to develop a housing project was refused. These plans to extend did not materialise and the land became the school sports field. By 1974 there were 65 pupils and school was considered to be over-crowded so extensions were again considered. In anticipation, a study was made of the historic Dead Sea Scrolls and the children produced a scroll depicting life in Sherburn in 1974 under the headings *"My Home", "School Life", "Village and Social Life", "Farming", "Food, Clothes and Entertainment"*. The 25 foot scroll was to be rolled and put into a container and placed in the wall of the proposed extension, but plans collapsed yet again following a £182 million government spending cut in Education which not only affected working conditions but hindered normal maintenance. National strikes and demands *"for less work and more pay"* were characteristic of the 1970's. In Sherburn, the population had increased to well over 700 and the village had changed from a farming to an industrial community that could boast of being the home of one of the country's leading steel firms with a 375 workforce and despite constant industrial unrest and the threat of crippling union action, was producing commercial buildings and winning valuable Middle East contracts. In early 1979, severe weather and strike action by tanker drivers created a national fuel crisis and in Sherburn school, heating was supplemented in the main building by electric radiators, working hours were extended through playtime and a quarter of an hour cut from lunch, so lessons could end at 2.30. On some days, the children had to take packed lunches because of strike action by NUPE staff at Filey Central Kitchen.

In October 1977, a mobile Elliott classroom was delivered in sections, put together the next day, and made ready for the top class to move into in the

New Year. The Infants moved back into the western classroom which Mr Sykes and his class had occupied since his arrival and the large room became 'the hall'. School governor Mrs Pat Barstow of Springfield Farm, officially opened the new classroom on 18 July 1978. During the summer holidays the wooden floors were sanded and polished and a new sterilising sink unit and Burco boiler were installed in the canteen.

Pupil achievements were recorded and in 1965 Melanie Gow won 2nd Prize for Handwriting in the Brooke Bond National Competition for the County of Yorkshire and Vanessa Skelton received a Special Merit Prize for Art. Pupils who passed the 11+ examination were: Anne Davison, Stephen Bean, Philip Dobson, Lynn Nesfield, Richard Heath, Graham Pickard, Melanie Gow (1965); Timothy Pickard, Stuart Dawson, Elissa Bean, (1966), Christine Bean, Kathleen Cracknell, Richard Duggleby (1967), Julie Gow (1968), Kevin Pickard, Andrew Pickard, Martin Flinton, Trevor Wiley (1969), Nigel Stephenson (1970), Brett Stephenson, (1972). On 27 July 1972, following the cessation of the 11+ exam, a meeting in school to discuss re-organisation of secondary education was addressed by Education Officer O'Reilly and Malcolm Liddle headmaster of Filey Secondary School outlined plans for the change-over to comprehensive education. The meeting was well attended and there was lively discussion. On 1 April 1974, County re-organisation came into effect and the East Riding ceased to exist and Sherburn school came within the Ryedale District Council area and under the authority of North Yorkshire County Council, Northallerton, with a divisional office at Scarborough.

Richard Sykes's first fund raising event was a slide show of his tours in Switzerland and Austria when parents and friends responded generously to a silver collection. The Autumn Fair in 1964 raised £75..10s and became a regular event to provide a Christmas party with tea that included fancy cakes from Woodheads van, games and a present from the tree for each child. The tradition began of exchanging Christmas cards via the school's internal letter box.

At Richard Sykes's first parents' meeting, future plans were discussed and questions invited and thereafter parents were involved whenever possible. They were invited to services at Harvest, Easter, Christmas and in July to end of term Open Day assembly when books were presented to pupils transferring to Filey or Norton and to the child in each class who had made the most progress during the year. In 1968, infant prize-winners were Louise Dexter (reading), Elaine Johnson (reliability), Richard Cundall (art), Adrian Pickard (models/craft); juniors: Carl Horsley and Patrick Umpleby, Neil Bassett (art) and Gillian Pickard (sports); top class: Ian Rackham (youngest pupil who kept up with top groups), Peter Dobson, Trevor Wiley (art) and Kevin Pickard (football); in 1970: infants Gary Bean and Trudie Marflitt; juniors Elaine Johnson and Richard Harrison, top class Sharon Moore; in

1973, infants: Deborah, Sally Stringer, Ian Harrison; juniors: Tracy Thistleton, Gary Marflitt; top class: David Wood, Andrew Gilbank. In 1981, each child was given a royal crown to commemorate the marriage on 29 July of Prince Charles and Lady Diana Spencer. The school's team of musicians played a selection of tunes then all the children sang *"I'm going to marry the girl next door"* written and composed by Mrs Ruth Botterill a retired teacher, in honour of the royal wedding. Two weeks before the wedding, there was anarchy on the streets of Britain's major cities as gangs of youths went on the rampage damaging property, looting, committing arson and injury to police. Suggested causes included unemployment, poor housing, racism, police harassment and some rioters confessed they were involved *"for no other reason than to enjoy the excitement"*. Richard Sykes in referring to those events, took the opportunity in his open day speech, to appeal to parents to support teachers' efforts to maintain discipline. As a deterrent to bad behaviour, Mr Sykes substituted Mr Newton's cane for an old plimsoll called *"Sally the Pump"* and although seldom used, was effective.

Staff and pupils attended a service in church on special days in the Church's calendar, such as Ash Wednesdays to mark the start of Lent, Ascension Day five weeks after Easter and All Saint's Day (1 November) to commemorate *'the faithful departed'*. For the first few years harvest gifts were shared between Kirbymoorside Children's' Orthopaedic Hospital and May Lodge National Children's Home, Scarborough. In later years, the children distributed gifts of fruit and vegetables to village pensioners.

In 1964, harvest readers were Philip Dobson, Andrea Seager and Graham Pickard and autumn verses were recited by Jane Simpson and Jonathan Galtry. At Christmas 1964, readers were Philip Dobson, Dorothy Scholes, Christine Bean, Julie Nesfield, Janet and Graham Pickard. Graham was the son of Dennis and Mary Pickard and was an exceptionally bright pupil. Three years later in the summer holidays of 1967, he died tragically after being knocked off his bicycle by a car as he was leaving a harvest field south of the village. At St Hilda's Carol Service in 1966, lessons were read by choir boys Peter and David Thistleton and on Christmas night, a group of children: Sally Bradford, Christopher, James and Richard Cundall, Caroline and Ian Mason and Barbara Jefferson, raised £2..6s..od for physically handicapped children by going round the village carol singing.

In 1975, the School and Church together organised a Festival Week from 13-21 September. There was a flower festival in church with each arrangement representing a passage from the New Testament. Sylvia Dudding whose husband Laurie was a signalman living in Station Cottages, was principal organiser helped by church members and the school children decorated the 1912 font beneath the tower. There was a musical evening in church, an arts and crafts exhibition, a display of bygones in school and the week ended with a social evening. That autumn the children planted daffodil bulbs donated by Cecil Wallis of Allison Wold Farm, near St Hilda's Church Lytch Gate and on land south-east of the crossroads.

At the annual Sports Day, the children competed in four teams Normans, Romans, Saxons and Vikings (see appendix 16). In 1969, proceeds of £12..11s..od were donated towards a new sports pavilion to be built in memory of Fred Lloyd "*Mazza*" Stead who died aged 55 a month earlier. The Football Club launched an appeal with a generous donation in appreciation of Mazza's years of service and PC Bob Waud, treasurer to the playing field committee, announced that funds had reached £400. By the following Spring, £1500 had been raised and that summer, 58 adults and children raised £210 in a 10-mile sponsored walk. Cynthia Skelton was the first lady to finish and 11-year old Kevin Stocks came fourth. Barbecues at Westfield Farm home of Mr & Mrs George Green, raised £500 (1970) £450 (1972) with turkey and ham suppers, music for dancing by The Panthers and the Paul Murray Disco and many other attractions.

Sherburn School had some talented footballers with exceptional results. In 1966 the year England won the World Cup for the first time by beating Germany 4-2, Sherburn's school team beat Bubwith County Primary 5-0 in the semi-final for the Asbestos Shield and in the final beat Leconfield County Primary 10-2. In November 1967 they beat Rillington 17-0 in a football friendly and reached the semi-final in the County Schools Knockout by beating Bubwith 4-1 at Middleton-on-the-Wolds, but lost 3-0 to South Cave. Other victories were: Pocklington Roman Catholic 8-0 and Rillington 9-1 (1970); Brompton-by-Sawdon 11-0 (1976) and in 1979 they won the village schools' Six-a-Side Tournament Shield. The children began travelling by coach each week for swimming lessons at Filey School and Mary and Harry Kedge presented the school with a Swimming Cup at a Mini-gala at Scarborough pool. By April 1977 out of 39 children, there were only 8 non-swimmers.

The school entered the Police Road Safety Quiz competing for the Newton Cup and came first in 1965 and second in 1966. National Cycling Proficiency Tests were taken annually and in 1983, Lee Metcalfe scored 100% and 11 pupils scored 94% and from 1965-83, the school was awarded a Road Safety Certificate each year because no pupils were involved in road accidents. There were few accidents at school but the climbing frame in the yard was a hazard. Andrea Holmes fell from the frame and needed 3 stitches in her forehead (1971), Tracy Pickering had her chin stitched (1974), Carol Walker needed stitches in a leg wound and Richard Brooks injured an elbow (1976). Jamie Berriman and Colin Daphne were hit by a cricket ball, Jamie on the nose, and both needed an X-ray (1981). The police regularly warned children about the dangers of playing on farms and showed safety films such as "*Never go with strangers*" and there were regular fire drills.

* * * * * * *

Each summer between 1965 and 1976, the top class went on trips alternately to London and Edinburgh. On 1 July 1965, 20 children and 2 teachers caught the 8 am train and arrived at King's Cross at 12.40. They spent a day and a half sight-seeing, saw the film *"The Sound of Music"* at the Palace Theatre and arrived home in the early hours. In 1966, they lodged at the *"Ardgowan Guest House"* in Newington, Edinburgh and a city tour included visits to the castle, St Gile's Cathedral, Greyfriars Kirk, Holyrood House, a picnic at King Arthur's Seat, a walk along the Royal Mile and they saw the Queen arrive at the Royal Lyceum Theatre. Next day they visited Forth Bridge (opened by the Queen on 4 September 1964). In 1967 they had four days in London staying at the King George V Memorial Hostel, Kensington and saw Lionel Bart's musical *"Oliver"* at the Piccadilly Theatre. In 1968, they travelled to Edinburgh on the *'Heart of Midlothian'* and as well as a city coach tour visited the burial place of King Robert the Bruce. In 1969 the London trip included a visit to the Airport, Runnymede and Windsor Castle. The highlight of the 1970 Edinburgh trip was a visit to the British Commonwealth Games. City trips ceased after 1976 but in his final year Mr Sykes took 15 children to Edinburgh.

Other outings from 1965-77 included York, Flamingo Park, a farm at Lebberston, Pickering, Helmsley and Reivaux Castles, Sewerby Park, Reighton Gap, the Malton Roman Museum, Castle Howard, Goathland and Whitby, Woodheads Bakery Scarborough and the top class attended a matinee performance of the York Pageant and saw the York Tattoo at the Knavesmire. When the Queen visited the Duchy of Lancaster Estates on 2 July 1975 and spent some time at Home Farm in Brompton-by-Sawdon, the children went by coach to see her and on 13 June 1977, Mrs Oulton and two children were in a party of official visitors to the Great Yorkshire show attended by the Queen. After a trip during the sunny summer of 1976, the headmaster wrote *"June 10 - School outing to Knaresborough. Party of 70 children and 8 adults left at 9.30 by Wallace Arnold coach. At Knaresborough the children picnicked and visited the Zoo, Dropping Well and Castle, returning home at 6 pm The weather was perfect!"* Mr Sykes' last school outing was on 22 July 1983 a glorious sunny day when all pupils and staff travelled by coach for a day on Filey beach.

The children had a day off when school was used on Polling Day and other days off included: the 700th Anniversary of Parliament and the 750th Anniversary of Magna Carta (5 July 1965); the Silver Wedding of the Queen and Prince Philip (20 November 1972), the marriage of Princess Anne and Capt Mark Phillips (1 November 1973) and for the European Economic Community elections (5 June 1975) when results were 17.5 million for and 8.5 million against. They were able to see special national events on the school's new TV such as the Investiture of Prince Charles at the age of 21 as Prince of Wales at Caernarfon Castle (1 July 1969), the 80th birthday celebrations of

Queen Elizabeth the Queen Mother (15 July 1980) and the official opening of the Humber Bridge by the Queen (17 July 1981).

For the Queen's Silver Jubilee celebrations in 1977 the children planted 100 willow trees around the village and festivities began with a united service at St Hilda's Church conducted by Rev Mark Simons, lessons were read by Richard Sykes and Michael Barstow (wardens) and the organist was Jack Briggs. Winners in a children's Fancy Dress Parade were: Nicola Dobson, Claire Stockill, Helen Pickering (prettiest); Nicholas Dobson, Angela and Colin Pickard, Dawn Bean (comical); Trudy Harrison, Vicky Rodgers, Mark Nettleton (original); Mark Pickard, Helen Woodall (consolation); and in the adults: Cynthia Skelton, George Stocks, Les Stockill, Mabel Cousins. The best decorated bicycles were by Claire Stockill, Dawn Foxton and Christopher and Andrew Hodgson. Sports winners were: Patricia Allison, Jeremy Cundall, Nicholas Dobson, Sarah Flinton, Dorothy Grayson, Andrea Holmes, Jane Horsley, Jane Newlove, Nigel Pickard, Helen and Richard Pickering, Michael and Kay Pickering, Peter Sotherby, Lee Steggle, Kevin and Michael Stocks, Christine and Julie Taylor, Richard and Nina Ward, Jackie and Michael Watts. Those taking part in a friendly tug-of-war included Philip Dobson, Barry, Kelvin, Henry and Teddy Foxton, David Cracknell and Johnny Walker. Tea was enjoyed by 400+ villagers in John Cundall's barn, then Sherburn Brass Band conducted by Roy Dalton, gave a concert with monologues by Yvonne Taylor and Roger Preston, the school children performed *"Salute the Queen"* and Richard Sykes and Alison Oulton presented 150 children with a jubilee mug and a silver crown (5/- or 25p). When darkness fell, a beacon was lit on Sherburn Wold followed by fireworks.

* * * * * * *

Richard Sykes loved books, history and sport and had an extensive knowledge of flowers, trees and birds, but his greatest passion was theatre, cinema and music. This was born in him when at the age of 8, he saw Gracie Field's film *"Sing as we go"* and in his autobiography *"The Song of the Sea"* he claims *"it was my first introduction to Gracie Fields and from that moment I was under her spell"*! Richard's book was not on public sale but he had sufficient copies printed for his friends. He saw all Gracie's movies, listened to her wireless broadcasts, bought her records, studied every detail of her life, wrote to her and attended many of her concerts. In 1965, he came face to face with his idol whilst on holiday in Italy. He took a boat trip from Sorrento to Capri, caught a bus and when it reached Gracie's home, he climbed off, went through the large wrought iron gates and in his own words *"I rang the doorbell, the Italian housekeeper answered and asked me to wait........ Gracie greeted me warmly, flaunting her broad Lancashire accent in that cheerful aggressive way..... It was a magic moment"*. After tea on the terrace, she signed his copy of her autobiography *"Sing as we go"* and he left with an invitation to return and thereafter, visited her several times.

Drama greatly influenced the curriculum and school produced Christmas Plays, Summer Pageants and colour films. At Christmas 1964, there were three plays *"Snow White and the Seven Dwarfs"* (infants), *"The Spick and Span Stone"* (juniors), *"The Wizard of Oz"* (top class); 1965 *"The Story of Peter Rabbit"* (infants), *"Down the Crocus Tunnel"* (juniors), *'Pinocchio'* (top class); 1966, *"Bobby Shaftoe"* (infants), *"Pearls for the Princess"* (juniors), *"Peter Pan"* (top class); 1967 *"The Two Lost Toys"* (infants), *"The Magic Snowman"* (juniors), *"Alice in Wonderland"* (top class); 1968, *"The Old Toys on Christmas Eve"* (infants), *"The Wizard who hated Christmas"* (juniors) and *"A pig in the Palace"* (top class) which was described as *"a miniature pantomime with glittering costumes, dashes of humour and good singing"*. At Christmas 1969, all 61 pupils performed *"It's a Ball"* telling Old Mother Hubbard's hard-luck story that turned out well through colourful scenes in an enchanted forest, rainbow land and Baron Rum-Tee-Foo's castle. Songs from popular musicals included *"Getting to know you"*, *"Somewhere Over the Rainbow"*, *"A Dream is a Wish Your Heart makes"*, *"I whistle a Happy Tune"* and *"Consider yourself one of Us"* and on 15 and 16 December 1975, all the children performed *"The Pied Piper of Hamelin"*. Christmas 1977 was slightly different with *"Follow the Star"* a Festival of Carols which raised £40 for the Treloar Trust. In 1979 a nativity play *"The Little Angel"* raised £90 for the Save the Children Fund and in December 1980, *"The Song of Caedmon"* was performed in Church to commemorate the 1300th anniversary of St Hilda's death. The 1981 play *"Only a Baby"* was performed in church and in 1982, *"A Medieval Christmas"* with hot mince pies and ginger wine raised £18 for school funds (see appendix 17).

Other charities supported by the school included Help the Aged, National Children's Homes, and the work of Mother Teresa of Calcutta. In 1979 when £53 was raised for the World Wildlife Fund in association with Brook Bond PG Tips, the school was awarded a Carousel Slide Projector at an informal ceremony attended by parents. That year was the *"International Year of the Child"*, and the school published an Anthology of Children's Verse containing pupils' poems written over the years 1964-79, and profits went to the Save the Children Fund. During Mr Sykes' last autumn term, the children collected £127 in five-pence pieces for school funds.

The first summer pageant *"Ten Sixty Six"* in 1966, marked the 900th anniversary of the Norman Conquest. For several weeks, parents were making colourful costumes and banners and the boys made shields, axes, swords and helmets whilst the girls knitted *"chain mail"* for Norman soldiers. Parents and friends loaned furniture, jewellery, sewing machines, a tape-recorder and helped with lighting and amplifying equipment and construction of the stage. Performances were on the School House lawn, admission was 1/6d (7.5p) and there were stalls, competitions and refreshments and despite gloomy weather 400 people attended over 3 July evenings. Mr Sykes filmed the pageant with sound and colour and scenes were taken on the Wolds and on Filey beach where a fishing boat was hired for the Vikings landing. The film's premier was on 14 October 1966 the anniversary of the Battle of Hastings and guests of honour were the children who left that summer: Elissa Bean, Vincent Brocklehurst, Stuart Dawson, Kelvin Foxton, Jonathan and Philip Galtry, Raymond Johnson, Timothy Pickard, Maureen Pickard, Howard Skelton, Ian Umpleby, Joan Walker. The 1967 pageant *"The Tudor Rose"* was based on the life of Queen Elizabeth I, and performed on 5 lovely warm evenings. Christine Bean played Queen Elizabeth and in one scene she *"rode majestically through Tilbury"* on Joey, a white pony led by the Queen's Page Richard Cundall and loaned by Mrs Zeila Cundall (see appendix 18). The film premiere was on 17 November 1967, the 409th anniversary of Queen Elizabeth I's accession in 1558. Some filming was done in St Hilda's Church, Scarborough Castle, the Tower of London and Hatfield House.

Richard Sykes claimed he found a stone dated 1869 on the school premises and so in Autumn 1968, staff and 69 pupils began to research local history and make plans to celebrate. Centenary week began on Sunday 15 June 1969 with a well attended service at St Hilda's Church when Ian Rackham read the lesson. On three evenings, the children performed an outdoor pageant *"The Sherburn Story"* in which two Victorian children find a bracelet on the site of an ancient Wolds settlement and in their imagination they see and relate the whole of Sherburn's history from the ancient Britons, through Roman, Saxon, Elizabethan and Victorian times. Other events included an exhibition of bygones and old photos, a reconstructed Victorian Room using furniture and heirlooms loaned by villagers, a Centenary Dinner at the East Riding Hotel attended by a large gathering of former pupils and friends who enjoyed an illustrated talk by Tony Brewster on his local archaeological discoveries. A souvenir book was produced containing village history written by the children and a floral display on the school hill featured the school's coat-of-arms designed by the children 5 years earlier for the badge on the school's red blazers. The film premier of *"The Sherburn Story"* began a five-day festival of events from 13 November 1980 to commemorate the 1300th anniversary of the death of St Hilda. Other school films included *"Robin Hood"* (1975), *"The Once and Future King"* (1976) and *"The Song of Hiawatha"* (1978) and the last one *"Exodus"* had its premier on the 12 March 1981, when the school was packed with people and the film declared *"a great success"* (see end of appendix 18). There were regular requests for the films to be shown at other schools, at teachers' meetings, at church meetings, Women's Institutes, Over 60's Clubs, various village organisations and at Theatre-in-the-Round in 1979 for a Young Peoples' Festival.

From time to time, the headmaster took the top class to Scarborough's Capitol Cinema (now a Bingo hall), and films they saw included *"Peter Pan"* (1966), *"The Ten Commandments"* (1967), *"Fantasia"* (1968), and *"The Ten Commandments"* (1973). There were visits to the theatre and in December 1975, for the first time, the whole school went by coach to Scarborough Spa where they saw *"Flibberty and the Penguin"* produced by students of the North Riding College. Thereafter, Christmas theatre visits included *"Hijack over Hygenia"* (Spa 1976), *"The Rose and the Ring"* (Royal Opera House 1977), *"Once upon a time"* (Theatre-in-the-Round 1978), *"Once more upon a time"* (1979), *"Simple Simon"* (1980), *"The Vanishing"* (1981) and *"Ghost Train to Cornelian Bay* (1982).

* * * * * * *

When Richard Sykes joined the Parish Council, issues under discussion included filling in the wells beneath the old pumps, piping in the West Beck along Vicarage Lane to prevent flooding, tidying the land south-east of the crossroads where the old Primitive-Methodist Chapel had been demolished and the possibility of using £500 from a defunct village hall building fund to pay for 33 street lights at £450 with a £140 running costs. A public meeting to discuss the lighting was badly attended, so those present organised a house-to-house ballot. The box contents were counted in the presence of Arthur L Duggleby clerk to the Parish Council and Percy Gilbank chairman and there were 376 in favour and 22 against. On 23 November 1966, the head master wrote *"The village street lighting was switched on this evening without ceremony"*. At the 1967 Parish Council AGM, following the removal of trees opposite the church where bungalows were being built, members resolved that the Coronation trees on the church side of the road must never be removed. Jack Skilbeck and Ron Bassett were chosen to represent the council on the board of school mangers. By the end of 1970, two bus shelters costing £280 were completed on High Street and paid for mainly from house-to-house collections.

Two months after Mr Sykes's arrival, Revd Thomas Wray died after being vicar since 1936. During the interregnum, the parish was in the care of Rural Dean R B Jackson, and at their first council meeting, members arranged for the overhaul of the organ, the repair of all broken windows, the sexton's hut, the Lytch Gate and the provision of litter baskets. The interior of the church and especially the brass, needed a thorough clean because of the presence of a large population of bats which Stan Clarke said had been there throughout his 14 years as sexton/cleaner and probably for much longer. Suggested remedies included placing a stuffed owl or live owl in the rafters to frighten the bats away but in the end flood lights were hired and kept on all night during the breeding season which reduced numbers considerably. Members of the congregation then set to and gave the place a thorough spring clean. That first summer after Thomas Wray's death, the garden fete was held at Springfield Farm, home of Michael and Pat Barstow and the school children organised a *'bathroom stall'* and each year thereafter. Sunday's Holy Communion moved to 9am after being at 8am for as long as anyone could remember.

Only one month after the organ overhaul, Percy Pinkney died aged 76 after being organist for 37 years, Church Council secretary for 32, and a member of the Brass Band for 38. He'd also served as church warden and parish councillor. Family mourners were Clifford and Raymond Pinkney (sons), Gladys and David Harrison (daughter and son-in-law). Percy's successor as organist was Peter Dunbar who'd just moved into the village to work in Cundalls' offices at Brewery House.

In October 1965, the Bishop of Selby instituted the Rev Eric Hardman as curate-in-charge and at a reception in school, Michael Barstow, PCC chairman, welcomed Mr Hardman and his wife *'Billie'* on behalf of the church council and congregation. In May 1968 the Bishop of Selby Rt Rev D N Sergeant spent a day in Sherburn and visited the school, Wards factory, several families and old people and attended the Women's Institute monthly meeting. Eric Hardman's successors were the Revd Frank Robinson (1972-74) and the Revd Mark Simons (1975-78). Mark was the last vicar of Sherburn because his successor Julian Armfelt (1978-83) was given the care of the parishes of Sherburn with East and West Heslerton and Yedingham with Knapton. On Ash Wednesday 1982 there was Holy Communion at 8am, a School Service at 10 am and Evensong at 7.30 pm and on 17 November 1982 St Hilda's Day, new metal lighting pendants in the Nave were dedicated. All these clergymen took a keen and active interest in school life.

Dr Wilfred Thistlethwaite retired in March 1965 after 40 years as GP in Sherburn and surrounding villages. His successors Dr Ian and Dr Marie Carrie moved, with their children Donald and Barbara, from Hull where they'd practised 13 years and *"Roseville"* was re-named *"Burnholme"* presumably because of the West Beck nearby. Dr Ian was born in Dundee and graduated from St Andrew's University in 1948 where he'd been president of the medical society and had represented the university in the athletics and rugby union. He enjoyed bee-keeping, gardening and sailing. At the Cricket and Football Club's sports day in Sherburn's new playing field on August Bank Holiday Monday 1965, both doctors judged the fancy dress and winners were Elaine Johnson, Jill Slack and Shirley Collier (under 5's) and Joan Walker, Carol Slack and Wendy Haxby (under 11's). Barry Foxton won the men's mile. The following year Dr Marie awarded prizes to Vanessa Skelton for the best decorated doll's pram and Paul Rackham for the best decorated bicycle. In 1967, Dr Ian awarded *"bonny baby"* prizes to: Allison Pickard, Lynda Pickard (under 1 year), Deborah Baron (1-2 years). In 1970, fancy dress winners were Jane Mortimer *"Beauty Queen"* (pretty), Ruth Currey *"Knitting Bee"* (original) and Eva Baker's children *"Love on the Dole"* (comic).

Dr Marie joined the Sherburn & District St John Ambulance Brigade led by Maggie Ridsdale assisted by District Nurse Jean Bradford. In June 1967, Rev H Ratcliffe, president, Staxton, welcomed County Officers, parents and visitors to a presentation ceremony in the Village Hall (see appendix 19). In June 1970 after a service in St Hilda's, County Commissioner Lord Westbury inspected the division at *"Burnholme"*. Margaret Ridsdale received a 2nd bar (25 years service), Dr Marie Carrie a medal (5 years) and Sheila Walker a Home Nursing certificate. Many school children were members and on 25 June 1971, seven girl cadets were given leave of absence from school to go to Hull where they were presented to Princess Anne the Brigade's president.

At the end of 1966, proposals to build a new fire-station and steel drill tower on Sherburn High Street met with opposition. Councillors Frank Ward and Pat Barstow thought the proposed building would not look right and the overall feeling was that the existing station was adequate. The Public Health Committee wanted the building to be re-sited and the flat roof and coloured wall panels altered but this was refused by the County Council who owned the land. That year, Ernest Pateman who joined Sherburn fire brigade in 1939, was awarded the Queen's Medal for long service.

In July 1967 the brigade was called out to High Mill Farm where spontaneous combustion caused hay in a 5-bay Dutch barn to burst into flames and 38 calves in an adjoining lean-to suffocated. Geoff Kershaw of Waterworks House, assistant farm manager and part-time fireman, was at Stony Haggs when the fire started and said: *"I could see the smoke coming from the direction of the farm, so I came back straight away"*. Filey brigade helped and the fire was soon under control but Sherburn crew remained on duty all night. That year, 134,000 farm animals were slaughtered following a serious epidemic of foot-and-mouth-disease.

The following Spring a shed on Charles Henderson's garden allotment next to the Vicarage caught fire. The structure was of corrugated iron, asbestos

---

Top Class c 1965: *Back:* Richard Sykes (head master), Stuart Dawson, Steve Bean, Kenneth Johnson, Richard Heath, Shaun Flinton, Mark Gilbank, Howard Skelton, Philip Dobson

Middle: Tim Pickard, Graham Pickard, Ian Umpleby, Vanessa Skelton, Melanie Gow,   ?   , Alison Pittam, Dorothy Scholes, Wendy Haxby, Ellisa Bean, Raymond Johnson, Kelvin Foxton

Front Row (sitting): Maureen Pickard, Lynn Nesfield, Ann Davison, Diane Oxtoby, Joan Walker

and timber and was a meeting place for Charles and his retired friends who met every day to talk and smoke and on fine days they brought their chairs out into the sunshine. Despite help from Filey brigade, the shed burnt to the ground. Charles was born in Sherburn, served in the 1914-18 war, worked for 12 years at Sherburn Brewery until its closure in the early 20's, then was groundsman at Ganton golf course for 40 years. He and his wife Emily were married for 61 years and Charles died at 86 in 1970 and Emily in 1984 at 96.

Sub-officer Ernie Patemen retired in 1973 and was succeeded by leading-fireman Jack Cousins. Fellow members that year were Bill Berriman, Derrick Collier, Colin Hotham, Harry Kedge, Tony Metcalfe, John Pickard and Roy Pickering. Tony Metcalfe who joined the brigade at 18, succeeded Jack Cousins as sub-officer in 1984 and retired in 1999 after 37 years. In February 1977, Ernie Pateman 63 died tragically whilst driving a 15 cwt Commer van belonging to his employers, the Muston & Yedingham Drainage Board, over an unmanned level crossing at Binnington. The van collided with the 2.16 pm passenger train from Scarborough to York and a witness saw Ernie get out of his van, open both gates, tie them back, return to his van and drive towards the line, but instead of stopping to allow the train to pass he kept going. Another witness said the van windows were steamed up. By the time the train driver saw the van there was no time to stop. Emergency service vehicles including Sherburn fire-engine, were towed by tractor across muddy fields and used lifting equipment to pull the van from under the train. A British Rail traffic assistant collapsed and died at the scene. The verdict was accidental death. Ernie and his wife Emily had no family but he was well loved by both children and adults. Emily's father William Matthews (died aged 76 in 1963), took up employment during the 1940's as a shepherd for Dickie Jackson at St Hilda's Farm and Emily's mother Ruth Matthews died aged 101 in the Ashfield Rest Home in June 1993. Ruth was a staunch Methodist, a founder member of the Women's Institute and for many years organised the annual autumn Sale of Work for the Blind in the Methodist schoolroom.

* * * * * * *

Juniors cc 1965: *Back:* Martin Haxby, Keith Mitchell, Neil Pickard, David Gilbank, Andrew Bean, Mrs V Watson (teacher)
Middle: Susan Pittam, Maureen Walker, Denise Harrison, Mary Pickard, Gary Axham, Peter Marston, Janet Pickard, Julie Gow, Sandra Pickard
Front (sitting): Kathleen Cracknell, Christine Bean, Christeen Thistleton, Pauline Bean, Julie Nesfield

In 1967, a change in village tradition began with the threat of the abolition of coursing the competitive chasing of hares by greyhounds. Although the sport was documented as long ago as 180AD by Greek historian Kynegetikos, the tradition did not begin in Sherburn until 1911 when local farmers began meeting casually to pit their dogs against each other for bets at Duggleby Wold and Sherburn Coursing Club was formed. Two of those farmers were school managers Richard Duggleby and Henry Prodham. The Dugglebys had been tenants of Duggleby Wold Farm for 80 years and spectators and officials gathered there for lunch on coursing days. When the Abolition Bill was introduced, Arthur Duggleby (b1892-d1979) son of Richard said *"Coursing is a good clean sport and usually only 4 or 5 hares are killed out of 30"*. George Prodham son of Henry said *"We shall oppose the Bill and I hope members will write to local MP's"*. Although the object of the chase was to exercise dogs rather than kill, hares were chased into the open and given only 60-80 yards start before dogs were released. Until well into the 1920's school closed on Coursing Day and older boys were employed as "bush beaters" to frighten the hares out into the open. In 1967, photography at meetings was prohibited without a licence, following the wide publication of the picture of two dogs tearing at a hare. The 2004 Hunting Act made coursing illegal in England and Scotland. Arthur Duggleby was Club secretary for 20 years until his retirement at 77 in 1968. Arthur worked in Cundalls' offices and was clerk to the Parish Council for many years.

One ardent member of Sherburn Coursing Club was Madge Ringrose (d 1974) who said *"I rode a little black donkey to course the hares when I was six and I've been an enthusiast ever since"*. Catherine Marjorie *'Madge'* Ringrose who was born at the Pigeon Pie in 1903 when her parents Ernest and Isabelle Ringrose were innkeepers, was educated at Scarborough Municipal and Malton St Andrew's Schools, and became a well-known horse woman throughout a wide area. She had stables at Low Mill and hunted with the Middleton and neighbouring clubs, competed in show jumping events and local point-to-points and played polo. She bred and trained grey hounds winning many prizes, her last prize was with her puppy *"Ring O' John"*

Infants c 1965: *Back:* Alison Brown (teacher), Gary Pickard, Richard Walker, Andrew Pickard, Peter Mattinson, Trevor Pickard, Ian Rackham, Paddy Umpleby, Pete Dobson, Chris Bean, Gary Dobson
Middle: Trevor Wiley, Kevin Pickard, Jonathan Galtry, Martin Flinton, Peter Mattinson, Howard Rogers, Carl Horsley, Margaret Gilbank
Front: Ann Pickering, Neil Bassett, Philip Galtry, Vincent Brocklehurst, Gill Pickard, Susan Scholes, Tina Foxton, Jane Simpson, Amanda Haxby, Andrea Worthy, Malcolm Thistleton, Kevin Stocks, Paul Harrison, Hazel Pickering

champion of the 1973 Huntingdon & District Coursing Club puppy stakes.

There was another threat to village tradition in 1967 when the Cricket Club had to drop out of the Hospital and Wold Newton Cup competitions. They'd been entering for many years but the previous season because the team was made up of schoolboys they failed to win a single match in the Beckett League. Peter Dunbar, chairman, said they had lost five good players in two seasons, one was Raymond Metcalfe, reputed to be the backbone of the team and one of the best bowlers. In his earlier days, when Raymond played for RAF Bawdsey and RAF Leconfield, he was described as *"a fast bowler of outstanding merit"*. Another loss was Roy Sadler who'd played for the club for 20 years and he said that sadly the days had gone when the game couldn't go on long enough, partly because of marriage and retirement amongst players but mainly through lack of interest. Six seasons passed before the situation changed when in 1973, Sherburn won the Dawson Cup by scoring 90 for 5 against Scalby's 87 all out. In the final over of an exciting game when only 5 runs were needed, Capt Dennis Marflitt hit the winning ball to the boundary bringing his score to 14 not out. Other scores were Stuart Dawson 8, Chris Ridsdale 11, Barry Foxton 34, David Nettleton 6, Sid Skilbeck (not out 10), Kevin Metcalfe 3. Chairman Peter Dunbar in his end of season report paid tribute to the players who after an interval of several seasons, gained re-election to Division C of the Beckett League. Barry Foxton had *"bowled admirably throughout the season"*, Captain Dennis Marflitt had *"set a fine example"* taking 13 catches, Stuart Dawson's batting included 2 centuries and Sid Skilbeck won the Chairman's Cup for the best bowling in 15 league matches, taking 14 wickets, making a total of 253 runs. Shaun Flinton was unbeaten 8 times in his 15 batting spells and Club Awards for league matches were: batting: Stuart Dawson, 16 innings, 3 not out, 725 runs, 114 highest score, 55.75 average; bowling: Barry Foxton, 192.2 overs, 57 maidens, 439 runs, 56 wickets, 7.84 averages.

At the Football Club's 1971 annual dinner, Mike Hotham said the season had been one of the best. They won the East Riding Senior Cup, were runners-up in League Division I, losing finalists in the League Cup; the 2nd XI finished in mid table and the juniors ended in 4th place. The Mazza Stead Memorial Trophy was presented by Mrs Mary Stead to Ken Metcalfe. That was the

---

Juniors c 1968 *Back:* Gary Dobson, Brett Stephenson, Barbara Smith (teacher), Patrick Umpleby, Richard Harrison
Timothy Mitchell, Christine Bean, John Brooks, Malcolm Thistleton, Paul Gilbank, Paul Harrison, David Walker
Jayne Horsley, Janice Gilbank, Louise Dexter, ? , Jacqueline Mouser, Sally Heath, Andrea Worthy

year when British Currency changed from £..s..d to decimalisation and several weeks beforehand Mr Sykes gave a course of evening classes in school for adults to prepare for the changeover.

* * * * * * *

The end of an era came in 1968, when Albert Marston, postmaster, and his wife Rhona and children Carol, Peter and Philip moved to York. At a Methodist Garden Party at *"Lyttle Dene"* the home of Mr & Mrs W E Bradford, Albert was presented with a fountain pen and pencil and Rhona with a bouquet by Ian Rackham. Albert said he would miss Sherburn for as well as being post master since the death of his father Albert Baker Marston in 1955, he'd been a parish councillor, was on the playing field committee, helped with the Reading Room, was a keen sportsman and musician and played the organ at both church and chapel and often returned to play for funerals. Several years later Albert and his family moved to Scarborough where he was manager for John Mitchell's Office Equipment Bureau. Albert was also musical director for the York and Scarborough Male Voice Choirs, the Scarborough Light Opera and Pickering Musical Societies and sang with the Take-Four Barbershop Quartet. He loved cricket and was wicket-keeper for Scarborough for 15 seasons. In 1988 Albert collapsed and died at the age of 63 during rehearsals with the Scarborough & District Male Voice Choir. His successors at the post office were Edward and Betty Stephenson who with their 4 children, moved from a dairy farm at Melbourne. After serving in the Royal Artillery in Egypt, Italy and Austria, Edward joined the Middlesborough police and reached the rank of sergeant, then left the force to take up farming. His grandmother was post-mistress at Cayton and two of his cousins were postmasters at Gristhorpe and Osgodby. Edward's ill health forced their spell at the post office to be short-lived and Jeffrey and Margaret Holmes and their children Mark and Andrea moved from the West Riding into the Post Office in 1970. One of their post ladies was Mrs Wilhelmina *"Mina"* Walker who for 17 years delivered mail around the village in an old pram nick-named *"Wells Fargo"*. Mina was up at 5.45 am and out every morning except Sunday in all weathers and was on her fourth pram when she retired on New Year's Eve 1986 when villagers gathered at the post office to wish her well and present her with a cheque. Her husband John Walker died aged 79 six months later.

Infants 1968: Alison Brown (teacher). *Back:* Linda Thompson, Shirley Collier, Trudie Marflitt, Janette Wiley, Joan Cussons, Pamela Duggleby, Julie Harrison, Carolyn Pickering, Elaine Pickering
Front: Martin Middle, Christopher Mouser, Philip Waud, Andrew Gilbank, Gary Bean, Desmond Bean, Duncan Law, Colin Pickard

In summer 1972, *"Hatrack"* a six-week low-flying exercise was carried out in the Derwent Valley by 100 RAF and Army personnel based at Weaverthorpe Station. Harrier Jump Jets from Lincolnshire simulated attacks on 24 inflated rubber tanks to work out new offensive and support tactics. Sqdn Ldr Stuart Penny paid tribute to the warm welcome and co-operation given by the people of Sherburn and said there had been only one registered complaint. There had however, been numerous un-registered complaints about animals, babies and old people being startled every day by loud low-flying jets and there were fears about the safety of the Church tower.

Another era ended in January 1973 with the death of Ronald Arthur Heath 51, only weeks after closing his butcher shop in St Hilda's Street for the last time. As well as playing in Sherburn Brass Band with his father and Uncle Harold, Ron was a member of the Ayton and Malton Art Societies. His mother Mary Elizabeth *"Lizzie"* Heath died 15 months later at 79 Langdale Avenue Victoria, Scarborough. The Heath family had supported the school for many years. Leslie and Diane Hodgson and their two children Christopher and Andrew moved into the premises from Slingsby in 1974 and started an electrical business.

The Brass Band in which the Heaths played disbanded during the 1960's, then in 1974 was revived by Stan Carr of Heslerton. Ray Dalton of Swinton was band leader, Lawrence Duggleby his deputy and players included Percy and Bill Gilbank, Bob Levitt, Jeffrey Holmes and his children Andrea and Mark, Mark Pickard, Sarah Flinton, Jerry Young (Malton), Rodney Preston, Pamela Duggleby, Jane Horsley, Graham Little and children from Ayton, Snainton, Brompton and Weaverthorpe. They practised every Wednesday in the Methodist schoolroom under the free tutorship of the Rev Mark Simons, vicar from 1974-79 and accomplished musician. In 1975, junior band members Pamela Duggleby, Mark and Andrea Holmes provided music for the Chapel Sunday School anniversary. Taking part were Mark Nettleton, Jane and Rosemary Newlove, Nigel and Mark Pickard, Deborah Baron, Janice Cousins, Julie and Sharon Taylor, Caroline Tolliday, Jane Pinder and Sarah Cousins. The Rev Harold Anfield praised the children for collecting £72 for mission and for coming 2nd in the Junior Rally. A year later Sunday School

---

Top Class c 1974: *Back:* Jamie Mitchell, Nigel Pickard, Jane Newlove, Andrew Simms, Tracy Thistleton, Dawn Foxton, Chris Hodgson, Ian Harrison, Michael Pickering
Middle: Gary Marflitt, Tracy Pickering, Trudie Harrison, Debra Baron, Mark Horsley, Jean Walker, Linda Pickard, Andrew Oldroyd
Front: Richard Collier, Paul Thompson, Lynn Umpleby, Rosemary Newlove, Julie Taylor, Martin Pickard, Andrew Pickering

prizewinners were Deborah Baron, Richard Brookes, Sarah Flinton, Mark Nettleton, Rosemary and Jane Newlove, Nigel and Mark Pickard, Jane Pinder, Richard and Nina Ward, Julie Taylor, Carolyn Tolliday. In 1976 the Band raised £160 with a concert organised by Mabel Cousins in aid of a heart machine for Scarborough Hospital.

Also during the 1970's, Sherburn had a Gym Club that met on Tuesday evening's in the Methodist Hall under the leadership of Gloria Axham and Margaret Wood. Members included Kim Kilvington, Jane Pinder, Julie Walker, Helen and Richard Pickering, Alison Pickard, Elaine and Richard Gillett, Caroline Axham, Trisha Skilbeck, Sharon Dennis, Nicola Dobson and Victoria Rodgers.

In 1974, Sherburn entered the tidy village competition organised by the Council for the Protection of Rural England and on Spring Bank Holiday, the parish council involved the school children in a sponsored litter collection. Every full bag earned 50p and 37 bags were collected in two hours. Trudie Marflitt 11, won a competition with her coloured felt-tip drawing of a dog burying bones bearing the caption: *"Even dogs bury litter. So why don't you?"* Andrew Gilbank 11 won a poetry competition and his opening lines were *"Remember you are a Womble and keep Sherburn clean. There will be no litter wherever we have been"*. That year the council considered re-naming St Hilda's Street to Langley Avenue in memory of Marmaduke Langley, Lord of the Manor in the early 1800's, because the 12 council houses opposite today's surgery were called St Hilda's Terrace and this caused confusion for postal deliveries. In the end, St Hilda's Terrace became part of St Hilda's Street. Council members included Richard Sykes, Pat Barstow, John Cundall, Tom Flinton, Hugh Mitchell, Jeffrey Holmes, Anne Collier, Mel Readman (clerk), Percy Gilbank and Arthur Stead (school governors), Winifred Foxton and Marion Charters (Ryedale Parish Council Assoc).

Another family era ended in 1983 with the death at 94 of Richard *"Dickie"* Jackson who'd been farming at St Hilda's Farm for most of the 20th century.

Whole School cc1983. *Back:* Alison Oulton (teacher), Colin Best, Colin Daphne, Paul Holmes, Ian Cade, Simon Cousins, Simon Dobson, Richard Sykes (head master), Tara Ward, Claire Howe, Nicholas Lickes, Barbara Smith (teacher)
Second: Nicola Dobson, Samantha Sedman, Lisa Gilbank, Kay Pickering, Trisha Skilbeck, Helen Armstrong, Alison Atkinson, Tracy Armstrong, Sharon Holmes
Third: Clare Stockill, Deborah Lickes, Helen Woodall, Marcus Gilbank, Jonathan Gillett, Mark Cousins, Joseph Simons, Dean Foxton, Alison Thompson
Front: Beverley Taylor, John Slack, Kelly Lickes, Gavin Metcalfe, Samantha Atkinson, Jamie Snowball, Kerry Metcalfe, Lynn Gosley, Katie Walker, Carl Berriman, Chris Cousins, Lorraine Shaw

Dickie's parents Richard and Annie who moved into the farm after school manager Henry Prodham retired, died in the early 30's. After *Dickie's* death, the farm was demolished and Wards bought the land. The name of Jackson first appeared in Sherburn parish records in 1718 when another Richard Jackson's daughter Sarah was baptised.

* * * * * * *

On Richard Sykes's last Open Day on July 1983, there was 100% attendance by parents and that year average pupil attendance was 93.7%, Clare Stockill and Samantha Sedman had no absences and Ian Cade, Simon Dobson and Trisha Skilbeck were absent twice. Numbers were dwindling and Mr Sykes predicted that by 1987 there would be only 24 pupils. Progress prizes were presented to Ian Cade, Mark and Simon Cousins, Simon Dobson, Sharon Holmes, Lorraine Shaw, Clare Stockill, Beverley Taylor. Leavers were Helen Armstrong, Colin Best, Nicola Dobson, Lisa Gilbank, Paul Holmes, Kay Pickering, Samantha Sedman, Trisha Skilbeck and Alison Thompson.

In his final open day speech Mr Sykes said: *"Responsibility is a much neglected word today when everyone is demanding rights. Nevertheless, our children have a responsibility for the future of the world, to maintain peace, stop pollution, preserve wild life and to learn from the mistakes of previous generations. So how can we help them? Here are some wise words taken from an old church plaque:*

If a child lives with criticism, he learns to condemn; if a child lives with hostility, he learns to fight. If a child lives with ridicule, he learns to by shy; if a child lives with shame, he learns to feel guilt. If a child lives with tolerance, he learns to be patient and if a child lives with encouragement, he learns to be confident. If a child lives with praise, he learns to appreciate, if a child lives with fairness, he learns to be just. If a child lives with security, he learns to have faith and if a child lives with acceptance, he learns how to love".

If teachers and parents could apply this wisdom, we would need no policemen, no social workers and no psychiatrists. I have tried to preserve in this school those elements which are the basic requirements of a responsible society. Finally, none of us knows what the future holds, and to those pupils who are moving to another school and to everyone here, I can give no better advice than that embraced in the words from Louise Haskins' poem: "I said to the man who stood at the Gate of the Year: 'Give me a light that I may tread safely into the unknown' and he replied: 'Go out into the darkness and put your hands into the hand of God. That shall be to you better than light and safer than a known way' ".

Richard Sykes retired nine days later on 27 July. The previous evening pupils, staff, parents governors and friends crowded into school to say farewell and present gifts in appreciation of his long service. Mr Sykes wrote in the log book: *"I leave this post, after 19 very happy years, grateful to parents, staff and pupils for their loyalty, friendship and encouragement"*. He moved into an apartment in Bridlington then later to a bungalow in Bempton. Gracie Fields died on 27 September 1979 and in his book *"The Song of the Sea"* Richard wrote *"I was stunned and heart-broken and tried hard to hide my sadness during lessons"*. Neither his reaction to her death nor his attendance at a Memorial Service in Rochdale Parish Church are recorded in his log book. Richard died suddenly aged 71 on Christmas Eve 1997 at his home in Bempton and at a thanksgiving service for his life at Octon Crematorium on 2 January, two of Gracie's records were played, *"Sally"* as the coffin entered the hall and *"Wish me luck as you wave me good-bye"* at the committal. He'd always said no-one would sing at his funeral but Gracie!

CHAPTER 7
GEOFFREY F HOWDLE 1983-2000

G EOFF HOWDLE was chosen out of three applicants and after leaving a teaching post at East Ayton County Primary School began his duties as headmaster of Sherburn School on 8 September 1983. He travelled each day from his home in Bridlington where he lived with his wife and children, and School House which had been the home of Sherburn's headmaster for over 60 years, was sold. There were 32 pupils and Geoff taught the older children, Barbara Smith the middle juniors and Alison Oulton continued as full-time Infants' teacher

Throughout the 1980's the teaching profession suffered long spells of political unrest about pay, working conditions and staff reductions. Schools nation-wide, were disrupted from time to time by strikes and although several local primary schools were affected, life at Sherburn school continued as normal. The eventual enforcement of staff reductions led to larger classes and the closure of many small primary schools. At a meeting of interested parties held in Staxton school on 23 June 1986, the decisions were made to allow Sherburn School to stay open, to close Ganton and Folkton and to build a new school at Staxton. Barbara Smith had to leave and at the last morning assembly before the 1986 summer holidays, was presented with flowers and a cut glass vase. When school re-opened in September, there were two full-time teachers in charge of Class I (lower school with 20 pupils) and Class II (upper school with 16). Six Ganton pupils were admitted and their head master John Found, joined the staff for one year. Staxton's new School opened in September 1988.

Subsequent part-time teachers included Mrs Janet Shipley 1990-1999, Miss Esther Preston 1996-98. Mrs A E Natschowney 1999 and supply teachers included Mrs Scott, Mrs Leyland Mrs Duggleby, Mrs Whittaker and Christine Thompson. Alison Oulton retired in Dec 1994 after 32 years and at a buffet evening attended by a large gathering of pupils, parents and friends, was presented with flowers and gift vouchers. Alison said *"I'm sad to be leaving and will miss the children and parents who have always been wonderfully supportive"*. Her successor was Mrs Carol Barnes of Seamer, who moved from a teaching post at Pickering Primary School. The school's first nursery assistants were Miss Alison Horne from 1995-98 and Mrs Joanne Harrison 1999 to 2000. By September 1999, pupil numbers had increased to 59, 18 in Class I (reception/year 1), 19 in Class II (years 2/3) and 22 in Class III (Years

4/5/6), qualifying the school for more teaching staff and Miss Katherine Crowther was appointed full-time and Mrs Anne Pratt part-time.

Mr Howdle's dining assistants included Mrs Gill Nettleton, Mrs Moyra Stockill, Mrs Maureen Walker, Mrs Janet Armstrong, Mrs Pam Foxton and Mrs Pauline Shaw. As well as serving dinners and in accordance with new regulations, these ladies supervised the children in the playground during the dinner hour. Teachers supervised children during morning and afternoon playtimes on a Rota basis. In 1997 Gordon Poole retired after delivering cooked meals for 30 years first from Filey during 1967-84 and then from the new school at West Heslerton from 1984-97. Anne Collier school secretary for 22 years, retired at Christmas 1998 and her successor was Miss Anna Massie.

Each Spring, two students came from the North Riding Education College for 2 weeks' teaching practice. Secondary pupils who came for a week's work experience in autumn included: Victoria Rodgers 1983, Hardy Brocklehurst 1984, Sharon Dennis 1986; Laura Scott 1987; Angela Arnell, Alison Atkinson 1989 + 92; Elizabeth Laws (Norton School) 1991; Lisa Gilbank, Della Shaw 1993; Karen Metcalfe 1994.

* * * * * * *

The main feature that made Mr Howdle's headship different from that of his predecessors' was the introduction or invasion, of computers into schools. Some historians claim computers began to develop after the first abacus was created in Babylon in 3000BC while others say that human beings were the world's first computers. Whichever is true, they've evolved over the centuries with the help of electricity (Benjamin Franklin 1780), telephone (Graham Bell 1876), wireless/telegraphy/radio (Guglielmo Marconi 1901) and photography/ television (John Logie Baird 1926). The first programmable computers were the Z1 (Konrad Zuse 1936), the ABC (Atansasoff & Berry 1942), IBM (1954), The Chip (Kilby & Noyces' Integrated Circuit 1958), Mouse & Windows (Douglas Englebart 1964), Microprocessor (Faggin, Hoff & Mazor 1971), Floppy (Alan Shugart & IBM 1971), Apple (1976/77), Word Processors (Rubenstein & Barnaby 1979), Microsoft (1981) with others in-between.

At Geoff Howdle's first Christmas of 1983, Wilf Ward founder of the village factory, donated £100 to start a computer fund. Collections in both pubs and a Boxing Day football match between Pigeon Pie regulars and the Sherburn 'has-beens', raised £382 and a bingo session raised £184. An ABC computer was delivered to school on 29 March 1984 and that day Mr Howdle was joined by head teachers from Folkton and Weaverthorpe in the first of a series of afternoon training sessions. In 1993 Word Processors (with training) replaced school typewriters, photo-copiers replaced ink duplicators and Sherburn's secretarial hours were increased to 8/week. During a weekend in May 1994, burglars stole the school's computer, video recorder and hi-fi system and again five months later they stole a lap-top, hi-fi system; video recorder and two printers. An alarm system was installed in 1996. Throughout 1998 Wards Social Club raised £1,000 for a new computer and printer and by 2000 there were ITC suites in every school.

Termly appointment sessions for parents to meet their child's teacher were introduced, team points certificates for class progress and after school clubs including cricket, gymnastics, net ball and chess were provided. Parents and villagers were welcomed into school to help with cookery, craft, music and reading and children were allowed to bring their own packed lunch. A press spotlight in June 1987, described the school as *"a central part of village life, a happy place with children looking after each other and older ones being tolerant and willing to look after younger ones at play time"*. The head teacher said *"I like to think our school has a family atmosphere where children are given every opportunity to reach their full potential"*. Mr Howdle, a quiet and gentle man, didn't need an instrument of punishment and three years after his arrival, corporal punishment was banned in state schools. In 1986, PC John Anderson, (Sherburn's last resident village policeman), visited school to question pupils about a broken fence and graffiti on school walls and again in 1988 about a broken school window and missing car badges. In 1994, *'Good Behaviour Certificates'* were introduced into school and a year later for the first time ever, 3 boys were excluded during dinner hour for the rest of the half term because of bad behaviour.

As well as services at Harvest, Christmas, Easter and at the end of summer term, parents were invited from time to time to morning assembly. Progress prizes continued to be awarded until 1994 but only to Class I and successful pupils included: Clare Howe, Samantha Atkinson (1984), Carl Berriman, Kelly Lickes (1985), Nicola Armstrong, Wayne Shaw (1986), Karen Metcalfe (1987 and 1988), Graham Ross (1889 and 1990), Donna Foxton (1991), Matthew Lickes (1992), Gemma Simms (1993), Adam Prest and Sarah Chadwick (1994).

In 1983 Lee Metcalfe, Simon Cousins, Nicholas Lickes, Simon Dobson and Ian Cade were chosen to play in the Scarborough 7-a-side football tournament for schools and beat Lindhead 2-0, Wheatcroft 2-0 and St Peter's 4-0 but were beaten by Newby 5-0 in the final. That season, Sherburn finished joint first with Staxton in the annual Village Schools Soccer Tournament. In 1984 they beat Folkton 2-0 and won the Challenge Shield in a 5-a-side football competition and in a 1986 six-a-side football tournament final, Jamie Snowball, Dean Foxton, Marcus Gilbank, John Slack, Robert Smith, Christopher Cousins and Gavin Metcalfe beat Brompton-by-Sawdon 1-0. In 1985, Simon Dobson and Nicholas Lickes were chosen to play in the Combined Village Schools Cricket team which scored 123 for 2 against Wheatcroft's 23 all out, 50 for 8 against Gladstone's 55 for 9 and 77 for 5 against Barrowcliff's 74 all out. Nicholas and Simon were also chosen to play in the final against Bramcote in the Esso Primary Schools Competition and although Bramcote won 107-6 against the Villages Team's 71, Simon scored 42 runs.

On the 8 May 1985, the 40th anniversary of 'Victory in Europe', Mrs Oulton organised a party with a wartime tea of potted meat sandwiches, the children wore 1940's clothes, played with 1940's whips 'n tops, skipping ropes, bowlers, marbles and sang wartime songs like: "I'll be seeing You, "We'll meet again", "There'll always be an England", and the famous "Lillie Marlene" sung by both German and British soldiers.

Also in 1985, 4th year juniors practised in a musical/recorder workshop at the North Riding College in readiness for the Scarborough Music Festival on 2/3 May at the Spa and the children wrote and illustrated their own poems for the Primary School Poetry Festival. Throughout the winter of 1987/8, John Chalcroft, St Hilda's Church organist, gave a series of free music lessons in school and at Christmas during the 1980's, the children sang carols and played recorder items at the Over 60's Club party. Several pupils took guitar lessons and in 1994 Tom Wright newly appointed leader of Sherburn Brass Band, started free individual brass tuition each Friday.

Competitions included a 'Keep Sherburn Tidy Poster Competition' (1985) organised by Margaret Wood. Winners were Michelle Coulson, Loraine Shaw, Mark Cousins (Class 1) and Kevin Metcalfe, Lynn Gosley, Karen Metcalfe (Class 2). Pupils who scored top marks in the 1985 Police Road Safety Quiz were Tara Ward, Sharon Holmes, Nicholas Lickes and Mark Cousins. Winners of the 1987 Easter competitions were Samantha Atkinson and Lee Jack (Easter card), Daniel Bibby and Karen Metcalfe (Easter garden), Dean Foxton, Katie Walker and Kerry Howe (decorated egg), Michelle Smith (Easter story). Dean Foxton, Christopher Cousins, Nicola Armstrong and Daniel Bibby read their own poems and Jamie Snowball, Samantha Atkinson and Nicola Armstrong read their own versions of "The Mysterious Egg". Readings from "The Easter Story" were by Gavin Metcalfe, Lynne Gosley, Lorraine Shaw, Katie Walker, Dean Foxton, Christopher Cousins, Kerry Metcalfe and Kelly Lickes. In 1989 Kerry Metcalfe, Katie Walker, Lynne Gosley and Christopher Cousins won the Wallis Trophy and Nicola Armstrong, Kelly Baxendale, William Freakley and Lynette Lickes finished joint 6th in the inter-school Road Safety Quiz. A "Dog Poster Competition" (1992) organised by Margaret Wood was won by Ian Allison, Stephen Armstrong, Lee and Ben Jack, Beth Rummel, Michelle Smith, Daniel and Marc Snowball. Between Easter and September 1999, in a national Walkers Crisp competition all 58 pupils ate the highest number of packets (20,150) by any school and were awarded 88 books for the school library and an autographed photo of England's footballer Michael Owen. On 5 January 2000, each pupil and member of staff were presented with a Millennium mug.

The Revd Paul Ockford vicar from 1983-93 was inducted the same year that Geoff Howdle was appointed. Paul was educated at Durham University and St Stephen's House, Oxford and served in the parishes of Streatham and Cheam, and Eastrington and Laxton near Goole. During Paul's ministry the tradition of flood-lighting the outside of the Church tower throughout the Christmas period began and the bell ropes were brought down so that the peel of eight bells could be operated at ground level. Paul maintained strong links between school and church and when he left, the Diocese sold the Vicarage and his successor Revd Pip Sharpe vicar from 1993-99, lived in his own home at Allerston. Pip who was one of the Church of England's first non-stipendiary priests was a retired headmaster and regularly gave voluntary classroom assistance. His successor, the Revd Christopher Hayes became the vicar of the Buckrose Carrs Benefice which combined the benefice of Rillington with Scampston, Wintringham and Thorpe Bassett and the benefice of Sherburn, East and West Heslerton with Yedingham and Knapton. The Bishop of Selby visited school in 1993 and 2000. School Governors included Percy Gilbank, Joan Briggs, Sandra Cade, Neville Akers, Sue Bradbury, Alan Massie, Anne Lickes, Ann Pickard, Ann Prince and Jane Pinder.

* * * * * * *

When Geoff Howdle arrived, only routine maintenance was necessary but the playground climbing frame which had caused several accidents was removed the Health & Safety Officer ordered all dustbins to be fenced off (1988), carpets were laid in the classrooms to reduce noise (1992) and inside toilets installed (1996) and a second mobile classroom was sited west of the first mobile classroom (2001).

Bad weather seldom affected attendance, but from 13-15 January 1987, the headmaster and several children were absent because of heavy snow and from 7-8 February 1991, roads were so bad, Heslerton school had to close and there were no school dinners. School did not have to close because of epidemic illness and there were few accidents. There was a case of worms, several cases of head lice (1986), colds and sickness (Jan-April 1988) and in December 1988, 50% of pupils were absent with 'flu. Mark Gilbank fell in the playground and cut his lip (1983) and Wayne Shaw broke a bone in the little finger of his left hand at dinner time (1989).

Mr Howdle's first Autumn Fair raised £158.31 (1983) and subsequent events raised money for charity as well as for school. A sponsored spell by the 32 children raised £197.87 (1984), a dinner dance £288.17 (1991), a National "Spell-a-thon" £191 for Mencap (1996), fashion show for school funds £287 and Comic Relief £64 (1997). A team of parents formed the Friends of Sherburn School (FOSS) and £1,400 was raised with a sponsored walk by a team of 'dads': Peter Mattinson, Michael and Kevin Stocks, Mike Suggitt, Des Bean, David Walker, Andrew Gilbank and Gary Marflitt who all completed the 79 miles of the Wolds Way in 23 hours, 55 minutes and 33 seconds. In 1999 for the first time, the Salvation Army Band played for *"Carols around the Christmas Tree"* now an annual event.

At Geoff Howdle's first Christmas the children presented *"Christmas News and Entertainment"* with readings on the Christmas Story and Christmas Legends, recorder music, carol singing and items by magicians, comedians and gymnasts. Subsequent performances were: *"In the Bleak Mid-Winter"* (1984 Ethiopian Famine Appeal £44); *"A Christmas Medley"* (1985); *"The Christmas Story"* (1986 Blue Peter £22.85); *"Christmas Candle, Christmas Lights"* (1987); *"Aladdin"* (1988 Blue Peter £27.20); Carol Concerts raised £22.36 for the Royal National Institute for the Blind (1989) and £20.94 for Children in Need (1990); a Nativity Play raised £22.30 (1991); *"A Christmas Presentation"* (1992); *"The Tale of Three Trees"* (1993); *"The Christmas Story"* (1995); *"Rock Around the Flock"* (1996); *"Rock the Baby"* (1997); (see appendix 20); *"The Inn Keeper's Story"* (1998); Carol Singing with St Hilda's Church members and Brass Band round the village (1999). Christmas theatre visits included *"The Adventures of Awful Knawful"* (Spa 1983), *"The Owl and the Pussycat"* (1984);*"Aladdin"* (1985) *"Worzel Gummidge"*(1986); *"Jack and the Giant"* (1987), *"The Wizard of Oz"* (1988); *"The Lion, the Witch and the Wardrobe"* (1989), *The Pied Piper"* (1990); *"Aesops Tales"* (1991); *"Dinosaurs and all that Rubbish"* (1992), no theatre visit 1993-1994, *"Grimms Tales"* (1995), *"The Champion of Pribanore"* (1996) and *"Honk"* (1997) both at Stephen Joseph Theatre, no visit 1998, a performance in school of *"Quack, Quack, Onk"* by a group of actors (1999) and *"Cinderella"* at York (2000).

Day coach trips included visits to Yorvik Viking Centre and York Minster (1984), Flamborough, Sewerby and Bridlington (1985), York Wildlife Centre, Roman Exhibition and Yorkshire Museum, York Minster Rose Window Exhibition and Murton Farming Museum (1986); York National Railway Museum (1987), half-day trips to Filey School Summer Fair (1988-91), a day at Hull Civil War Exhibition, Eden Camp and Beverley Army Transport Museum (1992); Oliver's Mount, the Millennium, Scarborough Lighthouse, Lifeboat and Castle (1993); Wood End Natural Museum and Art Gallery, Castle Howard (1994); Scarborough Sea Life Centre (1995); Ryedale Folk Museum and Dalby Forest (1997), York Railway Museum (1998), Halifax Eureka Museum (1999), a day in Bradford and a day in Hull (2000).

* * * * * * *

Village changes included the retirement in 1985, of Dr Marie Carrie who'd been Sherburn's GP for 20 years. At a large gathering of parishioners in the village hall, Marie was presented with a generous cheque from a collection in Sherburn and surrounding villages. When Marie's husband Dr Ian Carrie 52 died suddenly in 1978, she continued in practice and was joined by her son Dr Donald Carrie in 1981.

In 1988, Mrs Oulton was given leave of absence when her father Walter Evers Bradford 89 died after being garage proprietor for 65 years. Walter was a cousin of William Calvert Bell who taught at Sherburn School from 1904-12 and Walter and his wife Alys (nee Rank) were married at Wold Newton on 10 March 1926 and celebrated their Diamond Wedding two years before Walter's death

In August 1991, Frank Ward, local factory founder, died aged 76 at his home in Scalby. Despite the industrial unrest and gloomy economic climate of the 1970's and 80's when many businesses collapsed, Wards factory continued to expand and by the time Mr Frank died, had 1000+ employees and branches in Scotland and Europe. Less than a year later, the firm was forced into administration, but a London High Court decided Sherburn branch was still viable.

In May 1993, Margaret Wood died aged 68. Mrs Wood was special to the children through her support of the school and as Chapel Sunday School teacher. When the Woods moved to Sherburn in 1971, Margaret quickly became involved in the community, serving as a parish councillor, member of the Church Council, the village hall and playing field committees and the Yorkshire Countrywomen's Association. Each May she organised the annual Christian Aid House-to-House Collection and was presented to the Princess Royal at Castle Howard in recognition of her outstanding work for the Save the Children Fund. Margaret's husband Joe, a chiropodist, died in 1981 when the private air craft he was travelling in to Jersey, crashed into the Welsh mountains killing all four on board. The autumn before she died Margaret planted daffodil bulbs around the village with the help of the school children. Margaret had a deep Christian faith and a letter from her was read aloud at her funeral, thanking the people of Sherburn for their friendship and love. Arthur Stead, chairman and longest serving member of the parish council, planted 5 oak saplings in her memory at the north end of the churchyard and a seat was placed on the grass verge at the south-west corner of the churchyard.

During the summer holidays of 1993, the 'corner shop' closed when Tom and Betty Flinton retired after 26 years and the premises were re-named "Fourways". The Flintons succeeded Marion Charters who retired from district nursing in 1960 and took over the shop when Alfie Park died. The village was left with two shops Central Stores and the Post Office. Margaret and Jeffrey Holmes retired at Christmas 1993 after 23 years at the post office and everyone was invited to a two-day open house to enjoy wine and fruit cake. When Margaret and Jeffrey moved to Rillington, their successors at the post office were John and Rita Worthy.

Harry Cundall one of the county's best-known auctioneers and valuers died suddenly in 1994 in the garden of his home at High Mill. Joseph Cundall & Son was founded in the early 1900's and by 1987 had become Wells-Cundall with a chain of 18 offices throughout N-E Yorkshire. The business was sold to the Nation-wide Building Society then in 1992, Harry's younger brother John and a group of former partners, bought the firm back and began trading as Cundalls. Harry was a fellow of the Royal Institute of Chartered Surveyors and for many years was secretary to the Yorkshire Livestock Auctioneers Association, a member of the East Riding Central Association of Agricultural valuers, a JP and chairman of Malton magistrates. He allowed his land to be used for cross-country events to raise funds for the Riding for the Disabled Association and last but not least, Harry succeeded Richard Sykes as church-warden.

In 1998 Sherburn came third in the *'Best kept village'* competition. Judges said *"The whole village looked clean and tidy with some really attractive gardens. The Chapel was transformed by lovely flower pots and baskets, the row of cottages* (built 1857) *adjacent to the pump were a blaze of colour, the churchyard was immaculate and the village was outstandingly tidy"*.

* * * * * * *

Throughout Geoff Howdle's years as Sherburn's head teacher, as well as political, social and industrial unrest, Britain's schools had to face many sweeping changes. Only months after his arrival, Geoff began attending regular head teacher's courses and meetings with other head teachers, his teaching staff attended training courses, there were *'Baker'* training days, weekly staff meetings and *'cluster'* meetings with other schools. HM Inspectors were replaced by Ofsted (Office for standards in education) Inspectors, Classes I and II were re-named Key Stage 1 and Key Stage II, a national curriculum had to be strictly adhered to and policy documents produced for all subjects, with long term planning and aims and objectives, schools were invaded by advisers on all subjects and staff were trained to prepare pupils for the School Attainment Tests (SATs). Governors were divided into various committees, Finance & Staffing, Health & Safety, Curriculum, Staff Dismissal, Staff Appeals etc and were expected to engage in regular training. The northern classroom became the school office with piles of papers everywhere and there seemed hardly any time left for teaching.

On 8, 9 and 10 June 1997 Sherburn had its first Ofsted inspection. A team of Inspectors observed 23 lessons and found the quality of teaching to be satisfactory and often good or very good. The 52 pupils were achieving standards comparable with those expected for 7 and 11 year olds, they were well behaved and attendance was good. The report concluded that the school was providing value for money and pupils were enjoying a positive experience in a good environment with good working relationships and a good range of out of school activities. The Diocesan Inspectors commended the school for the pupils' moral and social development and its quality of collective Christian worship. There was room for improvement in the development of Information Technology and Design and Technology and inspectors suggested ways to maintain the school's progress by setting ambitious pupil targets. John Worthy, Chair of Governors predicted *"a bright and successful future"*. When school opened in September 1999 there were 59 children: 18 in Class 1 (reception/ year 1), 19 in Class 2 (yrs 2/3) and 22 in Class 3 (yrs 4/5/6).

In June 2002, at a party to celebrate the Queen's Golden Jubilee, each child received a Jubilee Medal from FOSS and a mug from the parish council. Winners of the *"Design a Crown"* competition were: Aiden Collins (Class 1) Abigail Gilbank (Class 2) and Nicola Suggitt (Class 3). Becci and Kathy Mattinson organised a World Cup raffle for school funds. That month, a local newspaper article by Paul Brook described Sherburn School as *"the hub of its rural community"* and said: *"The school's gates are bright blue....and inside, the school is just as bright and jolly. The friendly staff and cheerful children are part of a 'happy caring school that is keeping up with the times'"*. A play *'Moving On'* performed by the children portrayed the progress of mankind throughout the ages and carried the Christian message *"all these things have changed but God's love never changes"*. (see appendix 21).

Geoff Howdle, resigned in 2000 and Nigel Mainprize, deputy head of Barrowcliffe Junior School was acting head until Mrs Aileen Moss from Beverley was appointed in September 2001. Nine months later, Moyra Stockill had to leave after 23 years as caretaker because of the deteriorating health of her husband Les. The children presented Moyra with a *"splendid book"* containing their own art work and written contributions about her role as caretaker and she received a watch and flowers. Aileen Moss resigned in 2002 and was succeeded by Mrs Carol Barnes.

Whole School 1992. *Back:* Alison Oulton (teacher), Anne Collier (secretary), Robert Foxton, Michelle Smith, Lee Jack, Stephen Armstrong, Charlotte Neville, Kelly Johnson, Matthew Bradbury, Ian Allison, Geoff Howdle (head teacher), Alison Atkinson (work experience)
2nd: Marie Claire Bradbury, Christine Neill, Helen Neill, Sarah Pratt, Danielle Howe, Lyndsey Levitt, Michelle Jordan, Virginia Bradbury
3rd: Ashley and Mark and Daniel Snowball, Charlotte Cundall, Ben Jack, Beth Rummel, Frances and Hazel Neil, Rebecca Pratt, Sarah Chadwick, Shaun Ward, Ben Pollard
Front: Emma Ward, Natalie Wildish, Matthew Lickes, Martin Allison, Adam Prest, Daniel Bean, Hayley Prest, Gemma Simms, Donna Foxton, Emma Samples

CHAPTER 8
CAROL BARNES

When Carol Barnes began her duties as head teacher, Katherine Crowther took over the full-time teaching of KS1 and Anne Pratt part-time teaching of KS2 and the head teacher was allowed extra non-teaching time to cope with the ever-increasing volume of paperwork that constantly flows in and out of the school's busy office and secretary Monica Tye's hours were increased to 24/week. Former Caretaker Moyra Stockill died in December 2003 just over a year after her husband Les. Both were 61. The children created a garden in their memory on the school premises and the head teacher said *"Moyra was a dedicated member of staff who really did love and believe in the school. She and Les did so much"*. As well as being used as a quiet area, the garden provides an opportunity for the children to learn about plants and flowers and the school came third in the Ryedale in Bloom Competition.

In 2004, the school had it's second Ofsted inspection and the result was *"a glowing report"*. The school was described as providing *"good quality education and good value for money"*, pupils were *"achieving well"* and receiving *"consistently good teaching"*. County Councillor Murray Naylor, said: *"Governors, staff, parents and pupils should all be extremely pleased with Sherburn's OFSTED report. The head teacher deserves great praise for her leadership and her staff and the governing body also deserve commendation. All concerned with the leadership and management of the school deserve great praise"*.

The kitchen was adapted and Mrs Kim Pickard (nee Kilvington) was appointed the school's first cook. Healthy meals using fresh ingredients won the school the Jamie Oliver School Meals Award. A fruit and vegetable policy during break times and a breakfast club on some mornings are in place. French has been added to the Curriculum, *"Huff and Puff"* encourages playground exercise and *"Friday Friends"* gives older children an opportunity to be responsible for playing with groups of younger children during morning and dinner breaks. A *"walking bus"* enables pupils to walk safely to school instead

---

The whole school in 2001 with teachers from left to right Katherine Crowther, Nigel Mainprize (acting head teacher) Carol Barnes and Anne Pratt

of travelling by car and the column of children in bright yellow fluorescent jackets can be clearly seen winding its way from door to door and across busy St Hilda's Street, where 100 years ago a car would rarely be seen. In 2007, a group of teachers and parents took Years 4, 5 and 6 on a weekend residential trip enabling them to develop team building skills and enjoy outdoor activities like canoeing and horse riding.

Since the 2004 OFSTED, the annual SAT's results have placed Sherburn School in the top 5% in the country. But staff agree that school is not just about passing exams but about learning life's skills and to this end, a School Council has been formed so the children can take an active role in learning policies. A formal uniform with sweatshirts, fleeces and PE kits displaying the school name and logo, helps create a spirit of unity and encourages good standards of dress. Smudge the school rabbit is fed and cared for by the children to help develop a sense of responsibility towards animals. But one unchanging feature is the close link that exists between school and church with regular visits to help by the Rev Judy Duke, rector of the Buckrose Carrs Benefice who also leads Friday morning assembly. Both Judy's and Carol's predecessors would all rejoice that Sherburn School is still the centre of village life, still continues to maintain high standards of teaching and learning but more important, still nurtures and upholds the Christian values upon which the school was first founded.

APPENDICES

Appendix 1: Catechism (1666 Church of England's Book of Common Prayer) contains Questions which every child had to answer before they could be confirmed into the Christian faith at 11. They had to know the names of their God-parents, the promises made on their behalf at baptism and why, and learn by heart the Articles of Belief, i.e. The Lord's Prayer, Ten Commandments, Creed, and be able to explain the meaning of the Holy Sacraments of Baptism and the Supper of the Lord (Holy Communion).

Appendix 2: Vicarage Occupants - 1841: John MASON (35 vicar, born Ellerburn), wife Sarah (37, b Huddersfield), Hannah (5), John (4), James (1). Pupils (none born in Yorkshire): Geo LORING (11), Edmund WINN (10), Arthur SALTMARTHE (9), Geo WATTS (9), Alfred CRAYKE (9), John WOODALL (9), Chas WOODALL (8), Richard HOTHAM (8). Servants: Jane PATRICK (20), Ann LEAFE (15), Peter WILSON (15). 1851: John & Sarah MASON, James (10). Pupils: James ISBECK (13, Cambs), James DURLEY (11, Scalby), Bryan BURRELL (11, b Northumberland), Frank RAMSDEN (11, Hesthorpe), James WHITTAKER (10), Geo WHITTAKER (9, Bramham), Harry WILKINSON (8, Hope Hall, Bramham), Joseph ARMITAGE (10, Huddersfield), Ed WOODALL (8, Scarbro). Servants: Elizabeth KIDD (21, Wykeham), Fanny KNAGGS (18), groom Wm FOX (14). 1861: John & Sarah MASON, Hannah (25), John (24), James (20). Scholar Matthew Ridley CORBITT (10, Willington, Lincs), servants: Fanny BELL (29), Mary Ann GOODLEYS (23, Driffield), groom Henry LEE (13). 1871: John & Sarah MASON, daughter Hannah EARNSHAW (widow 35), pupils: Chas Ed BURRELL (15, Broom Park, Northumberland), Thos Clemmett FENWICK (13, Hetton Hall Park, Durham), John Raymond GARRETT (12, E Witton), Wm HOTHAM (11, Scoftworth, Notts), Bernard Geo Richard HALE (11, Bridlington), Wm Henry Fanshaw THORLD (11, Welham, Notts), Henry Leonard Gilpin BROWN (10, Scarbro), Fred Richard FENWICK (10, Kefton Hall, Durham), Thos Wm Carter (10, Edinburgh), Geo Douglas FINDLAY (10, Easter Hill, Lanark). Servants: Mary Ann PINKNEY (25 cook/domestic), Simeon LIGHTFOOT (21 groom), Sarah WRAY (17 maid, Scampston). 1881: Richard ELLIS (63 vicar, b Yedingham), wife Ann (57, b Hull), niece Rosa WILSON (15, Sunderland), servant Christina ADAMSON (18, Helperthorpe). 1891: Richard & Ann ELLIS, nieces: Rosa WILSON (25 pupil teacher, Sunderland), Mary WILSON (19, Scotland), boarder Hannah NEWTON (64

living on own means, Scarbro), servant Hannah ROWNTREE (21, Duggleby).
1901: Richard & Ann ELLIS, servant Jane BIELBY 20 (Knapton), visitor
Edith Emily EYRE (32, schoolmistress Derbyshire).

Appendix 3: Killer Epidemic: 1847: Mar: Richardson SMITH inf; May:
Richard OWSTON 10 wks, Harriet Humphreys SMITH 5 mths, John
MARSHALL 53 (Scarbro), Emma OWSTON 4 wks, Frances Mary
SMITHSON 30; June: William THOMPSON 6 (Flixton), Mary Ann
RICHMOND 11 mths (Scarbro, d Sherburn); July: Ann WILLIAMSON 34;
Aug: John BRIGHAM 4, Frances BRIGHAM 6, Hannah WAINES 17,
William Hotham GRAY 3; Sept: Margaret HARDY 3 mths, Elizabeth
OWSTON 2, Milcah HORSLEY 3, James STUART 3; Oct: Sarah MASON
3 wks, John STUART 2, Ann JACKSON 5, George BAKER 6 (Ruston), Robert
MASON 1, Charlotte MASON 3, Mary STUBBS 20 mths, Hannah COOKE
3, George BENNISON 29; Nov: Rachel & Robert HUGILL both 4, Mary
HUMFRAYES 2 mths; Dec: Thomas KENDALL 1, Emma SCRAFTON 1,
Jane BROWN 5, Ann HUMFRAYES 5. 1848: Jan: David BAKER 2 (Ruston),
Edward STUART 9 mths; Feb: William WILLIAMSON 38, William
WILLIAMSON 7, James WILLIAMSON 2, Martha HARDY 37, Ann
LIGHTFOOT 68; March: Emily CLARKSON 3 wks, James ATKINSON
inf, Tom KNAGGS 9 wks, Elizabeth GOWLAND 21 (E Heslerton), Ann Eliza
DAWSON 11 mths; Apr: Richard GOWLAND 28, Jane WREGGIT 53; May:
Esther BELL 38, George VASEY 70; Mary Ann OWSTON 7 wks; July: John
BOGG 49; Sept: Watson DICKINSON 1; Nov: Elizabeth WILLIAMSON
27; Dec: Elizabeth THOMPSON inf, Elizabeth ALLINSON 9 mths, Emma
ATKINSON inf.

Appendix 4: Love's Old Sweet Song (G Clifton Bingham)

Once in the dear dead days beyond recall
When on the world the mist began to fall
Out of the dreams that rose in happy throng
Low in our hearts, love sang an old sweet song
And in the dusk where fell the firelight's gleam
Softly it wove itself into a dream

Even today we hear love's song of yore
Deep in our hearts it dwells forevermore
Footsteps may falter, weary grow the way
Still we can hear it at the close of day
So till the end when life's dim shadows fall
Love will be found the sweets song of all : -

Chorus: Just a song at twilight, When the lights are low
And the flick'ring shadows softly come and go
Tho' the heart be weary, Sad the day and long
Still to us at twilight comes love's old song , comes love's old sweet song.

Appendix 5: WW1 Weddings (ref: PR/SHER 47). 1914: 17 Jan: John DIXON
24 brewer (Leeds) to Mabel HODGSON 18 (fathers: John DIXON brewer &
Robt HODGSON farmer); 15 Apr: Geo EMANUEL 28 Church Army Capt
to Charlotte CURREY 22 (Ambrose EMANUEL minister & Jonathan
CURREY grocer); 26 Dec: Herbert SIMPSON 28 (Rillington) to Eleanor

LIGHTFOOT 29 (Thos SIMPSON & Wm LIGHTFOOT shoemaker). 1915: 10 Apr: John Smith CURREY 26 joiner (Jonathan CURREY grocer) to Ellen Elizabeth WHYTE 34. 1916: 1 June: Fred GILLERY 32 clerk to Amy Gertrude HEATH 28 (Wm GILLERY & James Bell HEATH farmers); 8 July: Harold DUGGLEBY 35 to Mary Ella FOSTER 32 (Richard DUGGLEBY & John FOSTER farmers); 25 Nov: Geo Wm SCHOLES 31 to Edith BEAL 24 (E Acklam) (Hornby SCHOLES shepherd & John BEAL); 1917: 14 June: Arthur Cuthbert DUNN 21 2nd Lieut MGC to Kathleen SAWKILL 21 both of Ivy Cott (Fred Claude DUNN comm traveller & Anthony SAWKILL); 3 Dec: Geo Robt BOWES 49 (Hutton Buscel) (John BOWES) to Polly PICKARD 42 widow; 1918: none.

Appendix 6: Pupils with *Excellent, Very Good* or *Good* Attendance 1890-93: Georgina ALLEN; Lilian, Mary & Matilda ATKINSON; Harry & Thos G BAKER; Ada E BARKER, Guy D, Ida M, Sylvester, Thomas & Victoria BEAN, Eva & Wm BELL; Fred & Florence BLYTHE; Catherine, Edward, Florence & Wm BOGG; Florence, Fred, Patty, Robt & Rose BROWN; Florence & John CALAM; Mary CARTER; Chas, Herbert & Lucy CLARKE; John T, Lillian E, & Sam CLARKSON, Dora, Elizabeth, Geo L, John S, & Thos L CURREY; Chas, Elizabeth, Fred, James, Kate, Mary, Hannah, Jemma, Laura, Robt, Sara, & Wm DAWSON; Alice, Edmund, & Herbert DAY; Wm DICKINSON, Arthur, Blanche, Edward, Edwin, Harold & Harry DOBSON, Chas, Edgar, Flora, Harold, & Sydney DUGGLEBY; Leonard & Maud ELLIOTT; Edith, Emily, Jessie, Melton, Miriam & Thos G FORGE; Mary & John FOXTON; Harold FREER; John, Mary E, & Robt FULSTON; Fred & Wm GILLERY; Mary Jane HALL; John & Wm HARLAND; Amy, Arthur, & Hainsworth HEATH; Chas, Mary & Wm HENDERSON; Amy, Arthur & Ellen HICK; Jemima HILL; John & Thos HUGILL; Fred, Herbert & Thyra IRELAND; James, Richard & Wm JACKSON; Hilda & Wardell JOHNSON; Florence, Frances & Kate KELLINGTON, Edward & Richard KING; Eleanor, Frank & Rachel KNOX; Guy V & Wm H LAYCOCK; Edward, James, Sidney & Violet LEVITT; Charlotte, Eleanor & Mary LIGHTFOOT; Clara, Sarah & Walter LISTER; Lois A & Helena Blanche LOVEL; Amos & Ann MAGSON; Francis, & Gertrude METCALFE; Ellen & Harold OATES; Edwin, Maggie & Mary OWSTON; Agnes & Emily PATRICK; Lucy PEARSON; Arthur & Wm PICKERING; Albert, Harry & Wm PINCHER; Currey and John W PINKNEY; Martha POSTILL; Ada, Adam, Edward & Wm RAWDING; Beatrice REEVELEY; Emily, Elizabeth & Geo SCHOLES; Mary SCOTT; Geo & Mary SEWELL; John W & Maggie SHEPHERD; Arthur SLAUGHTER; Arthur E SPECK; Chas J STEAD; Hannah & Wm STONES; Elizabeth & Geo SWANN; Jessie &, Maria WATSON; Harry WARD; Albert, Alf & Elizabeth WELBORN. Year end March 1912: 100%:

Bertha BROWN; Herbert BEAN; Geo COUSINS; Blanche HICK; Chas Wilf HEATH; Geo JACKSON; John E & Gladys M METCALFE; John Allan NORTH; Olive M MILNER; Annie PICKARD. Absent once: Clarice BEECROFT; Florence & Agnes BASSETT; Doris & Wilf HART; John Baden PINKNEY. Absent twice: Elsie BRADFORD, Sarah Ellen & Emmeline BASSETT; Herbert DOBSON; Lilian DAWSON; Thos HART; Elizabeth HENDERSON; Wm W MILNER. Absent thrice: Evelyn BASSETT; George, Herbert & Eva JOHNSON; Ammeline METCALFE; Lucy POSTILL. Year end March 1928: 100%: Nellie DAWSON; John GILBANK; Maggie JACKSON; Ernest JOHNSON; Dorothy KNOX; Doris LEVITT; Fred METCALFE; Derrick MORTIMER; Gordon SKELTON; Sidney SIMPSON; Wm SCURR; Mabel STONES; Alf WALKER. Quarter end Sept 1929, out of 108 pupils, 28 boys and 23 girls had 100% attendance. Year end March 1930 out of 104 pupils 15 had 100% attendance: Annie BELL; Albert DAWSON; Annie & Phyllis ENGLAND; Edna GILLERY; William HESLETINE; Robert & Doris LEVITT; Fred METCALFE; Reggie ROGER; William SCURR; Adelaide SIMPSON; Arthur STEAD; Edgar SPANTON; Daisy WATSON;

Appendix 7: Sports June 1911: 50 yds under 5 boys: Thos CLARKE, Herbert HUGILL; girls: Emily HICK, Nellie STONES. 50 yds under 6 boys: Arthur PRODHAM, Fred WOODALL; girls: Pattie COCKERILL, Annie PICKARD. 75 yds under 7 boys: Geo PRODHAM, Geo COUSINS; girls: Margery RINGROSE, Hannah CLARKE. 75 yds under 8 boys: Christopher DAWSON, Herbert JOHNSON; girls: Winnie BRIGGS, Gladys HUNTER. 80 yds under 9 boys: Geoff RINGROSE, Geo LAWSON, girls: Elsie BEECROFT, Annie HENDERSON. 80 yds under 10 boys: Chas CLARKE, Geo JOHNSON; girls: Doris BRIGGS, Nellie BASSETT. 100 yds under 11 boys: Robt CLARKSON, Oliver PICKERING; girls: Clarice BEECROFT, Mildred COCKERILL. 100 yds under 12 boys: John METCALFE, Wm BRIGGS; girls: Sarah COUSINS, Isabella COATSWORTH. 100 yds under 14 boys: Harry MALLORY, Ed CALAM; girls: Sarah COUSINS, Gladys ATKINSON. 120 yds under 16 boys: Wm CURREY, Alfred SLEIGHTHOLME; girls: Rosa DUGGLEBY, Stella ATKINSON. Girls' Skipping under 9: Doris CLARKE (105), Elsie BEECROFT (98); under 12: Doris BRIGGS (126), Gladys WOODALL (121); under 15: Isabella COATSWORTH (222), Stella ATKINSON (176). Boys' 3-legged under 12: Robert CLARKSON & Ernest HEATH, Aubrey BROWN & Fred COUSINS; under 15: Harry ADAMS & Ed CALAM, Albert BAKER & Alec DAWSON. Boys' High jump under 15: Edgar BROWN, Harry MALLORY & Ed CALAM (divided). Girls' egg & spoon under 15: Nellie BASSETT, Elsie BEECROFT. Adults 100 yds flat: Herbert STONES, Fred STONES. 50 yds sack: T HAIKINGS, F DAWSON. 3-legged: H & S DUGGLEBY, T HAIKINGS & F MONKMAN. Donkey race: W CLARKE. Throwing cricket ball: F MONKMAN, F GILLERY. 50 yds (women over 30): Mrs BEECROFT, Mrs W MILLS. Obstacle: F MONKMAN, T HAIKINGS. Pony race under 18's: Chas FRYER, A SLEIGHTHOLME. Gent's quarter-mile slow cycle: C & S DUGGLEBY. Farm servants' 100 yds flat: S COLE, E ELLIS. Women 75 yds under 15: M STONES, M HODGSON. Mile cycle: C S DUGGLEBY, E SLEIGHTHOLME. Pig catching married women: Mrs LEVITT, consolation Mrs FOXTON. 60 yds men over 60: R DUGGLEBY, W CLARKE. Ladies quarter mile slow cycle: F DUGGLEBY, A SHARP. Singing comic song without smiling pig under arm: Mrs BEECROFT. Tug o'war: T STONES & H CLARKES' team. 100 yds men over 40: H BEECROFT, F BELT. Farm servants' mile cycle: W DAWSON, E ELLIS.

Appendix 8: 1914-18 Roll of Honour. William H ADAMS, Robert H BAKER, Thomas G BAKER, Arthur BASSETT, Herbert BASSETT, Thomas W BEAN, Sylvester BEAN, John H BEAN, William BELL, Walter E BRADFORD, Henry BRADFORD, Frederick BRASSLEAY, Edgar G BROWN, John BUTTERY, Edward CALAM, Sydney CALAM, Herbert CALAM, Harry V CLARKE, Samuel CLARKSON, Ernest R CLARKSON, Thomas W COPELAND, George L CURREY, T Stanley CURREY, William CURREY, Albert DAWSON, Harry DAWSON, John W DAWSON, Bernard W DOBSON, Harold C DOBSON, Edwin DOBSON, Edward DOBSON, Herbert DOBSON, Albert S DUGGLEBY, Edgar DUGGLEBY, Charles S DUGGLEBY, Arthur L DUGGLEBY, William P DUGGLEBY, Arthur C DUNN, Frank ELLIOTT, George EMANUEL, Claude FORGE, Thomas G FORGE, John F FORGE, Melton FORGE, George FOXTON, Charles FRYER, William GILLERY, Frederick GILLERY, John GILLERY, John HARLAND, Charles HENDERSON, William HENDERSON, William HESELTINE, Thomas HUGILL, Thomas JACKSON, Herbert JOHNSON, Charles W JAMES, Thomas KELLINGTON, Henry R LAYCOCK, Alfred LEVITT, Charles LEVITT, James LEVITT, John LEVITT, Lawrence LEVITT, Edward MALLORY, John E METCALFE, Francis W METCALFE, Sydney METCALFE, Herbert METCALFE, George MORTIMER, Thomas MILNER, Lawrence M MILNER, George E MONKMAN, Harry MUDD, Edwin OWSTON, Arthur C PINKNEY, Robert Percy PINKNEY, Thomas S PINKNEY, William C PINKNEY, Harry E POTTER, Thomas PUDSEY, A RICHARDSON, Ernest SCURR, Lawrence SELBY, George SKELTON, Charles H STEPHENSON, George H SLEIGHTHOLME, Ernest F SLEIGHTHOLME, Fred STONES, William STONES, Arthur TAYLOR, Alfred G TROHEAR, George WARD. Fourteen died: Frederick ATKINSON, Albert W BAKER, John W BAKER,

George BASSETT, John W CLARKE, Harry Y CUNDALL, William E DAWSON, John H DOBSON, William HARLAND, Edward HENDERSON, Amos MAGSON, Frederick Y SCOTT, Alfred P SLEIGHTHOLME, Richard SLEIGHTHOLME.

Appendix 9: Wykeham Military Hospital. The following signatures are from an autograph book found amongst the possessions of the late Lucie Metcalfe and published by kind permission from Raymond Metcalfe: Leslie STEWART 1915; A SCOTT 25 Sept 1916 18th S BMR; Harry SADLER Aug-Oct 1916 Royal Field Artillery; 13132 Pte H JOHNSON 7th E Lancs; Pte A C GOODMAN 1916 Royal Sussex Regt; L Cpl J MILLAR 27 Oct 1916 20th Kings L'pool Reg (wounded on Somme 30 July 1916); Sgt G H AGER 29 Aug 1917 16th RB; Cpl F W ADAMS 11 Oct 1916 2nd British Rifle Brigade; Sydney J DAVIES 10 Oct 1916 Glos Regt TT (wounded on Somme 24 July 1916); Rfm J McNAMARA 5th South Lancs; Sgt E H BROOKER 6 Nov 1917 RFA; C H HOPPER 12 Nov 1916; F H BELL 21 Dec 1916; Pte Harry CHAMPKIN 21 Nov 1916; 24th Manchesters; Pte F W CARNEY 1 Nov 1917 2nd Yorks Regt; Sgt J JEWETT 7 Dec 1916 6th KOYLI; J DICKSON 1st Royal Highlanders; L Cpl Alf WALTER Xmas 1916; 16th Royal Warwicks BEF; A MANSON 24 Sept 1918 Seaforth Highlanders; Rfm E FENNER 6 Jan 1917 6th Londons; Pte A KELMS 24 Oct 1917 2nd London RF; Gnr W HILL 5 July 1917 RGA; Cpl F DANIELS 5 July 1917 RGA; L Cpl T B GREVILLE 1 Sept 1918 Welsh Regt; 70242 L Cpl R FROST 2 Apr 1917 17th Sherwood Foresters; Cpl J T PORTER 11 Sept 1917 Liverpool Rifles; Pte W CAST 17th Sherwood Foresters; Pte Chas J CLOSE 19 Oct 1917 1st Scotts Guards; W J WELLS 10 Nov 1917 20th London Regt (wounded at Ypres 13 Aug 1917); Leslie STUART 1917; Pte E J CLARK (Nobby) 14 Nov 1917 2/4 Gloucesters (wounded at Ypres 27 Aug 1917); H A MYERS 1/6 Cameron Highlanders; Rfm W HORSLEY KRRC; D DONALDSON 20 May 1917 11th Royal Innisk Fus; Rfm J W HANNAH 24 Oct 1917 21st KRRC; Cpl BURKE 28 Jan 1918 1st Batt Irish Guards; Privates FOLLEN, FLEMING, FARRIS and Cpl ELSON; G R FLEMING 2nd R Scots; D HILLIER 9th Scottish Rifles; Cpl E DYKES 1st W Yorks.

Appendix 10: 1921 School Sports: 80 yds flat girls under 11: M Jackson, P Knox, R Skelton; boys: L Brassleay, W Pinkney, T Foxton. 120 yds girls 11 and over: N Kitching, M Ringrose, M Bradford; boys: W Perrin, J Simpson, R Greenley. Skipping girls under 11: M Calam, M Brassleay, N Copeland. Sack boys under 11: P Gilbank, T Foxton, R Foxton. Obstacle boys 11 and over: E Nesfield, A Garvey, A Outhart. Skipping girls 11 and over: M Bradford, E Finian, E Kirk. Potato girls 11 and over: E Jackson, M Bradford, E Finian. 'Late for school', mixed under 11: H Calam, M Johnson, Gillery. Boys' potato

11 and over: J Simpson, A Garvey, A Lomans. Boys' long jump under 11: H
Mortimer, L Brassleay, H Duggleby; over 11: A Garvey, E Nesfield, A Bramley.
3-legged: H Burrows/A Haykings, A Garvey/Brown. 'Balancing', girls 11 and
over: M Bradford, E Jackson. 'Blindfold': D Henderson/F Metcalfe, C Tacey/
M Bradford. Egg & Spoon: M Ringrose, M Kitching, M Watson. Slow cycle
11 and over girls: L Morrell, M Bradford, H Hick; boys: F Young, A Lomas.
Wheelbarrow: 1 R Greenley/A Lomas, 2 A Marston/P Shepherd. Whacking
donkey: A Garvey and Brown. Throwing cricket ball: W Perrin, O Henderson,
A Outhart. Skipping: E Jackson, N Kitching, M Woodall. Hair plaiting: C
Tacey/F Metcalfe, A Marston/Pinkney. Washing comp: C Tacey/F Metcalfe,
M Kirk/E Potter. Men cycle mile: Young, Hardy, Heath. 120 yds: Colley,
Morrison, Wright. Ladies slow cycle: Miss E Hick, Miss E B Duggleby, Miss
F E Duggleby. Single ladies 100 yds flat: Miss K Hollings, Miss P Miller, Miss
Zena Pinkney. Pillow fight: Edgar Brown, H Ineson. Obstacle: H Wright, H
Bean.

Appendix 11: 1919 Peace Sports. Girls 50yds under 7: Madge BRASSLEAY,
Lily WATSON, Violet LEVITT; under 9: Mona CALAM, Mary HUNTER,
Dorothy MUDD; 75yds under 11: Rosie PINKNEY, Maggie GILLERY, Mary
BRADFORD; 100yds under 14: Zena PINKNEY, Muriel METCALFE,
Annie FOXTON. Boys 60yds under 7: Tom HART, Ken HESELTINE, Les
JOHNSON; under 9: Raymond BEECROFT, John DAWSON, Francis
DOBSON; 75yds under 7: Harold DUGGLEBY, Chas DOBSON, Geo
EDMONDS; 100yds under 11: Les LAYCOCK, Wm HUDSON, Roland
FOXTON, 100yds under 14: Sid DAWSON, Gilbert DUNN, John PRATT.
Boys 3-legged: Wm HUNTER & John PRATT, Oliver HENDERSON & Tom
CLARK, Cliff STONES & Lewis HESELTINE. Girls Skipping under 14:
Kath WOODALL, Mary BRADFORD, Hilda HICK; under 8: Violet
LEVITT, Lilian BUTTERY, Madge BRASSLEAY. Girls 100yds 14-16: Sarah
HUNTER, Pattie COCKERILL, Winnie PINKNEY. Ladies 75yds: Miss Elsie
BEECROFT, Miss K HOLLINGS, Miss Sarah COUSINS. Ladies egg &
spoon: Miss Edith HICK, Miss NESFIELD, Mrs COPELAND. Cockerel-
catching: Miss Hilda COCKERILL. Married women 75yds: Mrs C
HENDERSON, Mrs E MINTOFT, Mrs J CLARKE. Mens 120yds: Claude
FORGE, T BEECROFT, Edwin OWSTON; quarter mile: Frank STEAD,
Claude FORGE, Stan CURREY. Mens high jump: Percy DUGGLEBY,
Edgar BROWN, Claude FORGE. Married men 75yds: Geo MORTIMER,
N COLLINSON, Arthur GILBANK. Servicemen/ex-Servicemen 100yds:
Claude FORGE, Wm STONES, Geo MORTIMER. Mile Bicycle: Ernest
HEATH, Percy DUGGLEBY, Chas DUGGLEBY. Bowling: J PENROSE,
John CALAM, Percy DUGGLEBY.

Appendix 12: Nia Bland (Scarborough) kindly translated the leaflet, presumably intended to undermine German morale, taken by Raymond P Metcalfe from the aircraft. One side reads: *"West Front: Krupp factory, Essen, shattered. The targets pictured show part of the Krupp factory after British air raids on the 5 & 12 March 1943. In each raid, approx 1000 tons of bombs were dropped whereas in an air raid over Coventry by the Luftwaffe on 4 Nov 1940 only 85 tons of bombs were dropped. During the British raids on 5 & 12 March 1943, 100 industrial/administrative buildings were either destroyed or made useless and water, gas and power services were put out of action".* The other side of the leaflet reads: *"South Front - Rommel trapped. In Tunisia, the army of Field Marshall Rommel holds a meagre bridgehead but without the bridge. They are enclosed in an unrelenting allied ring in the country and stand with their backs to the sea occupied by the British Mediterranean Fleet. Hitler's strategy on the South and East Fronts are the same and because large armies of German soldiers were pushed forward without the necessary supplies and ammunition, the positions covered were not held. Will Rommel's troops have better results than Paulus VI Division?"* Six photos enable the reader of the leaflet to *"Follow how the events in Tunisia develop with help from the OKW-Berichte reports and British broadcasts. Blow by Blow East Front: Annihilation of the VIth army at Stalingrad".* The 1st photo shows a column of prisoners and the caption: *"In 3 months at the entire East Front, the Russians took 349,000 German prisoners near Stalingrad"* the 2nd shows masses of corpses and reads: *"240,000 Germans of the VIth army were killed near Stalingrad. Within 3 months over 700,000 men fell in the East"*; photo 3 shows a group of German army leaders and reads: *"Field Marshall Paulus and his commandant General Schmidt during interrogation. Paulus and his staff capitulated 15 minutes after his headquarters came under fire";* the 4th photo shows a corpse, a prisoner, more army leaders and reads: *"One dead and one survivor. General Lieut Von Daniel (377 Inf.Div) captured. 24 German generals surrendered at Stalingrad"*; photo 5 shows badly damaged army vehicles and reads; *"In 3 months the Germans lost 7000 Panzer tanks and 17,000 canons/guns"*; the 6th photo is a close-up of prisoners and reads: *"General Lieut Sanne (4th Light Div) with survivors of his troop of Russian prisoners".*

Appendix 13: 1939-45 Roll of Honour. James Parker ALLISON, Thomas ALLISON, Thomas William ALLISON, Wilfred ALLISON, Fred ALLISON, Ronald BEAN, Harry Raymond BEECROFT, Francis Reginald BOLLAND, David BEAL, Reginald BEAN, Roy BAKER, Jack COUSINS, Charles Stanley CURREY, Harry Yates CUNDALL, John A CUNDALL, Laurence CLARK, Albert DAWSON, John DAWSON, George Edward EDMONDS, Ernest ELLIS, Claude FORGE, Francis FORGE, George Robert FOXTON, Thomas FOXTON, Dennis GILLERY, Roy GRICE, Barney HARRIS,

Kenneth HESELTINE, Nelson HESELTINE, Harold George HEATH, Ronald Arthur HEATH, Edward HUTCHINS, Leslie JOHNSON, George JACKSON, Harry KEDGE, John KEDGE, James KIRK, Albert MARSTON, Maurice MATTINSON, Cyril METCALFE, Fred METCALFE, Jack METCALFE, Raymond METCALFE, Kenneth MILNER, Jonathan MILNER, William Henry PINDER, Clifford PINKNEY, Cyril PINKNEY, Douglas PINKNEY, Raymond PINKNEY, William PINKNEY, Cecil PICKERING, Kenneth Gordon POTTER, Fred PUDSEY, Thomas PUDSEY, William SCURR, Sydney SHEPHERD, Fred STEAD, Harold Raymond THOMPSON, Colin Charles TAYLOR, Colin John VASEY, John WALKER, Fred WALKER, William WALKER, Lionel Maurice WEST, William WITTY, Geoffrey WRAY. Edith Julia ALLISON, Eva BOYES, Edna May GILLERY, Mary Elizabeth WITTY, Ellen Irene LAWSON, Margaret FOXTON. Two died: Thomas FOXTON, John SHIELDS-LEVITT

Appendix 14:1943 Sports. Flat races under 5 boys: Robin GRICE, Ken BEAN; under 8 boys: Peter STEAD, Geoffrey CURREY; 8 girls: Susan CLARKSON, Margaret PICKARD, under 10 boys: Alan PICKARD, Raymond PICKARD, girls: 10: Elna STEAD, Joyce DOUGLAS; Under 12 boys: Douglas PICKARD; Bill GILBANK; girls: Gertrude ATKINSON; Rowena HENDERSON; Boys under 13: Stubbs DOBSON, Godfrey HENDERSON; Girls under 14: Mabel CHURCH, Margaret WATSON. Sack boys under 8: Christopher GRICE, Geoffrey CURREY; under 10: Alan PICKARD, Raymond PICKARD. under 12: John PICKARD, Bill CLARKSON. Skipping girls under 8: Margaret PICKARD, Lillian MARFLITT; under 10: Joyce DAWSON, Elna STEAD; under 12: Rowena HENDERSON, Gertrude ATKINSON; under 14: Marjorie ATKINSON, Margaret WATSON. Boys' high jump: Godfrey HENDERSON, Clive BEAN, Roy BEAN. Slow cycle (open): Raymond METCALFE, Tom GILBANK. Mens 100yds: Ted HENDERSON, Charles PICKARD. 220yds: Ernie JOHNSON, Ted HENDERSON. Women's open: Miss Brenda TAYLOR, Miss Barbara KING.

Appendix 15: Newton mourners. Mrs L E Newton widow; Major J M Newton son (rep Mrs J M Newton Singapore); Mr & Mrs J Nash daughter/son-in-law; Mr & Mrs T M Newton brother/sister-in-law; Mrs H Fowler, Mrs T Myers sisters; Mr T Myers, Mr & Mrs C T Moore brothers-in-law/sister-in-law; Mr J Newton, Mr H R Leadley, nephews; Mr & Mrs G Newton, Mr F M Newton cousins. Others: Mrs J Thistleton, Mrs E Percival, Mr G M Stead, Mrs A Scholes, Mrs W Umpleby, Mrs H Foxton, Mrs L Dexter, Mrs A Dobson, Mr & Mrs W Gillings, Miss M Dexter, Mrs G Grice, Mrs H Mitchell, Mrs E Oxtoby; Mr R D Sykes, Mrs A Brown, Richard Heath, Philip Dobson, Dorothy Scholes, Ann Davison (teachers/pupils rep Sherburn School), Mr L Rollett, Mrs H

Wilkinson, Mr T S Mudd (rep Scarbro & Dist Football Assoc & Brompton Football Club), Mr A L Sellers (rep Scarbro & District Football League), Mr & Mrs G Newton (Burniston), Mr D Pickard (rep Sherburn Football Club), Mr R Sadler, Mr W A Beal (rep Mrs M Beal), Mr T Allison, Mrs M Charter (rep Mr J Charter), Mrs R Jackson, Mrs H Wray, Mrs R H Bean, Mrs L Henderson, Mrs E Henderson, Mrs R Mennel, Mrs E Pigg, Mrs L Gilbank, Mrs J Walker, Mrs R Bassett, Mrs W R Sadler, Miss L Hutton, Mrs H Adams, Mrs W Ward, Mrs F Ward, Mr & Mrs N R Burnett, Mrs R Dawson, Mrs J Cousins, Mrs J Poulter, Mr A Cousins, Mr & Mrs R Moss, Mrs H Marflitt, Miss S Robinson (rep Mr & Mrs E T Robinson), Mr Dick Robinson, Mr Alvin Addison, Mrs R Rackham, Mrs J Witty, Mrs A Pickard, Mr & Mrs N Bland, Mrs V Campbell, Mrs G Cousins, Mr & Mrs W Gilbank, Mrs T Flinton, Mrs G Hugill, Mrs P Harrison, Mrs G Harrison, Mr & Mrs S Stead, Mrs J Pickard, Mrs E Currey, Mrs D Taylor, Mrs W E Bradford, Mr & Mrs A Dyson, Mr & Mrs Sergeant, Miss Fryer (Ganton School), Mr Moore (Heslerton School), Mrs D Bogg, Mrs D Thompson, Mrs A Duggleby (rep Mr A L Duggleby clerk to Parish Council), Mrs J H Atkinson, Mrs F Kellington, Mr R P Metcalfe (rep Mr F L Stead sec to Football Club), Mrs F Atkinson, Mr & Mrs G White, Mr J Maynard, Mr T Marshall, Mr G Sissons, Mrs B Nesfield, Mrs F Stones, Mrs W Jackson, Mrs D Collier.

Appendix 16:1970 Sports. Boys High Jump: Nigel STEPHENSON; Carl HORSLEY; Paul MATTINSON. Girls: Gill PICKARD, Susan SCHOLES; Sally HEATH. Boys Flat 5 yrs: Nigel PICKARD; Gary MARFLITT, Andrew SIMMS. Girls 5yrs: Tracy THISTLETON, Jane NEWLOVE, Heather PICKERING. Boys 6yrs: Nigel PICKARD, Richard STRINGER, Gary MARFLITT. Girls 6yrs: Heather PICKERING, Tracy THISTLETON, Dawn FOXTON. Boys 7yrs: Philip WAUD, Malcolm COLLIN, Desmond BEAN. Girls 7yrs: Trudie MARFLITT, Pamela DUGGLEBY, Tracy THISTLETON. Boys 8yrs: Gary BEAN, George STRINGER, Philip WAUD. Girls 8yrs: Janice GILBANK, Julie HARRISON, Lynda THOMPSON. Boys 9yrs: Adrian PICKARD, Gary BEAN, Timothy MITCHELL. Girls 9yrs: Jayne HORSLEY, Elaine JOHNSON, Sally HEATH. Boys 10yrs: Paul GILBANK, Kevin STOCKS, Malcolm THISTLETON. Girls 10yrs: Jacqueline MOUSER, Janice GILBANK, Sharon MOORE. Boys 11yrs: Carl HORSLEY, Nigel STEPHENSON, Gary PICKARD. Girls 11yrs: Susan SCHOLES, Julie MOORE, Hazel PICKERING. Boys Potato 5yrs: Paul THOMPSON, Andrew SIMMS, Gary MARFLITT. Girls 5yrs: Tracy THISTLETON, Heather PICKERING, Carol WALKER. Boys 6yrs: Nigel PICKARD, Richard STRINGER, Paul THOMPSON. Girls 6yrs: Heather PICKERING, Dawn FOXTON, Tracy THISTLETON. Boys 7yrs: Gary BEAN, Duncan LAW, Richard STRINGER. Girls 7yrs: Pamela DUGGLEBY, Trudie MARFLITT,

Elaine PICKERING. Boys 8yrs: Gary BEAN, George STRINGER, Malcolm COLLIN. Girls 8yrs: Janice GILBANK, Lynda THOMPSON, Julie HARRISON. Girls Skipping 9yrs: Elaine JOHNSON, Sally HEATH, Jayne HORSLEY. 10yrs: Jacqueline MOUSER, Sally HEATH, Janice GILBANK. 11yrs: Susan SCHOLES, Gill PICKARD, Julie MOORE. Boys Sack 9yrs: Gary BEAN, Brett STEPHENSON, Gary PICKARD. 10yrs: Kevin STOCKS, Paul GILBANK, Gary DOBSON. 11yrs: Ian RACKHAM, Gary PICKARD, Nigel STEPHENSON. Boys Obstacle 7yrs: Gary BEAN, Nigel STEPHENSON, Timothy MITCHELL. 9yrs: Kevin STOCKS, Paul GILBANK, Gary DOBSON. 11yrs: Nigel STEPHENSON, Gary PICKARD, Ian RACKHAM. Girls 11yrs: Susan SCHOLES, Sharon MOORE, Gill PICKARD. Cricket Ball: Neil BASSETT, Kevin STOCKS, Ian RACKHAM. Slow Bicycle: Nigel STEPHENSON, Richard WALKER, Paul GILBANK. Relay under 9: Duncan LAW, Shirley COLLIER, Gary BEAN. Over 9: Ian RACKHAM, Julie MOORE, Malcolm THISTLETON.

Appendix 17: Christmas Plays. 1965 INFANTS: *The Story of Peter Rabbit*, narrator Carl Horsley; Hazel Pickering (soloist) *Mrs Rabbit*. JUNIORS: *Down the Crocus Tunnel*, Jane Simpson *Betty*, Peter Dobson *Robin*, Peter Marston *Fairy King*, Pauline Bean *Fairy Queen*, Andrew Pickard *Overseer of Elves*. TOP CLASS: *Pinocchio*, Ian Umpleby *Pinocchio*, Timothy Pickard *Geppetto the Woodcarver'*, Stuart Dawson *Jiminy Cricket*, Julie Nesfield *Blue Fairy*.
1966 INFANTS: *Bobby Shaftoe*, narrator Malcolm Thistleton; *Bobby Shaftoe* Timothy Mitchell; *Crew Members*: Wm O'Brien, Richard Walker, Paul Gilbank, John Brooks; *Eskimos*; Gary Dobson, Paul Harrison, Patrick Umpleby, Christopher Bean, Adrian Pickard; *Polar Bears*: Philip Galtry, Garry Pickard, Joan Cussons, Louise Dexter, David Pratt; *Snowflakes*: Elaine Johnson, Sally Heath, Lynda Thompson; *Gypsies*: Andrea Worthy, Richard Harrison, Janice Gilbank, Jayne Horsley. JUNIORS: *Pearls for the Princess*, Margaret Gilbank *Princess Iona*; Mary Brooks *Lady-in-Waiting*; Tina Foxton *Lady of the Valley*; Ian Rackham *Pixie*; Howard Rogers *Green Echo*; Trevor Wiley *Red Echo*; Hazel Pickering *Yellow Echo*; Susan Scholes *Pink Echo*; Martin Flinton *Purple Echo*; Peter and Paul Mattinson, Trevor Pickard, Neil Bassett, Carl Horsley, Kevin Stocks *Valley Echoes*; Jonathan Galtry, Andrew Pickard *Woodcutters*; Gillian Pickard *Girl*; Peter Dobson *Boy*. TOP CLASS: *Peter Pan; Mr Darling* Richard Duggleby; *Mrs Darling* Janet Pickard; *Wendy* Julie Nesfield; *John* Keith Mitchell; *Michael* Andrew Bean; *Nana the dog* Kathleen Cracknell; *Peter Pan* Kevin Pickard; *Mermaids*: Denise Harrison, Jane Simpson; *Captain Hook* Peter Marston; *Mr Smee* Gary Axham; *Pirates*: Neil Pickard, Julie Gow, Mary Pickard; *Crocodile* David Gilbank; *Tiger Lily* Christeen Thistleton; *Indians*: Pauline Bean, Christine Bean, Sandra Pickard, Maureen Walker.

Peter Pan – 1965.

1967 INFANTS: *The Two Lost Toys.* Richard Cundall *Father Christmas*; *Tippy* Janice Gilbank; *Tubby* Richard Harrison; *Elves:* Timothy Mitchell, Adrian Pickard; *Dolly* Elaine Johnson; *Golly* Jayne Horsley; *June* Sally Heath; *Jeremy* John Brooks; *Moonbeam Fairies*: Lynda Thompson, Pamela Duggleby, Julie Harrison; *Squirrels*: Louise Dexter, Christopher Mouser, Janette Wiley; *Rabbits*: Gary Bean, Joan Cussons, Shirley Collier; *Owlets*: Philip Marston, Desmond Bean, Andrew Gilbank; *Cat* Jacqueline Mouser. JUNIORS: *The Magic Snowman.* narrator Howard Rogers; *Snowman* Carl Horsley; *Snow Queen* Susan Scholes; *Amanda* Gillian Pickard; *Peter* Christopher Bean; *John* Gary Pickard, *Jill* Ann Pickering, *Paul* Gary Dobson; *Children*: Richard Walker, Paul Harrison, Kevin Stocks, William O'Brian, Peter and Paul Mattinson; *Gardener* Neil Bassett, *Cat*, Patrick Umpleby, *Robins*: Malcolm Thistleton, Paul Gilbank; *Frost Fairies*: Hazel Pickering, Andrea Worthy. TOP CLASS: *Alice in Wonderland*; *Alice* Jane Simpson; *White Rabbit* Pauline Oldroyd; *Footmen*: Trevor Pickard, Andrew Bean; *Duchess* Tina Foxton; *Cook* Mary Brooks; *Cheshire Cat* Margaret Gilbank; *March Hare* Ian Rackham; *Mad Hatter* Peter Marston; *Dormouse* Jane Mortimer; *2 of Hearts* Neil Pickard; *3 of Hearts* Martin Flinton; *4 of Hearts* Pauline Bean; *5 of Hearts* Kevin Pickard; *7 of Hearts* Trevor Wiley; *Queen of*

Alice in Wonderland – 1967.

Hearts Julie Gow; *King of Hearts* David Gilbank; *Knave of Hearts* Andrew Pickard; *Executioner* Peter Dobson.

1968 INFANTS: *Old Toys on Christmas Eve.* Gary Bean *Santa Claus*, Janette Wiley *Old Doll*, Lynda Thompson *Teddy*, Joan Cussons *Horse;* Julie Harrison, Pamela Duggleby *Golliwogs*, Shirley Collier *Puppy*, Philip Waud *Policeman*, Trudy Marflitt *Girl*, Christopher Mouser *Boy*, Andrew Gilbank *Elephant*, Carolyn Pickering *New Doll*, Martin Middle *Cowboy,* Elaine Pickering *Fairy*, Angela Pickard *Nurse*; Duncan Law *Robin*; Desmond Bean, Colin Pickard *Rabbits*. JUNIORS: *The Wizard who hated Christmas.* Paul Gilbank *Wizard Willikins*, Timothy Mitchell *Father Christmas*, Brett Stephenson *Old Man*; John Brooks, Richard Walker Paul Harrison, Adrian Pickard, Gary Dobson, Patrick Umpleby *Goblins;* Louise Dexter, Jacqueline Mouser, Jayne Horsley, Malcolm Thistleton, Christopher Bean, Richard Harrison *Children*; Andrea Worthy, Sally Heath, Elaine Johnson, Janice Gilbank, Carole Batty *Fairies*. TOP CLASS: *A pig in the Palace.* Jane Simpson *Fairy Goodenough*, Peter Dobson *Witch Watt*, Hazel Pickering *Wotamess*, Gillian Pickard *Princess Marianne*, Gary Pickard *Pig*, Ian Rackham *Prince Charming*; Kevin Pickard, Andrew Pickard, Neil Bassett *Footmen*; Mary Brooks, Richard Bettison, Martin Flinton, Tina Foxton, Margaret Gilbank, Carl Horsley, Peter and Paul Mattinson, Jane Mortimer, Trevor Pickard, Ann Pickering, Howard Rogers, Kevin Stocks Nigel Stephenson, Susan Scholes, Trevor Wiley *Guests.*

1969 (all 61 pupils) *It's a Ball: Good Fairy* Sharon Moore; *Mother Hubbard* Hazel Pickering; *Children:* Gary Dobson, Tracy Thistleton, Paul Thompson, Richard Collier, Adrian and Angela Pickard, George Stringer, Martin Middle; *Idle Jack* Howard Rogers; *Simple Simon* Brett Stephenson; *Marian,* Janette Wiley; *Snow Fairies:* Jacqueline Mouser, Susan Scholes, Janice Gilbank, Jayne Horsley; *Animals:* Christopher Mouser, Desmond Bean, Elaine Pickering, Frank Newlove, Andrew Oldroyd, Richard Stringer; *Robin Hood* Ian Rackham; *Little John* Nigel Stephenson; *Much Miller's son* Gary Pickard; *Friar Tuck* Neil Bassett; *Robin's men* Timothy Mitchell, Kevin Stocks; *Pedlar* Christopher Bean; *Knight* Paul Gilbank; *Knight's Page* Colin Pickard; *Rainbow Fairies:* Shirley Collier, Lynda Thompson, Trudy Marflitt, Pamela Duggleby, Julie Harrison, Carolyn Pickering, Elaine Johnson; *Baron's Page* Philip Waud; *Baron Rum-Tee-Foo* Carl Horsley; *Baron's daughters:* Gillian Pickard, Louise Dexter; *Heralds* Gary Bean, Andrew Gilbank; *Ball Guests:* Andrew Cussons, Duncan Law, Richard and Paul Harrison, Richard Walker, Peter and Paul Mattinson, John Brooks, Patrick Umpleby, Malcolm Thistleton, Ann Pickering, Judith Marsden Andrea Worthy. Joan Cussons, Sally Heath.

A Pig in a Palace – 1968.

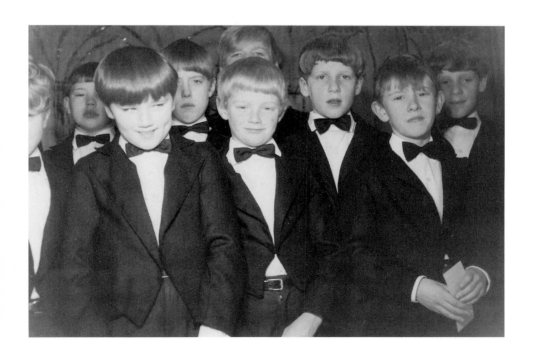

It's a Ball – 1969.

It's a Ball – 1969.

1975 (all 59 pupils) *The Pied Piper of Hamelin* : *Pied Piper* Nigel Pickard, *Willi* Paul Thompson, *Klaus* Gary Marflitt, *Mrs Becker* Jane Newlove, *Mrs Fleischer* Julie Taylor, *Mrs Schultz* Trudy Harrison, *Mr Fleischer* Jamie Mitchell, *Councillor Schmidt* Ian Harrison, *Mrs Hoffmann* Rosemary Newlove, *Councillor Reiter* Richard Collier, *Mayor Schultz* Christopher Hodgson, *Townspeople:* Deborah Baron, Dawn Foxton, Mark Horsley, Michael and Tracy Pickering, Linda Pickard, Andrew Pickering, Martin Pickard, Anthony Rackham, Tracy Thistleton, Lynn Umpleby, Carol Walker; *Children:* Dawn Bean, Darren and Theresa Bean, Nicola Best, Lee Cade, Sarah Cousins, Philip Holtby, Kim Kilvington, Alison Pickard, Julie Simms, Anita Shaw, Sharon Taylor, Gary Walker; *Rats:* Joanne Bean, Jamie Berriman, Richard Brooks, Linda and Sarah Flinton, Richard Gillett, Mark Nettleton, Helen Pickering, Sharon Pickard, Mark Pickard, Victoria and Michael Rodgers.

Appendix 18: 1966 Pageant (All 62 pupils). *Ten Sixty-Six: Saxon Heralds*: Neil and Andrew Pickard; *Edward the Confessor* Richard Duggleby; *Queen Edith* Joan Walker; *Earl of Wessex* Ian Umpleby; *Gyrth* Kevin Pickard; *Leofwine* Raymond Johnson, *Archbishop of York* Kelvin Foxton; *Saxon*

Piper of Hamelin – 1975.

Piper of Hamelin – 1975.

soldiers: Gary Axham, Keith Mitchell, Howard Skelton, Trevor Wiley; *Saxon peasants*: Pauline Bean, Mary Brooks, Christine Bean, Kathleen Cracknell, Louise Dexter, Gary Dobson, Philip Galtry, Sally Heath, Denise Harrison, Paul Harrison, Carl Horsley, Elaine Johnson, Timothy Mitchell, Julie Nesfield, Mary Pickard, Adrian and Gary Pickard, Hazel Pickering, Ian Rackham, Susan Scholes, Jane Simpson, Kevin Stocks, Malcolm Thistleton, Maureen Walker. *Duke of Normandy* Stuart Dawson, *Odo Bishop of Bayeux* Peter Marston, *Count Eustace* Jonathan Galtry, *Queen Matilda* Elissa Bean, *Page* Trevor Pickard, *Monk* Andrew Bean; *Norman Knights*: Timothy Pickard, David Gilbank, Martin Flinton, Peter Dobson; *Court Ladies*: Tina Foxton, Margaret Gilbank, Julie Gow, Maureen and Sandra Pickard, Janet Pickard, Christine Thistleton; *Norman Peasants*: Neil Bassett, Christopher Bean, John Brooks, Janice Gilbank, Paul Gilbank, Richard Harrison, Jayne Horsley, Peter and Paul Mattinson, Gillian Pickard, Ann Pickering, Howard Rogers, Patrick Umpleby, Andrea Worthy, Richard Walker.

Ten Sixty-Six – 1966.

Ten Sixty-Six – 1966.

Ten Sixty-Six – 1966.

1967 *The Tudor Rose* (all 66 pupils). *Queen Elizabeth I*, Christine Bean; *Queen's page* Richard Cundall; *Yoeman of the Guard* Malcolm Thistleton, Patrick Umpleby; *William Cecil Lord Burghley* Martin Flinton; *Katherine Ashley* Janet Pickard; *Court Ladies*: Julie Nesfield, Christeen Thistleton, Tina Foxton, Margaret Gilbank, Stephanie Oldroyd; *Robert Dudley Early of Leicester* Peter Marston; *Sir Francis Drake* Ian Rackham; *Sir Walter Raleigh* Trevor Wiley, *Robert Dereveux Earl of Essex* Richard Duggleby, *Will Shakespeare* Peter Dobson; *Bishop of Carlisle* Gary Axham; *Soldiers:* Neil Bassett, Carl Horsley, Peter Mattinson, Keith Mitchell, Neil and Andrew Pickard, Howard Rogers, Kevin Stocks. *Sailors:* Andrew Bean, David Gilbank, Raymond Johnson, Paul Mattinson. Kevin Pickard, Trevor Pickard. *London Citizens:* Pauline Bean, Mary and John Brooks, Shirley Collier, Joan Cussons, Kathleen Cracknell, Pamela Duggleby, Gary Dobson, Paul Gilbank, Julie Gow. Denise Harrison, Paul and Richard Harrison, Julie Harrison, Elaine Johnson, Philip Marston, Christopher Mouser, Pauline Oldroyd, Gillian Pickard, Hazel Pickering, Ann Pickering, Mary Pickard, Sandra Pickard, David Pratt, Susan Scholes, Jane Simpson, Lynda Thompson, Maureen Walker. Janette Wiley. *Dancers*: Christopher Bean, Louise Dexter, Janice Gilbank, Jayne Horsley, Sally Heath, Timothy Mitchell, Jacqueline Mouser, William O'Brian, Adrian and Gary Pickard, Richard Walker, Andrea Worthy.

The Tudor Rose – 1967.

1969 *The Sherburn Story* (all 61 pupils): *Victorian Children* Janette Wiley, Gary Bean, *Ancient Britons*: John Brooks, Joan Cussons, Louise Dexter, Paul Gilbank, Christopher Mouser, Martin Middle, Andrea Worthy, Richard Walker; *Merwin the Druid* Christopher Bean; *Roman Centurion* Carl Horsley; *Standard Bearer* Howard Rogers; *Roman Soldiers:* Trevor Pickard, Malcolm Thistleton, Paul and Peter Mattinson; *Saxon Thegn* Ian Rackham; *Villagers*: Mary Brooks, Shirley Collier, Guy Charlesworth, Pamela Duggleby, Andrew and Janice Gilbank, Julie Harrison, Paul Harrison, Sally Heath, Elaine Johnson, Duncan Law, Trudy Marflitt, Timothy Mitchell, Frank Newlove, Gary, Adrian and Angela Pickard, Colin Pickard, Carolyn Pickering, Elaine Pickering, Susan Scholes, Jane Simpson, Brett Stephenson, Lynda Thompson, Patrick Umpleby, Philip Waud; *King Edwin of Northumbria* Andrew Pickard; *Queen Ethelburga* Gillian Pickard, *Paulinus a monk* Neil Bassett; *St Hilda Abbess of Whitby* Tina Foxton; *Nuns:* Jane Mortimer, Jacqueline Mouser, Jayne Horsley, Ann Pickering; *Monks:* Richard Harrison, Desmond Bean; *Vikings:* Martin Flinton, Christopher Bean, Nigel Stephenson, Kevin Pickard, Kevin Stocks, Trevor Wiley; *Norman soldiers:* Gary and Peter Dobson; *Lord of the Manor* Richard Bettison; *Lady of the Manor* Hazel Pickering; *Crusaders:* Martin Flinton, Peter Dobson; *Outlaws:* Ian Rackham, Kevin Pickard; *Mary*

The Sherburn Story – 1969.

The Sherburn Story – 1969.

Queen of Scots Ann Pickering; *Tudor Earls:* Carl Horsley, Brett Stephenson; *Dick Turpin* Trevor Wiley; *Toll Gate Keeper* Kevin Stocks; *Chimney Sweep's Boy* Gary Pickard; *Victorian Gentlemen:* Andrew Pickard, Nigel Stephenson, Peter and Paul Mattinson; *Queen Victoria,* Margaret Gilbank.

1981 *Exodus* (all 37 pupils). *Jacob* Mark Pickard; Joseph Richard Gillett; *Benjamin* Colin Best; *Judah* Richard Pickering; *Simeon* Michael Rodgers; *Reuben* Darren Bean; *Levi* Nicholas Worthy; *Dan* Mark Nettleton; *Asher* Jamie Berriman; *Naphtali* Adrian Evans; *Gad* Gary Walker; *Zebulun* Simon Cousins; *Issachar* Paul Holmes; *a stranger* Ian Cade; *Ishmaelite merchants* Sarah Pickard, Nicola Best, Sarah Cousins; *Potiphar Captain of Pharaoh's Guard* Philip Holtby; *Potiphar's wife* Anita Shaw; *Pharaoh of Egypt* Nicholas Dobson; *Pharaoh's Wife* Sharon Taylor; *Guards* Sharon Dennis, Emma Wright; *A Priest of the Temple* Elaine Gillett; *Keeper of Slaves* Sarah Flinton; *Slaves in the Market* Joanne Bean, Theresa Bean, Sharon Pickard; *Crowd* Andrew Mattinson, Simon Dobson, Nicholas Lickes, Carl Evans, Mark Cousins, Lisa Gilbank, Samantha Sedman, Trisha Skilbeck, Nicola Dobson, Kay Pickering, Alison Atkinson, Clare Stockill, Sharon Holmes, Claire Howe, Jonathan Gillett, Helen Woodall, Victoria Mattinson

Exodus – 1981.

Exodus – 1981.

Exodus – 1981.

Appendix 19: 1967 St John's Awards. Preliminary Home Nursing: Elizabeth BURTON, Mary DUGGLEBY, Jane HUMPHREYS, Lynda & Charles OUTHART, Susan PICKARD, Dorothy SCHOLES, Susan THOMPSON, Sheila & Joan WALKER, Valerie & Carol WITTY, Stephen WOODHOUSE; Junior Certificates: Sandra BURTON, Gina Marie FLINTON, Christopher & Mary Ann OUTHART, Anita Jane RIDSDALE, Keith Frederick STEPHENSON; Basic First Aid: Stephen BEAN, Barry FOXTON, Susan PICKARD, Geoffrey & Christopher RIDSDALE, Dorothy SCHOLES, Sheila & Joan WALKER; Adult Initial Course; Marian BENNISON, Yvonne SHAW, Susan STEPHENSON, Sheila WITTY; Adult First Aid: John NAPTHINE, Kenneth PRATT, Susan RIDSDALE, Susan STEPHENSON, Sheila WITTY. 1970: Newly Qualified: Hazel BROWN; Mary Ann MOAT, Elizabeth POTTS, Jane RIDSDALE; Road/Home Safety: Pauline BEAN, Hazel BROWN, Mary Ann MOAT, Christopher OUTHET, Elizabeth POTTS, Jane RIDSDALE, Dorothy SCHOLES, Ian UMPLEBY; Sheila & Joan WALKER, Valerie WITTY; Basic First Aid: Hazel BROWN, Mary Ann MOAT, Elizabeth POTTS, Jane RIDSDALE; Adult First Aid: Joan WALKER, Mrs M ATKINSON.

Appendix 20: Christmas Plays. 1986 *The Christmas Story* (all 36 pupils): Nicola Armstrong (Mary), Wayne Shaw (Joseph), Jayne Smith (Angel Gabriel), Bryan Atkinson (Innkeeper), Lynette Lickes (Elizabeth). Paul Moore (shepherd), Karl Skelton (Balthazar), Kevin Metcalfe (Gaspar), Daniel Bibby (Melchoir). Solos and Duets by Samantha Atkinson, Christopher Cousins, Dean Foxton, Marcus Gilbank, Lynne Gosley. Susannah Irving, Kelly Lickes, Kerry Metcalfe, Gavin Metcalfe, Marc Skelton, John Slack, Lorraine Shaw, James Snowball. Recorders: Samantha Atkinson, Carl Berriman, Christopher Cousins. Dean Foxton, Lynne Gosley, Gavin Metcalfe, Kelly Metcalfe, Kerry Metcalfe, Lorraine Shaw, John Slack, Marc Skelton, Robert Smith, Katie Walker.

1997 *Rock the Baby* (all 51 pupils): Marie Suggitt (Mary); Martin Marflitt, James Chadwick (Joseph); Lisa Thompson (Angel Gabriel); Rebecca Mattinson, Sophie Pickard, Adam Temple, Emma Samples (Innkeepers); Lee Harrison (Herod); Stuart Stocks (Soldier); Adam Prest, Liam Colling, Kristen Temple (Wise Men); Christopher Mattinson, Emma Ward, Jamie Pollard, Sarah Chadwick (Shepherds); Adam and Matthew Harrison, Jonathan Davies, Kieran Artley (Sheep), Helen Thompson, Kelly Hunter, Kimberly Moston, Nicola Suggitt (Angels); Luke Walker, Jonathan Pickard, Tom Haldenby, Stuart Pickard (Animals); Rachel Bellwood, Kelly Colling (Narrators); Laura Mattinson, James Harrison (Band); Terri Calvert, Bethany Davies, Thomas Gilbank, Rachel Harrison, Ben Hakin, Liam Hunter, Julie and Roxy Lawson, Aimee Lickes, Zoe Marflitt, Kathy Mattinson, Eleanor Mennell, Emma and Natalie Moston, Philip Pickard, Stephanie Samples, Daniel Stocks, Daniel Simpson, Ryan Walker, (Carol Singers).

Appendix 21: *Moving On* (all children) Class 1: Naomi Temple (narrator/Victorian Child), Abigail Gilbank (business woman/Victorian child), Ashley Adams (Mr Biro/toy soldier), Ben Scott (shopkeeper), Leanne Pickering, Emily Hardwick (dolls), Chelsey Howe (Victorian Doll), Max Lawson, Ben Simpson (Jack-in-a-Box), Jack Roland, Kieran Colling (soldiers), Aimee Walker (Mrs Bell/a doll), Jessica Metcalfe (baby doll), Jack Pickard (toy soldier), Jamie Thompson (motor bike rider), Kirsty Howe and Damon Hakin (Victorian Girl and Boy). Class 2: James Harrison (Jonathan), Helen Thompson, Nicola Suggitt, Kelly Hunter (Zone Gnomes), Dan Simpson (Caveman), Zoe Marflitt (Cave woman), Thomas Gilbank (Gaffer), Tom Haldenby (Slosher), Lovette Dixon (Conductor), Jenny Bromley (Mizz Fizz), Liam Hunter, Jack Elliss (bodyguards), Matthew Harrison, Liam Hunter Thomas Gilbank (Transport Zone), Adam Harrison, Stuart Pickard, Ben Hakin, Jenny Bromley, Jordan Walker, Jonathan Pickard, Jack Ellis, Hilary Tortice, Lovette Dixon (builders). Class 3: Aimee Lickes (Rachel), Christopher Mattinson (Jesus), Laura Mattinson (Megabyte), Becci and Kathy Mattinson (Zone Gnomes), Cassie Tortice (photographer), Liam Colling (Gallileo/Robot), Marie Suggitt (Donna),

Jamie Pollard (Mario), Elliott Sturrock (Professor), Stephanie Samples, Rachel Harrison, Kristen Temple, Laura Dixon, Lisa Thompson (fashion models), Daniel and Stuart Stocks, Philip Pickard, Holly Walker (Machine/Scientists/ Photographers). Stage Management by Lee Harrison and Martin Marflitt. The play is about Jonathan and Rachel, brother and sister, preparing to move house and deciding what to take and what to leave. Megabyte and Zone Gnomes appear out of their crashed computer and take them through various zones to help them make the right choices. In the end the children realise that all achievements are worthless unless they are able to love one another.